SHAPING THE NEW SOCIAL WORK

SOCIAL WORK AND SOCIAL ISSUES
COLUMBIA UNIVERSITY SCHOOL OF SOCIAL WORK

SHAPING THE
NEW SOCIAL WORK

Alfred J. Kahn, Editor

Columbia University Press
New York & London

The Columbia University School of Social Work Publication Series, "Social Work and Social Issues," is concerned with the implications of social work practice and social welfare policy for solving problems. Each volume is an independent work. The Series is intended to contribute to the knowledge base of social work education, to facilitate communication with related disciplines, and to serve as a background for public policy discussion. Other books in the series are

SHIRLEY JENKINS, *editor*
Social Security in International Perspective   1969

GEORGE BRAGER and HARRY SPECHT
Community Organizing   1973

LIBRARY OF CONGRESS CATALOGING IN PUBLICATION DATA

Kahn, Alfred J   1919–
  Shaping the new social work.

  (Social work and social issues series)
  Includes bibliographical references.
  1. Social service—United States—Addresses, essays, lectures.   2. Social work as a profession—Addresses, essays, lectures.   I. Title.
HV91.K29   361'.973   73-4189

THE CONTRIBUTORS

Alfred J. Kahn, Professor, Columbia University School of Social Work

Ralph Dolgoff, Educational Program Specialist, Council on Social Work Education, New York

George Getzel, Instructor, Hunter College School of Social Work, New York

Charles Grosser, Professor, Columbia University School of Social Work, New York

Arnold Gurin, Dean, Florence Heller Graduate School for Advanced Studies in Social Welfare, Brandeis University, Waltham, Massachusetts

Sheila B. Kamerman, Research Associate and Project Director, Columbia University School of Social Work, New York

Carol H. Meyer, Professor, Columbia University School of Social Work, New York

Judith Nelsen, Lecturer, Hunter College School of Social Work, New York

Norman A. Polansky, Professor, School of Social Work and Department of Sociology, University of Georgia, Athens

Willard C. Richan, Associate Dean and Professor, School of Social Administration, Temple University, Philadelphia

PREFACE

Late in the 1950s, a diverse group of social workers collaborated on what was to be one of the more widely read professional volumes of the following decade—*Issues in American Social Work*,[1] a volume still being used as text and reference. Yet all would agree, given the intervening events, that while many of the old *issues* remain, there also are new questions to be discussed. Moreover, it may at this moment be useful to focus more sharply —not on *all* issues facing *all* of social work but, rather, on issues which may in their resolution point to the future of social work practice.

Why? Because the antipoverty war of the 1960s, the civil rights revolution which provided its backdrop, the search for participation at the local level, and the exploration of new cultural forms as part of the revolt against (or of?) alienation or against the corporate state (depending on one's ideological orientation) led some social workers and agencies in the mid-1960s and early 1970s largely to a focus on power, control, structure, organization, staffing. The assumption was that good practice would follow. Yet this has not occurred. The milieu has provided a context for greater flexibility in theoretical base and organizational form, yet it is far from certain that there has been a practice renaissance. One can, indeed, complain about the lack of social invention and progress in technique. In fact, there are those who predict a demise of the profession on the grounds that too much has been given up and not enough substituted.

Convinced that social work practice has much to do to answer the call of its time, we here choose to focus on problems of practice. Yet our emphasis is not necessarily technical. The premise is one

[1] Alfred J. Kahn, ed., *Issues in American Social Work* (New York: Columbia University Press, 1959).

which I found occasion to formulate during six years as national chairman, Division of Practice and Knowledge, National Association of Social Workers: *practice enacts policy*. What the practitioner does, how he relates to clients, the way in which he exercises discretion, the priorities he places upon his time, the details of his role structuring are all ways of setting the direction, content, milieu, and atmosphere of programs. The practitioner sets, modifies or negates policy in his every action. He often settles what programs mean and do to or for people. Thus, the questions which unify this series of explorations are the following: Given the emerging social issues and policies of the 1970s, what can and should be the response of social work practice? To what extent are we poised for accomplishment?

In such perspective, the introductory essay discusses the social milieu of the 1970s and the policy consequences it might inspire, relevant to social work practice. Co-authors were called upon to decide independently whether the characterizations are accurate and the derivations sound. Readers will carry similar responsibility. In this instance, both agreement and disagreement can stimulate needed progress for practice.

The chapters have been prepared by authors of standing as social work scholars and practice-innovators. The points of reference are the 1959 *Issues* book, this brief preface, and the editor's effort, in the first essay, to state a conceptual frame of reference. Each author as an expert in his or her own right has been free to deal with the elements of the framework and to define a personal stance. The editor, in issuing invitations to collaborate, avoided political, theoretical, or moral consensus.

From the first chapter, dealing with the nature of the milieu, the volume turns to conceptions of new ways of organizing direct service (Meyer) or changing the system (Grosser). Polansky confronts specifically and uniquely the possible social work response to the characteristic individual malaise of our time, loneliness, and offers both policy and service strategies.

We then turn back to the question of knowledge base. Four young scholars (Kamerman, Dolgoff, Getzel, and Nelsen) collaborate in a review of the social and behavioral science armamentarium, illustrating their thesis of the need for specialization.

The final two papers look at the profession and its institutional bases. Richan seeks a role for the organized social work profession in the light of our policy thrusts and the nature of our times. Gurin examines more specifically the future of social work education. In my own final comments, I note some remaining gaps, react to several of the themes which emerged, and point to issues needing discussion. Here I speak personally, expecting both collaborators and readers to join the future debate from the base of their personal experience.

ALFRED J. KAHN
Columbia University
1973

CONTENTS

SHAPING THE NEW SOCIAL WORK

Alfred J. Kahn

❀

A POLICY BASE FOR SOCIAL WORK PRACTICE: SOCIETAL PERSPECTIVES

We want to influence the direction of American social work at a most complex time. Our "reluctant" welfare state, in which social work is embedded, expanded for three decades before it became clear to a large proportion of the profession that the chosen paths would not necessarily lead all the way to cherished goals. There were even those who argued that we were pointed in the wrong direction.

As the debate is joined or as social workers independently seek increased "relevance," more attention is devoted to societal perspectives. Surely, social work is affected by, and would be responsive to, its general social context. Yet, he who looks ahead today toward improving social services and enhancing the social "sector" generally, finds it difficult both to identify and to achieve some consensus about basic facts and about guiding concepts. Long-held premises come into question. New ideas, foreign to the liberal thoughtways of an era that extended from the New Deal to the Great Society, now seem worthy of serious consideration.

As the first Nixon term came to an end, some observers argued that the basic Great Society social services strategies had failed, and many social workers agreed. Others complained that the investment had been too small and the time horizon too brief, only to be reminded of the absolute increases in expenditures even while the Vietnam war was being escalated.

Certainly, American reformers, who began to look to government for solution of social problems and the enrichment of daily living late in the nineteenth century, and who became fully committed to governmental intervention during the New Deal, are suddenly uncertain about their chosen instrument. Perhaps, as Daniel P. Moynihan has alleged, Washington is better at collecting money than at developing services. Perhaps, as Milton Friedman has long argued, effective and efficient services really do require the resort to market mechanisms. Perhaps, as critics from the New Left proclaim, large-scale organization, the bureaucratization of the welfare state, is self-defeating in two ways: it cannot avoid serving as an instrument of a military-industrial complex with very different goals; within the several related governmental bureaucracies organizational boundary maintenance overwhelms any humanity that may have existed in the initial program conception.

Almost simultaneously, or certainly within a brief period, analysts swing from stressing the dominance of our life by large, bureaucratized organizations to emphasizing the emergence of the postindustrial society as the key contextual component in setting the parameters. They fluctuate from placing great weight on the shifting relations among generations (who sets the norms?) to seeing the causal nexus in the relative adaptability of different forms of "consciousness," defined by Charles Reich as "a total configuration in any individual making up his total perception of reality." [1] They assign great significance to cybernation, only to announce that "community control" is possible, emerging, and the key shaper of things to come. They note that individuals, in learning how to work with and manipulate bureaucracies, can sustain their integrity and initiative (Toffler's "ad-hocracy") [2] while describing new pace setters as so much alike that one doubts that their "revolution" enhances freedom. [3] They bemoan both the transience and constant novelty which defeat the individual in his search for buoys in a swirling ocean and the rigid overorganization and stratified status system said to give him no breathing space at all!

For some these perspectives are too narrow. If the warnings derived from computer simulations reported by the ecology-minded Club of Rome [4] are correct (and is not the evidence impressive?), current population levels and economic activity are excessive. Projections of the consequences of the interplay among population, food supply, natural resources, industrial production, and pollution all lead to predictions of inevitable world collapse unless the world can quickly choose a policy of equilibrium. But in a world political arena this can only mean major redistribution of wealth and income within societies, a shift of productivity away from factory manufacturing to services, an immediate slowing of growth in industrialized countries so that developing countries may reach a viable level for stabilizing, and so on. Surely such policies could come only from major shifts in values, concepts of rights and freedom, and national morality. A world capable of planning on this level would be in many ways unrecognizable.

In this "age of acceleration," several analysts have noted, even images of reality seem to change more rapidly than ever before. Yet images must be discussed, evaluated, ranked, since assessment of the experience with government, choice of approaches to provision and to rights, and emphases in selection of priority programs derive in part from a concept of what is "going on" (and in part from valuations). One must depict the "civilization" if one would deal with its "discontents." Without intellectual tools the task cannot be approached.

Faddism, cultism, controversy about basic facts mark all attempts to characterize the social scene, to state how one might look at America today in thinking about the social sector, social welfare, social services, or social work—whatever the political perspective —in the reshaping of a "relevant" and effective social practice. Yet the advocate of social welfare policies and the molder of social practice must face the contradictions and must decide what to make of it all. Otherwise, *ad hoc* programming takes over, repeating a periodic history of professional drifting in which service priorities, program philosophies, and manpower strategies are based on inconsistent, or at least on unarticulated, premises and do not come close to solving urgent social problems, coping with serious individual needs, or enriching community life.

The ways in which practitioners view their clients, exercise discretion, set up access to programs, define goal hierarchies, and so on, become ways of formulating the operative policies of agencies. These are as potent as announced ideology, direction, content, or constraint. Yet these practitioner perspectives derive from a definition of the social scene in which the practice takes place. In short, because practice does enact policy, whether latent policy or a carefully articulated and debated direction, and because policy, in turn, is an outgrowth of a convergence of reality assessment, application of values, and the relative power and potency of interested parties, the issue of how one sees the social scene cannot be forgone in any practice-oriented effort. Social welfare partakes of a long tradition of humanistic values and the Judaeo-Christian heritage and has a continuing line of value stances and preferences which are relatively clear. It is possible to raise a banner, seek allies, advocate support —but only if one understands the present and emerging life experiences of constituencies and offers with conviction a meaningful direction. This at least must be the perspective of a responsible profession which would maximize planfulness and rationality.

Thus we return, for brief elaboration, to several emerging perspectives on the social scene to ask: on what world view can social practice base a policy?

As the point of departure we note what appear to be firm and basic, even though variously interpreted and even differently named by different observers:

1. The American welfare state is committed to demand management of the economy through monetary and fiscal policy and the way in which governmental budget priorities are set. Different administrations vary in their goals and techniques, but even Republicans accept neo-Keynesian strategies, and President Nixon undertook wage-and-price-control measures not risked by his Democrat predecessors.

2. Ours is a national society, made national by governmental power, communication, the nature of the economy, and the mobility of the people.

3. Cybernation is growing in importance, and with it analytic, decision-making, and management techniques (operations research, systems analysis) which it makes possible. Cybernation has long-range implications for our labor force needs and even for location of residences and factories. This phenomenon, in turn, is subsumed under a larger development: the increased importance of knowledge and theory in human organization and decision-making.

4. The components of the "social minimum," assured or partially

guaranteed by the American welfare state, generally increase—but slowly—and there is some reversal. This process has not been based in recent years on significant redistribution of income or wealth among the major income groups in the population.

5. Given its affluence, the society has more institutional and programmatic choices before it, more "degrees of freedom" than ever before, at least in the short run, even if the Club of Rome is right. We can, too, begin to consider less "growth" and a more civilized "equilibrium." Values can be articulated and implemented—if we so choose.

6. In small ways one may also see the emergence of an international society, supported by new patterns of investment and corporate control and by many other phenomena, including communication and transportation developments and increased affluence in many parts of the world.

These are the backdrops which have high significance once urbanization and industrialization are accepted as the fundamental givens. The attacks on poverty and racism, central and symptomatic problems of our age, are best planned in such perspective. In addition, we note, several other phenomena appear to have new, timely significance for the social welfare system in general and social work practice in particular. Here the generalizations and interpretations are often in dispute.

Reacting to Big Organizations and Distant Government

If Toffler is correct in interpreting current research, large-scale organization and rigid bureaucratization—with their defined hierarchies and clearly demarcated roles—have reached their outer limits from the point of view of their effects on workers and executives. One could hardly argue, however, in the age of conglomerates, that bigness is dysfunctional economically. Indeed, international boundaries have in recent years given way to permit even large corporate entities to be internationally owned. Operationally, however, creativity, responsiveness, initiative, seem to demand a

breaking away from the traditional bureaucratic model for work organizations, with its emphasis on hierarchy and specialization, so as
to create permanent or *ad hoc* work groups which can be more flexible and task-oriented. The individual with decision-making or deci-
sion-influencing responsibility does appear to need an environment
in which his perceptions and observations are not prestructured by
organizational position, in which his responses can be relatively autonomous, and in which he can contribute to new initiatives; that is,
if the organization seeks more than the maintenance of the *status
quo*. As cybernation increases, even the line worker must exercise
considerable judgment and can no longer be located in an organizational hierarchy like the one appropriate for a traditional assembly
line. The craftsman rather than the assembly-line worker of Chap-
lin's *Modern Times* is his counterpart.

Thus, while bureaucratic organization dominates industry, its effects must be contained or countermanded in new ways. What of
highly bureaucratized education, recreation, religion, health, general
social services? What is or can be the human response to a market
economy which would structure leisure, culture, and recreation via
the book-of-the-month, theater-of-the-month, flower-of-the-month,
candy-of-the-month, cheese-of-the-month, British magazine-of-the-
month, and so on? What of education in which students feel no in-
dividuality, or religion which seems unable to respond to unique-
ness?

Government, of course, has become the primary example of
bigness. Power has moved to Washington, most major personal services (as well as most supports for business, labor, and consumer
protection) derive from Washington, and the scale of the operation
demands a large, complex organization of many layers. Government
is the biggest producer, the biggest purchaser, the greatest influence
on quality, price, and accessibility.[5] Where states and localities retain their prerogatives or expand their roles, their scale, too, often
remains so large and their apparatus so elaborate as to seem beyond
the influence and even beyond the communication range of the individual consumer.

The response is a search for planned decentralization which does
not sacrifice the possibility of central policy where appropriate. The

debate rages between "administrative decentralization" (decentralization for service delivery within over-all central political control) and "political decentralization" (giving more responsibilities and financial power to local governments, including what are now neighborhoods in large cities). Block grants, general and special revenue sharing, planning grants, incentives to "repackage" categorical programs on the lower level now characterize federal and state governments. The federal government itself has developed regional structures for some of its human service programs and is considering reallocating some of "the action." For some purposes, Washington bypasses states and deals with cities or even smaller entities. States bypass cities and deal with communities. Cities experiment with smaller units and consider neighborhood government, but some experts predict that the major tiers will be Washington, the states, the community—with cities weakened.

Everywhere, but especially in the human services (the "social services," as the term is used internationally), there is renewed preoccupation with service delivery, and its main feature is planned decentralization. Parallel and closely related developments involve a stepped-up consumerism: providing more detailed information to consumers about their rights and about the quality of products and services; and creating mechanisms whereby they may monitor services and have impact on what is delivered and how. Activists appeal to members of many professions and to workers in many industries to monitor their own enterprises and to disclose the facts when the public good is subverted.

One need not be in a position fully to predict exactly how far these processes will go, and one need not ignore the need for increased centralization, too, in some realms as a companion (not contradictory) development, to see their significance for social welfare. The tendency toward modification of rigid bureaucracy with new, more individualized and responsive work units and work rules, whether "ad-hocracies" à la Toffler or new primary group outlets and mechanisms as conceptualized by observers such as Litwak and Meyer,[6] faces us with (*a*) the question of whether we in social work know enough about people to contribute to the process and (*b*) the challenge to help those for whom the discontinuities and *lack* of structure [7] pose personal problems. The movements toward decentralization and reorganized service delivery challenge our fundamental modes of proffesional service organization, our view of what belongs to experts and to consumers, and the way in which different services are brought together on the local level.

Government, Markets, and the Private Sector

Issues of organization and service delivery apply both to large government and to large voluntary sectors. There are those who urge that a major effort be made to decrease the reliance on government per se and to employ the market increasingly as a coordinating device so as to assure service responsiveness. In this view, consumerism can be more effective in dealing with nonpublic organizations than with government departments. Forces of supply and demand can both increase efficiency and maximize responsiveness. The market coordinates and enhances accountability because only active demand generates and sustains service, and when consumers turn away it becomes readily apparent. Besides, it is argued, the private sector, with its many components, can create or sustain diversity and avoid overcentralization of power. A return to selective "reprivatization," in Peter Drucker's sense, is thus part of the same thrust as is decentralization.

It is unclear whether serious effort actually will be made to decrease governmental activity and enterprise. It does seem apparent, however, that social services will expand and will offer widespread opportunities which will be attractive to the private sector. The postindustrial or consumer society devotes more than half its manpower to services. Some of these are services which none would separate from the market place: tailoring, real estate brokerage, travel agencies, plumbing, beauty culture, and so on. However, the dedication of the society to a social minimum, to a new standard of social justice, to achieving solidarity through shared and mutual enrichment, yields a far higher degree of expectation than ever before of social or human services, available as rights or near rights. For this is the nature of the institution called "social welfare," or what is called the "social sector" in the "consumer" or "service" or "welfare" or "postindustrial" state: considerations of social justice and solidarity, and the knowledge of what it takes to rear competent citizens, lead to commitment to a social minimum and to the recognition of certain rights, needs, and entitlements, justiciable to different degrees. Demand management of the economy is accepted as the means to finance and protect the guaranteed minimum of food, shelter, clothing, service, and these new rights. The individual's access to services is not determined by his ability to command them in the market place, because it is held that the interests of the larger society are at stake in his being assured these consumption guarantees.

Social services are thus nonmarket services in the sense that the individual's access is determined by broader social policy. Nonetheless, a range of intermediary devices is available: providing cash to the needy so that they too may command the product, which is then delivered in the market; providing a voucher, which allows choice of purveyor; performance contracting, an arrangement under which payment to a supplier of services depends upon results (how much did the child learn to read?); delivering service through a public agency; subsidizing a voluntary agency to deliver services to all those who are eligible; partially subsidizing the voluntary agency, and so on. The market may, in short, be used to improve delivery and coordination, but not to determine rights or shares in a welfare state.

Historically, certain social services have been publicly organized and operated, being considered inappropriate for the voluntary sector (correctional institutions) or as not eligible for subsidy (elementary education). (The issue was that private elementary education, often church-related, could not be subsidized federally without "establishing" a religion, and until the "solution" of 1965, subsidizing consumers, not agencies, it was not possible politically to subsidize public elementary schools federally without helping the private ones.[8]) Others have tended to be reserved for the voluntary sectarian and nonsectarian agencies on the assumption that they could assure necessary diversity and more effective individualization than public agencies. A few have been organized by nonprofit organizations and profit-making proprietary agencies to appeal to those who wanted to buy services other than what were offered to the general public (proprietary hospitals) or were not guaranteed to all (private medical care).

Now, with the raising of the service threshold, services long unattractive to private business interests command their attention. The arrival of Medicare in 1965 led to multiple expansion of private nursing homes. The day care expansion of the 1970s aroused the interest of a number of franchise firms (but, later, the profitability of such programs became questionable as expected federal funding evaporated). The interest of service reformers in the potential values of competition has even recaptured some elementary education for market-place competition via voucher experiments. Positioning has begun for the evolving debate on medical service systems as new proposals for coverage appear. In the housing field, some would interpret the past history as evidence that the market cannot house any of the below-the-median-income group, so that a publicly operated public social utility needs to be provided. Others are convinced that adequate incentives for the private sector will be found.

Whatever the resolution of the specific debates—Will franchised day care not shortchange children? Is medicine not too strong a monopoly to respond to market forces?—it does appear likely that the social service expansion of the postindustrial society will involve a more complex public-nonprofit-profit mix than ever before. Traditional formulas for allocation of tasks tumble before the scale of demand, experience which negates structures, and the search to incorporate the advantages of competition and diversity.[9] Some of the hesitation about the voluntary social welfare sector and its elitist control will be resolved by public capitalization of new types of voluntary agencies in the form of publicly financed community corporations deriving from the federal antipoverty, Model Cities, and manpower programs of the 1960s and 1970s.

Social welfare personnel will no longer, in the future, be spared the issue of where would be the best location for their service, and the criteria are likely to be somewhat more related to output than in the past. If there is evidence that the market will create services (while the consumer is subsidized) and that in some qualitative sense this is more desirable than the traditional pattern in which government operates, or supports and subsidizes, voluntary organizations, it is likely that the device will be employed. "Performance contracting" may even take hold in some few programs. At the very least, then, social welfare personnel must prepare to work in new kinds of locations and to interrelate services under these several auspices. They must expect evaluations by consumers and by government, and should be prepared to cope with market-type delivery systems. All the while, services will expand in type and significance as the society shifts its attention from increasing productivity to improving human life styles.

Identity, Primary Groups, Integrity

Moynihan, writing about urban policy in 1969, and Reich, in 1970, despite their different ideological perspectives are preoccupied with "a sense of the failure of community." [10] While Reich's star declined almost as rapidly as it rose, the problem of community and its role in one's sense of identity remains of central concern. Decentralization, neighborhood government, and the "community control" movement treat this phenomenon, in part, but are also responsive to political strategies which see particularism (separatism of ethnic or interest groups) as a more likely vehicle for redistributing political, economic, and social power than are centralization and universalism.

Decentralization of services and community control of some programs, neighborhood government, and resource sharing from higher to lower political jurisdictions would also do much to facilitate identification with "place" and to restore the sense of ability to cope with additional aspects of one's environment. They would permit a measure of program diversity and the developing of appropriate devices to enhance service adaptability and assure user access. One is tempted, however, to predict that the process would inevitably be made self-limiting by: (a) the necessity of sustaining a national community and certain overriding policies, when joined to the political realities in which power is related to purse strings; (b) the fact that economy of scale places some constraints on decentralization; (c) as well as the fact that decentralization is wasteful in administrative costs in the instance of standardized programs (social insurance); and that (*d*) professional associations and unions are dominated by "cosmopolitans" who are unwilling to permit a degree of decentralization which would weaken their ability to organize and negotiate for large constituencies.

Yet the loss of community has other elements as well, and the social service network may make a unique contribution which is identifiable apart from the political and organizational strategies mentioned above. The crisis in individual identity, deriving as it does from a number of sources, reflects at least in part the failure of the family and other primary groups to cope with a bureaucratized, often centralized, inadequately individualized, and sometimes transitory environment. Where the individual lacks a primary group base, there is an erosion of "social community." Or, if the preceding overstresses the impersonal, large-scale organization, and Toffler is right, individuals may be suffering from excessive transience in jobs, relationships, place, and are in crisis because of the "death of permanence." In this sense, physical mobility statistics, data about divorce and separation, and facts about product disposability (of paper plates, for instance, and rapid, "built-in" obsolescence of many products) are part of one picture. Large proportions of our children have lived in divorced, separated, or never-stabilized families; and large numbers of our adults have experienced several marriages after "trial" (nonconsecrated) relationships. There is everywhere a desperate search for stability and meaning in an environment in which deep and satisfying relationships are hard to sustain. And, indeed, to return to Moynihan and Reich, it may very well be that a crisis of primary groups is truly reflected in the lack of community norms, which brings about high crime rates, a failure of efforts to keep streets clean because citizens do not cooperate, and so on.

Without necessarily either eschewing the institutional and governmental reforms described above or adopting them all, advocates of a responsive social welfare system may ask whether there are policies and programs which might contribute to primary relationships in a desirable way. If Erikson and others are correct in the view that essential human qualities derive from primary group experiences, and if our society continues—despite its many institutional changes—to value a modal personality which has identity and integrity and is characterized by a capacity for creativity, it becomes essential to seek ways either to bolster traditional institutional outlets for primary relationships or to find new ones.

On a policy level, issues of women's roles, parental rights and responsibilities, ease of abortion, separation, and divorce must be debated. The availability and nature of child care resources affect parental patterns, as does assignment of social insurance entitlements to a mother at home. The nature of "home life" education in the school, as it shapes norms, becomes significant.

Policies guide the enactment of programs, but creative programs do not appear of themselves. Social welfare personnel face a social invention challenge if they would bolster the old or offer new institutional outlets for primary relationships. (Of course, in the sense here intended, "invention" may imply discovering and supporting solutions which community members have evolved for themselves.) In this field where policy and program meet, there must be progress in inventing new forms and winning support for them, while new service personnel are attracted to, and prepared for, their tasks. To illustrate, there might be: diversified, universal day care and early childhood programs, ranging from brief "baby parking" to all-day programs; homemakers and home helps to serve many needs; communal eating resources and substitute homes (semicommunes?); new extended families of unrelated people (communes?): multipurpose centers for adolescents; multipurpose centers for retired people; family vacation resources; neighborhood information centers; school-based breakfast and lunch programs; hostels for adolescents, in the city and as vacation resources; library homework-aid centers, particularly for young people moving beyond their parents' experience, and so on.

We are here in the realm of public social utilities, of urban amenities essential to man in our modern culture. The right of access should be universal, whether to all individuals who wish to exercise the option or to those of specified status: retired people, preschoolers, and so forth. Since these are social welfare resources, the community must seek to maximize access; fees, if charged, should vary with the user's income and be sought to help finance programs, not to determine who may utilize a basic facility.

The primary group crisis continues to take its toll. While new policies and social inventions are—or should be—preventive, our urban and rural settlements are full of casualties: the lost and alienated, the addicted, the antisocial, the mentally disturbed, those who cannot learn, those who do not feel or enjoy, those who cannot construct and sustain satisfying relationships. When institutional failures and social policy dilemmas come to the forefront, societies are tempted to underplay efforts to aid the maladjusted or sick individual in favor of "more basic remedies." Such impulse has not been lacking in American social welfare and in the American social work profession during the past decade. Many agencies and individuals have not been diverted from their work, and in some fields of practice resources have even increased. In general, however, the glamour has been elsewhere, as have been the appropriations.[11]

Now, facing the scale of casualties where the developmental environment leaves many standing naked, cold, and alone in a social milieu lacking sustenance, the issue for social welfare programmers and practitioners, as for policy-makers, is whether a reasonable balance can be struck between direct case services to those needing help, income-maintenance programs, and the general social policies and public social utilities needed by all consumers. One cannot write off the thousands of casualties without paying a huge price in dollars, suffering, and transmitted pathology.[12]

But mere continuation and even expansion of current services would not be adequate. What can social work practice offer which is responsive in its behavioral and social science underpinnings—and therefore in its interventive modalities—to the social context and dynamics of individual deficits, maladaptation, and pathology? Surely some of the present failures of general social services are organizational failures: a true network of services does not exist, yet only well-articulated, sustained interventions could hope to be effective. However, other failures must relate to outmoded interventive approaches, to treatment based on incorrect theoretical premises, to technique which has an inaccurate perception of patients-clients.

Unless social work practice experiences the significant renewal which now is due, it will continue to be of limited "relevance."

Help, Provision, and Advocacy

The welfare or service state, we have noted, employs demand management, legislative policy, and considerable revenue as it seeks to assure a social minimum, implement some concepts of social justice, enhance personal and group development, and offer specific help to the underprivileged and the deviant. The components of state activity to attain such ends are called "social welfare" policies and programs or the "social sector." The guarantee and accountability are in the province of government, but voluntary nonprofit and profit sectors and the market itself may be instruments of such purpose, so long as they do not determine entitlements and access. Early twentieth-century beginnings developed into extensive welfare state enterprises in a postindustrial society which has so mastered industrial and agricultural productivity as to be able to devote well over half of its manpower to profit and nonprofit services. (Of course, the situation would be different if national boundaries were less important, but political facts in this realm do not seem destined for short-range change. The world does not yet recognize that productivity and distribution mechanisms do not meet the needs of, or reach the majority of, mankind. Those nations which have conquered productivity thus move into a postindustrial phase while others cannot feed their peoples.) Industrialization, urbanization, and population growth create new needs for service and amenity, lest productivity always be purchased at the price of a less-human life style.

What types of services implement such purposes? What does the welfare society do beyond implementing policies and passing laws to protect individual rights, assure justice and equity? First there is *developmental provision:* the resources, services, amenities, the universally available public social utilities that are the core of the guaranteed minimum of goods and services a society defines as essential to survival. There are components in income maintenance (largely social insurance), education, health, housing, cultural activity and recreation, perhaps transportation, which are indispensable to life in current urbanized societies.

Secondly, because rights and entitlements are many and complex, because government is large and many-layered, and because the voluntary sector is fragmented and often operates like free enterprise, the social sector must organize special means of *access.* Access services include information, advice, referral, complaint machinery, ombudsmen, legal services, and the like.

Finally, there are the *helping services:* public assistance where the problem is a budget deficit, rehabilitation, counseling, guidance, and therapy, as well as supplemental and substitute services ranging from homemakers and home helps to foster care, adoption, training schools, residential treatment centers, day care, budgeting help, family life education, provision of food stamps, home furnishings, prosthetic devices, tutoring, public housing, and so on.

Historically, when welfare state ideology was not widespread and when *laissez faire* coped with poverty and deviance via the Poor Law, the emphasis was neither upon developmental provision nor upon access. Individualized "helping services," available via means tests and moral assessments, sorted out those who would be guided and given interim aid and those whose treatment would be basically punitive. All those seeking help experienced a significant degree of coercion since the assumption was that he who faltered was either culpable or inferior. In any case, social welfare programs could not endanger the prevailing motivational system of an expanding industrialism. Social work, a profession within social welfare, was born in this tradition. As it grew and gained some of the attributes of a knowledge-based and value-conscious discipline, it specialized in individualized services. Moral judgment gave way to social assessment and diagnosis. The component of concern for the individual, for "the least of these," grew. But even diagnostic and assessment processes are value-laden and not free of institutional purpose. Sometimes—too often—the victim was "blamed."[13] Society helped people to adjust and to function, and social work was one of its instruments.

A sensitive practice learns from experience, particularly a practice anchored in a religious and humanistic ethic and always involved through voluntary and church-related programs in softening the blows of broader public neglect and creating exceptions to punitive and obviously unjust provision. Thus, in the early twentieth century and again during the great depression of the 1930s social work played a leading role in refocusing social welfare from individualized helping alone to the efforts at institutional reform and social provision. During the antipoverty and urban crisis efforts of the 1960s there was a redirection within the helping services from personal guidance and therapy to job counseling, training, placement. People were offered the chance to acquire the skills and goals which are the pathway to "opportunity." Then, as the antipoverty effort added its political action phase, there was included the large grassroots organizing component (an evolution out of community organization's coordinating and "enabling" precedents). Finally, direct practice itself, guided by an ideology which understood that the welfare state's rights and entitlements are indeed a new form of property, and that stratification led to a degree of unjust deprivation, began to accent a component of access called *advocacy*. In reality, advocacy, too, had long had its roots in social work and was internationally recognizable as a liaison service, but in political context and through the employment of indigenous personnel it developed both militancy and sophistication in practice.

But case advocacy, seriously pursued, leads to the discovery that some problems cannot be coped with because of inadequacies of provision and institutional failings. It also raises the question of whether efficiency does not demand that some problems be dealt with "wholesale." In short, case advocacy leads to class advocacy as well.

As implied earlier, current sophistication does not permit one to argue for a concept of social welfare, institutionally, which would concern itself with improvement and implementation of developmental provision, while ignoring the also valid case for institutional and legal reform. Nor do universal provision, available as a right, and institutionally directed social action substitute for access services and individualized helping services. Finally, while political milieu and strategy or the dominant ethic may at a given moment accentuate one or another component, none is ever redundant or obsolete.

Long-range social reform may be read as "pie in the sky" by a family needing food stamps today; personal casework help may seem to be a "Band-Aid" to those who need a warm and clean apartment; access services are a diversion if referral is made to an agency with a waiting list; class advocacy may exploit people who need personal help today; case advocacy may discriminate against those without champions. Counseling is hollow if a family needs income. Passing laws will not help tonight's anguish of the man with an anxiety attack.

The issues for a socially oriented profession, for social work concerned as it always has been with person-in-situation, with the personal-institutional interaction [14] are (*a*) whether one profession can encompass all these components and (*b*) whether it can find a way to achieve balance and set priorities at a given moment. Both are difficult.

In short, social welfare strategies are dysfunctional if some of the above components are eliminated, even though there may be short-run priorities and emphases (money, policy, institutional change, helping, access, and so forth). Social work, a social welfare profession but not *all* of social welfare, cannot forgo asking which of all this can be "packaged" by one profession, one system of education, by one ethic and body of knowledge. As the 1970s began, social work was in apparent disarray on the issue: the energies and strategies essential to sound social and political action relating to poverty and racism appeared so to dominate schools, professional associations, and accrediting bodies that the substantive requirements of professional strategy, educational policy, scientific development, and practice advancement were in major eclipse. Social workers passed "relevant" resolutions, supported sound causes, and had a good institutional record on the dominant issues of the day; but there was little evidence that their professional practice was growing, improving, or achieving the quality possible and necessary if an over-all mission as broad as is implied above were to be implemented.[15]

The response to this situation takes two directions. To assure that all of the components have adequate attention, there are some who would see social work as a two-track but unified profession, and they cite the precedent of medicine (medicine and public health) and psychology (clinical or research specialties). The social work tracks are variously defined as: (*a*) direct-service treatment (individual, group, and even community approaches); and (*b*) planning, program development, and administration. Others would organize three tracks: (*a*) direct service; (*b*) planning, program development, and administration; (*c*) grass-roots organizing. The proponents of these conceptions of social work and their several variations generally assume that all social workers can be educated in one system of schools, sharing a common core, and can work together on broader professional issues and in social action through one professional association.

The alternative view, less common now than it was a decade ago, before organizing and planning had their extensive developments, is to question the traditional boundaries and to redefine the social work practitioner. In this view the social worker is capable of direct-service work and advocacy, of a planning contribution and its individualization. Some practitioners may emphasize one component more than the other, but the role is deemed inclusive. Ideologically appealing, the perspective requires evidence that the range of knowledge and skill implied is not excessive and that the patterns of activity covered by the two- or three-track concept do not imply different personality types and predilections. These latter are assumptions difficult to sustain. The existing experiments do not impress. Yet, for lack of resolution, social work finds decision-making difficult.

Targets and Technique

Perhaps because it would like to think of itself as one of the more socially conscious professions—or because it now contains strong representation from underprivileged minorities and operates on the front line of suffering and deprivation—these latter preoccupations are often defined within social work as reflecting excessive professionalism.

The society is too often dominated by technique,[16] redefining problems in accord with technique-based categories. Social priorities are set so that available technique may be used. We build ever faster automobiles and roads on which they may travel at high speed, despite safety hazards and the availability of mass transportation, in part, at least, because the feat is possible. We organize agencies around the task of processing and supervising child placement because that is a specialty, despite the evidence that such organization is not a good way to help families. We make people choose between medical and nonmedical help because each has its own principles of organization, even though the need is for a mix. We create a network of family-helping agencies on the a priori principle that they are and therefore may always be characterized by the casework method.

There are, therefore, those who would reorganize social work training and redefine its expertise on a problem-focused principle, allowing flexible employment of individual and group-helping measures, institutional and policy intervention, self-help stimulation, planning-policy input, and social provision as circumstances may warrant. Conceptually interesting and experimentally seen as viable, this approach may be the way to seek freedom from technique. An alternative, closely related, is to focus on service fields, to become expert in their development and administration. Social work has yet to clarify the commonality of value, knowledge, and skill that would characterize all those in social work and justify turning specific problems or new service fields over to them. Nor is it clear which social problems are to be social work's special domain, in this sense. More basically, even problem definition and conceptualization reflect a value stance, a goal, a *policy*. What is the policy perspective from which social workers are to view deviance, suffering, inequality, dis-ease, conflict, deprivation, or even failure to thrive? Is this not the crucial matter? Does it, then, not define the role clusters and their related knowledge and skill requirements? Social work should and must free itself from dominance by technique and from method dimensions, but it cannot avoid a policy stance from which it may elaborate its practice. While the problem has been put by Harriet Bartlett, among others,[17] there is no satisfactory answer generally accepted by social workers and their institutions.

A shift from a method focus to a problem focus, or a field-of-service focus, however extensive, remains an intraprofessional solution.

There are those who would turn the spotlight on "the community" as problem-definer and solution-finder. In some places and in some fields, certainly in many programs with which social work is associated, consumerism, activism, decentralization, separatism, and community control have all been potent movements with sometimes significant impact on personnel and programs. The debate rages about the phenomenon, its significance, and its validity. We suggest that the needed democratization of social welfare and the general strengthening of consumerism in American society do not relieve professional workers of the need to give leadership where they are expert, to bear witness where they are knowledgeable, to influence where they have opinions, to carry responsibility where they have sanction. Community participation, however valid and significant, does not wipe out all questions and issues on the professional agenda. Specht is right: surely a profession cannot live without individualism, too.[18]

The authors of the papers in this collection discuss in a number of ways the policy base of social work practice and the implications of a particular perspective. They knew from the very structuring of the enterprise and the hypotheses about the current scene that their editor believes that social work as a central (if weak and low-status), emerging profession in the welfare state must suit its role to the requirements of the society and to the roles being otherwise filled. A democratic, humanistic perspective does not permit ruthless sacrifice of people today to goals of ideologists, political leaders, and governments which make promises about tomorrow. It does not recognize violence, curtailment of individual rights or liberties, or the engendering of intergroup hatred as essential to communal progress in the United States, despite many institutional failings and a crisis of confidence in legitimate institutions. Nor does such society accept as valid the allegation that intergenerational interests are so completely at odds as to make collaboration impossible. It knows that redistributional and equitable distributional policies within the basic framework of the current social system, or as a democratically determined evolution out of that system, can enhance the lives of the majority and erase major inequities and injustices. It understands that with the rest of the world we must quickly face the challenge of attaining increased justice between developed and underdeveloped lands and must engage in much joint planning to attain global equilibrium, lest the projections of the Club of Rome prove completely true.

Such direction requires active citizens and legitimate social action. Social workers, as citizens and as organized professionals, may play roles in such enterprises. The welfare state, however, needs more from them. It requires expert professionals, committed to democratic and humanistic values, expert in specific knowledge areas, and skilled for well-defined enterprises. The welfare state, in short, needs leaders, administrators, social inventors, planners, organizers, direct-service practitioners. Social work's traditions, personnel, and professional core leave it positioned for many of these roles if it proves able to update its professional repertoire, strive for greater excellence, and recognize that the well-performed task however technical needs no apology. The welfare state needs politics—but it also needs planning. Neither is meaningful sans ethics, and both must be realized via expertise and skill.

Notes

[1] The popularity and rapid eclipse of Reich illustrate the acceleration of intellectual faddism in our time, generally an age of acceleration. See Charles A. Reich, *The Greening of America* (New York: Random House, 1970).

[2] Alvin Toffler, *Future Shock* (New York: Random House, 1970).

[3] Reich, *op. cit.*, p. 209.

[4] See Danella H. Meadows *et al.*, *The Limits to Growth* (New York: Universe Books, 1972). The Club of Rome is a small, international group exploring worldwide problems from the premise of interdependence of nations and systems.

[5] In 1969, for example, with a gross national product of $932.3 billion, federal government purchases totaled $102 billion; state and local government purchases, $112.7 billion; personal consumption expenditures, $576 billion; and gross private investment, $141.7 billion. *Toward Balanced Growth: Quantity with Quality*, report of the National Goals Research Staff (Washington, D.C.: Government Printing Office, 1970), p. 175.

[6] Eugene Litwak and Henry J. Meyer, "A Balance Theory of Coordination between Bureaucratic Organizations and Community Primary Groups," *Administrative Science Quarterly*, XI (1966), 31–58; also re-

printed in Edwin J. Thomas, ed., *Behavioral Science for Social Workers* (New York: Free Press, 1967), pp. 246–62.

[7] Peter F. Drucker, *The Age of Discontinuity* (New York: Harper and Row, 1969), Chap. XI.

[8] See James Sundquist, *Politics and Policy* (Washington, D.C.: Brookings Institution, 1968; paperback).

[9] For several positions on the "public-voluntary-proprietary" issue, see Alfred J. Kahn, *Social Policy and Social Services* (New York: Random House, 1973; paperback).

[10] The phrasing is that of James Q. Wilson, "The Urban Unease: Community vs. City," *The Public Interest*, No. 12 (1968), p. 25. See Daniel P. Moynihan, ed., *Toward a National Urban Policy* (New York: Basic Books, 1970), p. 334, or Reich: "*Absence of Community*. America is one vast, terrifying anti-community. The great organizations to which most people give their working day and the apartments and suburbs to which they return at night are equally places of loneliness and alienation." (*op. cit.*, p. 7.)

[11] See Alfred J. Kahn, "Do Social Services Have a Future in New York?" *City Almanac*, New School for Social Research, constituting the issue for February, 1971, Vol. V, No. 5. Yet, even as we go to press, there is evidence of renewed interest among social work students in becoming more competent in offering expert personal help. Casework text sales are said to be booming.

[12] For proposals, see Alfred J. Kahn, "Public Social Services: the Next Phase," *Public Welfare*, XXX, No. 1 (1972) 15–24.

[13] William Ryan, *Blaming the Victim* (New York: Pantheon Books, 1971).

[14] For elaboration and for the notion that social work has stressed the integrative view, see Kahn, "The Function of Social Work in the Modern World," in Kahn, ed., *Issues in American Social Work* (New York: Columbia University Press, 1959), pp. 3–38.

[15] For the view that activism, anti-individualism (or better, repression of individual judgment and autonomy), communalism (the group is more likely to be right), and environmental determinism (the problem is the "system," "structure," "elite," but never is us) have all but destroyed social work professionalism and undermined the profession's key functions, see Harry Specht, "Deprofessionalization of Social Work," *Social Work*, XVII, No. 2 (1972), 3–15. Specht believes that unless the unexpected occurs, social work will rapidly be superseded, deserted, or both.

[16] Jacques Ellul, *The Technological Society* (New York: Alfred A. Knopf, Inc., 1964).

[17] Harriet Bartlett, *The Common Base of Social Work Practice* (New York: National Association of Social Workers, 1970).

[18] Specht, *op. cit.*

Carol H. Meyer
❦

DIRECT SERVICES IN NEW
AND OLD CONTEXTS

In these times of global uncertainty, there are only a few alternatives available for social work practitioners who are forced by events to reexamine what they do. Some may bide their time, assuming that the transitional period will end and all will be back to normal again. Others may rely on the "truths" and "insights" of Toffler,[1] Reich,[2] and Illitch[3] as examples of the base line for the future of practice. The distance in time and thought between the older, scientific and the newer, phenomenological emphasis may be too great, and one might question whether the move from old to new would necessarily represent progress. Between these two extreme positions are those social workers who have not thought through the implications of sweeping changes for their practice, since they have not been aware of strain, either because they have been able to learn, adapt to, and manage new practice roles, or because they have been so busy carrying the conflicting burdens of practice that they have not thought much about it.

Whatever the outcome, all must be able to concur in some measure in their view of the world in which practice has to rest. On the whole, professional social work practitioners would have to agree that in some areas of practice there is evidence of cultural lag, while in others, perhaps in an attempt to keep *au courant*, there is evidence of nondifferentiated, scatter-shot approaches to human problems within the social welfare parameter. The source of either commitment may be due to anxiety in the face of change, rigidity in the face of challenge, radicalism in the face of authoritarian establishments, or "pop" inventions in the face of institutional breakdown. Whatever may be their adaptations to the uncertain outcomes, all must be able to attack the issues in rational and intellectual terms.

The Search for Models

Thomas Kuhn asks what causes a profession or a subgroup to abandon one tradition for another. By what process does a new candidate for a paradigm (an exemplar, or pattern) replace its predecessor? He suggests that actions are possible only so long as the paradigm is taken for granted, and that, "therefore, paradigm testing occurs only after persistent failure to solve a noteworthy puzzle has given rise to crisis. And even then it occurs only after the sense of crisis has evoked an alternate candidate for the paradigm." [4] Was Kuhn tuned into the "noteworthy puzzle" that social work practice has been trying to solve for over a half century? The specializations of social casework, group work, and community organization have examined the puzzle, but have not acquired a generic view of the puzzle, much less a coordinated plan for its solution.

Social casework has had as its reference the medical-disease model as originated in Richmond's *Social Diagnosis*,[5] elaborated into a psychosocial formulation in Hamilton's *Theory and Practice of Social Casework*,[6] and further refined as methodology in Hollis's *Casework: a Psychosocial Therapy*.[7] Along quite a different route, the ideas of function and process moved from Taft's *A Functional Approach to Family Casework*,[8] to Robinson's *A Changing Psychology in Social Casework*,[9] to Smalley's *Theory for Social Work Practice*.[10] A third line of effort identified in Perlman's *Casework: a Problem-solving Process*[11] tackled the puzzle in a more eclectic and yet more unitary fashion. Then, more recently, followed Thomas's "Behavioral Modification and Casework," [12] a tightly reasoned formulation that derived from a completely different perception of individual development. Models, paradigms, concepts, ideas, beliefs, and sometimes fads—social casework thought seriously undertook to solve the puzzle, albeit not always with outstanding success. Carel Germain comments:

Following upon our commitment in the ending years of the last century, science and the philosophy of science moved on in new ways and new directions and with new perspectives whereas social casework remained committed to a view of science and the scientific method that became outmoded both in the light of science itself and of the changing human condition. Yet it can and does construct metaphors based on scientific concepts and in doing so must utilize new concepts and themes in science and not those no longer acceptable to science itself.[13]

Social group work has its distinguished theorists, including Konopka,[14] Coyle,[15] Wilson,[16] Vinter, [17] and Schwartz,[18] all of whom approached the puzzle from a particular perspective. Some viewed it as developmental or therapeutic; others viewed it as a process of negotiation between client and agency service. And yet the puzzle remained unsolved. Community organization, coming late into professional practice, has had a great deal of intellectual activity in recent years. Through its prominent theorists, Brager,[19] Morris,[20] and Ross,[21] for example, its perspective has ranged from the organization of established community groups to grass-roots organizing and social planning, and still there has been no solution to the puzzle.

We would not expect total and final solutions, of course, but it must be faced that within the professional family there is little agreement about the validity of our several approaches, the communities we serve are unclear about what we do, and the public at large has given social work an uncertain mandate. This professional confusion will not be so easy to dissolve either, because we are dealing with different paradigms in casework, group work, and community organization. We cannot assess a unified practice in theory or in action, because one does not exist.

The fact that there is not a unitary practice, the modes of which all participants in professional social work could agree upon, does not seem to be the most serious problem in the field. A profession can survive for centuries and yet contain a range of contradictory theories, propositions of uneven weight, conflicting ideologies, and methods and techniques that vary from the staid, tried-and-true to the hit-and-miss. Look at medicine, with its expertise ranging from complicated organ transplantation to acupuncture. And look at law, seemingly able to contain strict constructionist Supreme Court justices and poverty lawyers in the same profession. It is not the search for an all-encompassing paradigm that is in question but rather the search for a rationale, a context that would provide for different kinds and levels of practice interventions and yet would allow for differences in special interests, in the accumulation of specialized knowledge and the development of particular skills, and above all, in meeting differentiated human need as defined within the boundaries of social welfare. It is intellectual inquiry that will connect social work practice with the people to whom it is obligated; it is rational thinking that will supplant isms of any kind, be they traditionalisms or radicalisms; it is empirical evidence that will offer the proof of practice performed. The field of social work might need a series of paradigms for the range of its work, but the present plight seems to be that in large measure there either are no paradigms functioning at all, or there are paradigms of such limited dimensions that they cannot apply to the breadth of social welfare's concerns.

The Challenge of Crisis

As Kuhn suggests, however, a profession does not seek new ways or new contexts until it feels the challenge of crisis. The 1960s made clear the challenge, for causes were taken to the street, and professional social work practice suffered recriminations aplenty for its supposed lack of relevance, its cloistered methodological commitments, its avoidance of political action, and the accusation that it was part of the problem because it was not part of the solution. Traditional practice was shaken up, and the crisis was felt by everyone. By 1972 the political climate had changed; action retrenched, and one could detect a "turn inward" among students, for example. Whether this reaction was due to the lack of durability of intense feelings, frustration in the face of unyielding institutions, or temporary surrender during a period of political reaction, one cannot easily determine. The fact is, however, that outright public attacks on social work have not softened appreciably, as evidenced in official disinterest and disapproval expressed through massive budget cuts for all social work programs in practice and education. Also, there continue to be sporadic challenges from increasing numbers of organized groups of Chicanos, blacks, and Puerto Ricans, both those served and those not served by social workers. Further, there is a rise of self-help groups like Birth Right, Mothers Anonymous, Synanon, encounter groups, and so on, all seeming to say that they can do better by themselves than social workers have been able to do for them. Finally, lack of clarity and mastery of the issue of differential roles of social work manpower has provided an outlet for public agency administrators and private agency boards who seem to prefer nonprofessional (or undergraduate) workers even when professionals are available. Is it only because nonprofessionals cost less? Is it really because young professional practitioners are too militant these days? Or is it because agencies find it hard to differentiate what indeed the two levels of staff can do when they carry out practice tasks?

In light of these challenges and the questions they reflect, what would be most convincing to social work practitioners, educators, and administrators of the need to rethink the solutions to the human puzzle? Would it be accumulated data? Or a new consciousness about social work's professionalism and its self-serving aspects? Or a polemical argument about values and commitment? Perhaps all of these are needed, but in addition, and most particularly, there should be a call for intellectual inquiry and a hard look at the evidence.

The contexts of social work practice are a mélange of values, knowledge, skills, commitments, and patterns of service. To the extent that these contexts remain out of touch with the world as it is, the world will have little need of social workers. New contexts, arising from the old and taking their cues from the ways of the world, will, on the contrary, alert society to a modern practice whose expertise derives in part from hard expert knowledge, in part from being aware of what clients need and want, and in part from being a socially oriented profession that is dedicated to individualizing human services for people with problems in living.

Four issues continue to plague the practice of social work as it seeks new contexts: the uncertain purposes of social work practice; the limited uses of empirical knowledge; the restrictions imposed by the medical disease model; and the constraints upon service delivery.

The Uncertain Purposes
of Social Work Practice

All professions exist for purposes defined by society, and social work, perhaps the one most responsive to social mandate, is foundering in the networks of many mixed messages. In order to demonstrate a coherent and socially condoned practice, sooner or later it will be necessary to define the purposes to which we put our knowledge, skills, and practice wisdom. Without a sense of purpose, all social work processes are nondifferentiated from other helping processes, ranging from those provided by psychiatry, psychology, and the ministry to community self-help groups and problem-focused groups of people who share similar afflictions. In Kahn's "view of the world," *everyone* is suffering from a sense of rootlessness and alienation in a society of whirling transience and impermanence. We are all victims of failing institutions and we have developed a hardened cynicism that reflects a massive credibility gap between rising expectations and social provision. Primary groups are failing, and we are left by society to invent spontaneous supports for our lives, supports that are themselves transient—and fragmented. If this view is even approximately true, then the human troubles of our society surely are broader in scope and more pervasive than a mere profession plying its trade can expect to cope with.

Yet, society needs to partialize its efforts, and social work practice has been allocated responsibility for "social services." The reality of the times in America suggests that these services will continue to be case services, despite the fact that it is all too evident that a more equitable distribution of jobs and income, planned housing, adequate health care and nutrition, a stimulating program of education, sufficient and imaginative leisure-time provisions, and more livable cities would make case services the lesser thrust in social welfare. However, since case services are presently the chief entree into improved social welfare, it will be through the direct and indirect management of these services that social work practitioners will make their stab at improving the human condition.

Social control as a purpose of social work practice is not an idea that would sit well within the value system of the profession; yet the effectiveness of practice is so often judged by numbers of cases closed, families off relief, patients out of hospitals, children placed indiscriminately in foster care, and offenders sent to correctional facilities, that one must at times wonder if the chief aim of social work practice is to make things tidy for social institutions. Perhaps this is the very mandate that society has held out. Perhaps this has come about because of the structure of the agencies in which social workers practice—the courts, schools, public welfare departments, hospitals, and so forth. Despite the desire of young workers to see their roles differently, we are living in a highly charged society, and social institutions that use social workers often exert absolute power over the life styles of their clientele. To the degree that hospitals and clinics affirm therapeutic and remedial goals, social workers may find kinder hosts in such settings, but too often the practice role is defined by the hospital as aiding the patient to adapt to institutional requirements. Sometimes those demands are arbitrary and unreasonable, having to do with bureaucratic rules, questions of professional authority and misunderstandings. In recent years, through systems formulations and broadening of practice roles, social workers have come to perceive the possibilities of helping clients negotiate those aspects of institutions that are contradictory to their well-being and autonomy so that social control might diminish as even an unconscious objective of social work practice.

Then there are noninstitutional aspects of social control that appear to derive from practice wisdom, theoretical formulations, and ideologies created not by institutional requisites, but by the field of social work itself. In voluntary family and child welfare agencies, for example, where the direction of practice does not rely upon goals defined by other professional disciplines or legal mandates, social workers are, in effect, in charge of their own purposes. What purposes, then, are served by maintaining obstacles to the family visiting of children in placement? What part of society has ruled that a homemaker should report to the social worker about the intimate life of a family? Whose standard determines that a poor family is "multiproblemed" and not amenable to high-quality services?

Do such goals of practice derive from practice wisdom or from

Social Darwinism? Has professional expertise, without our realizing it, led us to the brink of social control? If so, it will not have been the first time. In the early twentieth century the settlement movement promoted hard work and healthful activity when "good" and "evil" were the significant constructs.[22] After the Second World War, therapy was the modal intervention when "sick" and "well" were the constructs by which the case was viewed. In the 1950s, before *The Other America* [23] set off a rediscovery of poverty, socialization of "multiproblem" families became an accommodating intervention when those families were a burden to the community and did not fit into known clinical classifications.[24] Was this once again a practice function that would mold the recipient group into the proper behavior? The 1960s brought their own form of behavioral "disorder," and perhaps it was not coincidental that behavioral modification became a popular mode of practice.

Constructs of any kind focus our vision; thus we must at least be aware of the myths and metaphors we use, for they are fictions that might serve as the basis of an idea. But when the fictions are mistaken for reality, we tend to clasp them as our truth. Are these constructs of "good" and "bad," "sick" and "well," "multiproblem," "hard-to-reach" all so different? Has practice functioned at one and the same time as educative, socializing, moralizing, and therapeutic? Is it social control in many guises of the poor, the deviant, the "problem" group, so that they do not disturb the *status quo* of middle-class morality? To the degree that social work practice continues to seek definitions of this order and to develop practice modalities to cure the "sick" and socialize the multiproblemed, the field will be straddling its ambivalence forever. Are we not, really, talking about the poor when we talk about a multiproblemed client? The song from *Finian's Rainbow* [25] explains:

> When a rich man doesn't want to work, he's a *bon-vivant*,
> But when a poor man doesn't want to work, he's a loafer,
> He's a lounger, he's a lazy good-for-nothing, he's a jerk.

The fact is that purposes vary within social work practice itself. For example, social workers deal with the problems of psychosocially endowed clients as they are defined by the clients themselves, but they use a different standard of motivation for help when work-ing with less-well-endowed clients. It remains at the least a sign of ambivalence in purpose when clients who go to public agencies when they are in trouble with society confront a practice that is of a different order than that met by clients who go with contained problems to voluntary agencies. It would seem that there must be a better, overriding construct that will unify social work practice.

There are other possibilities, and to the degree that social work practice will keep pace with society, new purposes will become more determining of practice. When these new purposes develop, or at least when they become integrated into the professional con-sciousness, they undoubtedly will influence practice processes, just as, indeed, our past use of processes has been influenced by our prior assumptions of goals. Not only social workers but also social agen-cies have been permanently affected by the turmoil of the 1960s. Even if the political scene in America were to keep turning back-ward, no institution would ever again be the same, once having ex-perienced the overt and covert power in the concept of community participation. Will there ever again be an American university that excludes students from its decision-making bodies? Will there ever again be a board of directors of a hospital or social agency that will not include representation from its constituent community? Will any political party, corporation, construction company, union, bank, or educational system survive long without increasing the ratio of its minority personnel?

Consider the effects upon professional decisions that derive from expertise in a child placement agency, for example. The decision to place a child and the authority to set the ground rules before, dur-ing, and after that experience have been enjoyed in the past almost totally by social workers. Will the newly formed Foster Parents As-sociation not make a difference to the mode of practice?

This Association is not merely a group of foster parents who are invited annually to the Christmas party at the agency; it has within it the potential power and possibly the inclination to effect changes in the actual behavior of the social worker responsible for supervis-ing placements. And what outcomes might be foreseen if natural parents organized themselves to clarify their legal rights to visit children and to have services on their own behalf while their children are in placement? And when mental patients, parents of school children, and young community residents organize, all demanding services as they define them, what effect will they have upon practice? Social work will have to move with seven-league boots in order to find a purpose that would govern these threads of interest. It hardly seems likely that social workers will continue to straddle those impossible goals of help and social control. It will no longer be possible to be the benevolent policemen of social institutions, and *at the same time* the link between service and help and the client constituencies. Social work has long suffered from this ambivalent purpose, but it might yet be saved from continuing embarrassment by allowing itself to listen to its clients define the terms of service provision, if not the actual modes of help.

The idea of consumerism has become commonplace in America, whether it be through the efforts of Ralph Nader, local consumer protection agencies, or consumer groups themselves. All are asking for a part in improving products and services. Consumerism is everywhere, and social workers, to the extent that they are exposed to the public view, will not be the last to hear demands upon their skills and knowledge. Consumerism will test our mettle; the people we serve will let us know whether or not they are being served as they really want.

With purposes no longer haunted by the specter of social control, there is a host of alternative approaches available in the social work practice repertoire: help in accordance with client wants rather than defined needs, [26] crisis-oriented brief services; [27] planned short-term treatment; [28] problem-solving processes; [29] use of group processes to negotiate systems; [30] individualization to countermand institutional impersonality; [31] diagnostically oriented casework help, task development, group experiences, and so on. The extension of options of service in accordance with individual client life styles and value choices seems to be a crucial concept to weave into the fabric of new contexts for social work practice. But even yet we have not completed our exploration into the commitment to the old in attempting to solve the "noteworthy puzzle." So many questions are raised that it is not enough to debate propositions, to provide an array of helping modes, and to affirm new goals. There is more that defines the boundaries of practice, and we must probe more deeply.

The Limited Uses of Empirical Knowledge

In 1959, Alfred Kadushin [32] sounded a hopeful note about the future of research and the development of the knowledge base in social work. In 1959 it seemed that social work was on the right track, pursuing its own knowledge of social processes and selectively utilizing derivative knowledge from the social and behavioral sciences. Yet, although research methodology proliferated in the ensuing years, it did not seem that the practice that evolved derived from cumulative empirical knowledge to any large extent. True, there has been a major research thrust in these years, with perhaps an overweening emphasis upon evaluative rather than basic research, but the field still seems to be plagued by halting research methodology, and more significantly by the amazing lack of replication of studies. Perhaps the knowledge explosion has overwhelmed those who would try to keep up with new data and to sift sound from unsound findings. To affirm that there is more research is not to say that it is all of equal validity nor is it to say that the field at large makes use of its findings.

Is it possible that social work's lack of reliance upon systematic, empirical work has something to do with the field's uncertain value commitments and its multiple perceptions as to what exactly the field of social work is uniquely, and what precisely one ought to be expert about in his practice? For example, if the profession had an agreed-upon arena of practice, such as in child welfare, and this were defined to the satisfaction of all the constituents involved, there would be self-evident, researchable possibilities, the results of which would undoubtedly be binding upon practice. But the fact is that the field has not settled upon even a compromise view of child welfare, much less the purposes of social work practice in that area. Thus, the existing research is disregarded on ideological grounds, on the basis of value preferences rather than on empirical evidence.

To illustrate, reputable studies have appeared about children in foster care, such as Weinstein's *The Self-Image of the Foster Child*.[33] If the author's recommendations had been followed, the nature and methods of working with children in placement would have been changed. The work was published in 1960 and is now out of print; and the methods of working with children in foster care still do not reflect the implications of that study. Other, perhaps more important, studies have dealt with other aspects of children in placement and out of placement, with day care as a social provision, with the selection of foster parents, and so on and so forth. While we are not here evaluating particular research, it would seem that there are other considerations besides the power of knowledge derived empirically. There are considerations on the level of values that derive, for instance, from the shortage of foster homes, the debate as to whether placement is inherently better than maintenance of a child in his deficient own home or in group care, and the lack of skilled child welfare workers to carry out the mandates of any program. Such "real" policy issues as well as purely ideological ones continue to exert powerful control over practice, despite the emergence of new knowledge.

Perhaps, also, one must confront the philosophical idea that in truth, empirically assembled knowledge, the study of events now past, holds decreasing interest in a world that moves so quickly and is viewed as existential. Perhaps there is no *fin de siècle* statement possible any more; perhaps we exist in a world where language and not its substance is the controlling variable. Maybe thus we can account for fads and instant experts, and rhetorical demands for change without knowledge of change for what and to what purpose. It is also possible that in a systems perspective, which must surely be an accommodation to the complexity of the world, the bombardment of our senses through multimedia stimuli and jet travel that reduces time and space, has made some kinds of research and use of empirical data almost dysfunctional. For every problem explored through research done on one or two levels of interaction, there is always the question: "But what if another intervening variable were introduced?" Partializing is no longer as helpful a concept as "cross-sectioning," so that we will be assured of including all the elements of a problem in the piece we study. But do we have the capacity for such a prismatic view that would enable us to detect exactly all the necessary components of a single phenomenon?

Reliance upon empirical data has not been a hallmark of professional social work practice, partly because of our tools and objectives of research, but also, perhaps, because we have not yet agreed upon the goals and boundaries of social work practice.

The Constraints of the Medical Model

For a humanistic practice profession it is obvious that direct knowledge of people, obtained through repeated observations and face-to-face contact, must underlie the work that is done by the professional involved. The quality of any practice is assessed by what is actually done, whether building bridges, performing surgery, or presenting a case in court. Theories of practice are never ends in themselves, and extensive or intensive background knowledge only has value when it is put to use. Otherwise, its aquisition would be merely an academic pursuit. Traditionally in social casework, and more recently in group work, this direct experience with clients has been called "clinical" experience. According to Webster's dictionary, "clinical" implies direct attention *at the bedside of a patient*. Considering the fact that the diagnostic theme is derivative from medicine, as is the notion of treatment, the concept of clinical knowledge has not been alien to the structure of social work practice. However, it has been limiting of both knowledge and practice to the degree that it has tended to confine social caseworkers to "the bedside" more or less, and thus they have not been fully conscious of the real life style of clients. This limitation has made it difficult in recent years to wrest practitioners from the clinic to the world "outside," to entice them to assess psychosocial problems in nonmedical contexts, to view health and adaptation as well as pathology, and to enable them to place as high a value upon modes of *help* as upon the more constricting, goal-directed concept of *treatment*.

Apart from the limitations upon modes of help, concentration on clinical entities has proved to be less fruitful today than in previous decades when there seemed to be greater certainty as to the etiology of disease states than can be supported through current research efforts. A pathological state like schizophrenia once flagged immediate treatment prescriptions to social work practitioners, since the condition was assumed to be clinically definable and thus dictated specific practice interventions. Today, there is much research along contradictory lines of thought as to the meaning of schizophrenia,[34] investigating its etiology in biochemistry, family relationships, genealogy, and in the confused state of the world itself. Alcoholism is under similar inquiry, even to the point where it is thought to be no disease at all, but a condition of life induced by particular social configurations. Drug addiction we know as the classic example of pathology that few people know anything definitively about so far as etiology and cure are concerned. While some might think that the source of drug addiction is in the poppy fields of Turkey and the cure is avoidance by means of methadone, physical incarceration, or in encounter groups, there has hardly been a notable role for social work practice in determining cause or cure or, in fact, in helping addicts. As for our once pleasant association with classical neurosis, the middle-aged neurotics with symptoms who were raised in the post-Victorian era may have either used up all the couches provided by psychoanalysts, or by now found a workable accommodation to life. In any event, one would be hard pressed to define the anomie, malaise, and alienation found in our cities and towns as due to psychic pressures alone, deriving primarily from neurotic roots defined in original Freudian terms.

Clinical certainties have vanished, along with some other cherished truths, values, traditions, and behaviors. Despite the presence of their remnants, it would appear unlikely in 1973 that the dysfunctional psychosocial manifestations in the world could be totally explained by theories of neurosis or psychosis, particularly as they are uncovered in the narrow clinical context. The core of social work practice can no longer be directed to the vanishing breed of clients from which we gained our certainty.

Yet, we have available a general ego psychology that has provided constructs such as coping and adaptation which have made possible a view of personality that is open to environmental influences, as indeed it affects environment. It would seem that the modern uses of this psychological framework have made possible social work's consideration of development, growth, and health, necessitating less preoccupation with intrapsychic conflict, symptoms, and psychopathology, and thus less restraint placed upon practice by clinical determinants. Furthermore, the appearance of interpersonal constructs, particularly as described by family therapists and communication theorists, has made possible explanatory notions that are no longer restricted to clinical entities.

Current literature, practice examples, and revised graduate school curricula seem to suggest that the day of the medical model is over, or at least that there is a concerted effort to replace it. However, it is likely that the transition to a newer context for practice will continue to be arduous for the profession of social work for two reasons. First, old allegiances do not just dissolve, even when confronted with new demands and new knowledge, and new languages do not necessarily indicate new contexts. Second, antidiagnostic practice modalities described as "new" solutions to conceptual problems will not take root unless they rest in knowledge and tested experience. It would appear that the only way out of becoming overwhelmed with new modalities, and with no framework in which to place them, is to reconceptualize the framework itself; it would never do for a profession, even one as young as social work, to utilize competing approaches based upon ideology alone. We seem to be beyond the struggle between the old and the new, and so our search proceeds.

The Constraints upon Service Delivery

A professional practice that is defined by its knowledge of theories, its methods, processes, modalities, and techniques, is meaningless to all but its own practictioners if it is not delivered appropriately to those who need its services. A public health-medical example comes to mind. It is many years since the Salk and Sabine medications were discovered and polio was found to be completely preventable. Yet in 1971 over three million American children[35] did not have access to this simple, cheap, foolproof method of preventing polio.

Moving to a social work practice example, we can use a relatively simple procedure, like helping an adolescent, unmarried mother return to school after the birth of her baby, and to work out some child-caring arrangements. In neither example is the problem simple; we are referring only to the helping system. Once the Salk vaccine was discovered, and once the resources for the support of a young, single mother's needs were identified, the actual process of help itself would not be excessively complex. Yet, if there are *x* thousands of young, single mothers in this country and social workers serve a mere 2 percent of them, then 98 percent are not served. Assuming that even half of that number do not want social work services, the 2 percent hardly makes a dent on the half that might want service.

The most refined techniques of working with unmarried mothers are relatively insignificant if social work practitioners are so located that they do not see most of the girls even to offer the service. If only a fraction of the unmarried mothers would ever be known to clinical workers, or if the problem is seen primarily in terms of the girl's decision to keep or place the baby, so that only the merest fraction of willing girls become clients, then it would be fair to say that the population-at-risk is actually unserved. Is one answer to broaden the agency's boundaries so as to serve all young, single women in a defined community? Or, barring structural change in traditional agencies and clinics, would it be more serving of client need to locate practitioners in well-baby clinics, or maternity wards, where the need of such mothers would be apparent? Professionally defined problems are not always commensurate with the actual existence of problems.

Despite the cumulative record of clients served by a variety of agencies, raw numbers have little meaning outside their epidemiological context. To some extent, the way in which social work practice counts its cases has to do with the way in which agencies define their boundaries. However, there are other limiting factors to the stand taken by practitioners, having to do with ambivalent purposes, limited use of empirical knowledge, and constrictions in the clinical context. In some fashion, this all adds up to the view of the world assumed by social workers. Were we to conceive of the population at large as in need of individualizing human services because of the depersonalization and bureaucratization of a life that is full of personal strain, then we would have to assess present social work services against quite a large population parameter. Or, were we to assess our services against a narrower population-at-risk, we would still find our services matched against a large gap. The way we do count case services is usually constrained by the cases we know, the ones that are already within the agency's boundary—the ones we have screened in, perhaps because they suit our methodology, our sense of professional status, or even our personal tastes. This selection process makes for successful work and often for very busy social workers, but it does not deliver case services to the unknown numbers of people in need of service, who for one reason or another have not been screened into the system. Nor does it make a mark for social work practice in the society at large that expects social work to be expert in its practice, but also accountable in its coverage of any defined client group. In the search for new contexts, the pressures created by demands for quantity as well as quality will have the most powerful effect.

The Strains in Coping with the "New"— Manpower and Knowledge

Whatever the causes of resistance to change and whatever the distance between the way the world seems to turn and the convolutions of social work practice, there is one reality that has to be confronted, willingly or not. The practice of social work as taught by educators, managed by administrators, and carried out by practitioners will continue to be overwhelmed by the manpower "numbers game" and inundated by "new" approaches added to the present armamentarium. Just as the field was caught unawares and ultimately seemed to turn inward as a result of the attacks upon practice in the 1960s, so the impact of greater demand in quantity of service and in range of practice modalities could tend to paralyze the field in the 1970s . . . unless.

Let us specify the problem. An illustration might be found in the separation of eligibility investigation from the delivery of service.

Today, a state with a large urban population might set the desirable caseload for an individual worker at sixty-five families. In child welfare, where protective service demands intensive casework, fifteen or twenty families may be the standard. We are forced to ponder, then, what arrangements will be made when "separation" of eligibility from the service function becomes a reality—if it ever does. The impact of social work practice will be truly felt at the point where the ordinary, middle-class citizen needing help from a social worker will begin to expect the public agency to attend to his needs as well as to those of the citizen who receives public assistance. What, then, will the "numbers game" do to the sixty-five-family caseload? As a matter of fact, what indeed can the practitioner do now with such a caseload?

Another example: assuming that the practice of social work were to become modal for services combined with other bureaucratic functions, and social workers were viewed by the community as necessary for survival in the urban society, would there ever be enough professional social workers to carry out this mandate? And to the extent that the medical-disease model remains as the primary context, will professionals ever be able to let in lesser skilled and knowledgeable workers to help carry out the mandate? Further assuming, in another example, that social work practice were to be regarded as a requisite discipline in community mental health, or home-care medical treatment, how large would a caseload have to be before the practitioner groaned under its weight?

Finally, if in this decade it came to pass that social work practitioners were able to carve out individualizing helping roles in day care centers, well-baby centers, public schools, housing complexes, and other developmental institutions and social utilities, the "numbers game" would defeat us before we began—if we continued to use the medical-disease model of practice under whatever guise. Perhaps, as we find in 1973, the apparent return to traditional methods is not so much reflective of a change in commitment as of lack of confidence in being able to grasp all the threads of practice and weave them into a whole network of practice ideas.

Parallel to the stress brought about by questions of manpower deployment and demands for services is that brought on by the often enticing presence of new practice modes. The attempt to paste on anything new to existing conceptualizations in an effort to modernize practice ultimately will frustrate even the highest-minded, most flexible, and strongest practitioners, administrators, and educators among us. "What, do family treatment when I already have twenty-five individual cases plus one group of adolescents?" Pity the poor practitioner. What else will we ask him to do? The educator who has crammed the practice sequence full to overflowing with theories about working with individuals of all ages, on all levels of psychosexual development, illustrative of all known clinically defined problems with various levels of ego strength, in all fields that define the ways those individuals are worked with, may indeed freeze when confronted with the necessity to teach as well theories of group process, the varied kinds of groups, new knowledge about family treatment and how it differs from traditional casework and group work. Then add theories of advocacy, crisis intervention, brief treatment, social brokerage, community processes, work with self-help groups and with agency structures in need of change—the mind boggles.

In a normal two-year program of graduate education enough is enough, and we have not yet even introduced the problems of working with nonprofessional social workers in typical social work practice. No, it will not do. The whole is greater than the sum of its parts, and merely adding all that is new will not solve our intellectual tensions any more than adding more and more graduates to the scene will solve the manpower problem. For each demonstration of success will create further demands, and indeed the boundaries of social work practice are at this moment not sufficiently defined for our field to say that we need x number of workers to do a certain kind of job.

How to use nonprofessional manpower is probably the most serious question confronting social work practice. It is uniquely a threat to the front-line practitioner, who will have to remodel his practice to permit others to enter his world of expertise. One finds cavalier acceptance of new uses of manpower among administrators, perhaps for unfortunate reasons. Among those who teach and those who devise programs there seems to be little support for the benighted practitioner who must make the accommodations. The educational continuum remains a continuum of mystery and challenge. The concern that the entrance of the worker with a bachelor's degree in social work will create a Gresham's Law of social work practice, and "bad" workers will drive out "good" is a reflection of the idea that he is conceived of as bad and the worker with a master's degree as good. This polarity can be avoided by facing the fact that there are complementary roles to be played; but again, these will depend upon new perceptions of practice. Like new knowledge and new practice modalities, new manpower strategies will depend upon how practice is conceptualized. It will be quite impossible to take the therapeutic, medical-diagnostic, linear cause-effect model of practice and paste upon it a manpower strategy that will go beyond using nonprofessional manpower as aides, messengers, record keepers, friendly visitors, and the like. Something new cannot be added: something different has to be devised.

Tangential to the manpower deployment issue, but not to be viewed in the same context, is the question of the relationship of social work practice to indigenous self-help groups. It may prove to be a test of the humanistic (as opposed to the professional) commitment of social workers as to whether or not there will be a working relationship between these helping efforts. Is the Fortune Society, a self-help group of ex-prisoners, for example, to be part of the social work effort to help ex-prisoners live in the world with a degree of success? If so, there will be no hierarchy involved, because the Fortune Society would win "in men's eyes." There would have to be a differential allocation of tasks, and social workers would have to be clear about their purposes so that it would be possible to sit down with the Fortune Society and come to agreement about the tasks in which each group would be most expert.

All of these new demands, be they for quantity services, flexibility in using new modes of service, or acceptance of other than professional practitioners—both nonprofessional workers and self-help groups—point to a new road to travel. Only new contexts will keep the field from being as overwhelmed by change as the clients with whom we would hope to work. The reconceptualization of practice is the least that can be done, for we have found that adding on without intrinsic change can be in itself an overwhelming experience.

The usual way out of the dilemmas posed here is for the field to assert that there are enough problems for a range of approaches to suit every occasion and to reflect every ideology. It would appear that this atomized view of practice expresses where social work practice is at present. Yet, it is hard to avoid the thought that far from being a solution, this begs the question. How will social workers be deployed and, indeed, how will they be educated for the range of problems encountered by the field? Will there be a therapeutic case/group worker specialist for pathological clients, and a wide-ranging helper/individualizing generalist for "normal" clients? Who will man the treatment facilities while the social work practitioner is in the streets? In other words, what of the "real" case problems that require intensive case or group treatment if the field attends to the consumerism issues that reflect the more commonplace concerns of the ordinary person?

If we were to continue to dichotomize along these linear lines, we would continue to maintain hierarchies in practice, where some few therapeutic practitioners would go in one direction, treating the smallest number of clients in traditional and perhaps outmoded ways. At the same time, the social workers would be trying to cope with the everyday problems of people and would be struggling to devise tasks for themselves and for the nonprofessional workers. No, to pose the dilemma in this way is to force a split in practice.

There seems to be some hope that the creation of a generic core of practice—bringing together group work, casework, and community organization—would somehow solve the present dilemmas. Of course, the field cannot any longer define itself along methodological boundaries; but without a different context for practice, it is possible that the bringing together of these specialties would upon analysis turn out to be doing just that. It might prove to be a bringing together of reluctant lovers into a connubial bed, only to find that when the marriage broker has gone and the lights are out, one has kicked the other out of bed. Furthermore, through a series of intimate bargaining sessions they have agreed to act as a couple in public, but in private one is sleeping in the bed and one on the sofa.

Casework and group work might fool the world for some time, but the marriage would indeed become complicated by the entrance of community organization methods. Where would C.O. sleep? Perhaps, in order to keep the family secret, C.O. would keep watch at the window to alert them all to the presence of onlookers. Out of this family neurosis, building quietly because none of the intimates really wants to be a family, it is not inconceivable to imagine that outside, the neighborhood wise man, who never went to college, and his little hippie friend, a flower child and an ex-member of VISTA, unencumbered by traditional arguments, are actually taking over the helping function in the street below.

Transitional crises indeed contain the seeds of threat or promise.

A Systems Framework

It would be insufficient to reconceptualize a practice by merely placing it in a systems framework. Many issues would be left unresolved by simply renaming phenomena and relocating practitioners in its scheme. The transition from linear to systemic thinking involves fundamental changes in practice, particularly in the perception of the "case" or the unit of attention and in the utilization of manpower. We have commented upon both these elements of practice as being crucial to the viability of social work in the modern world; a systems framework makes possible at last a context that could provide for quantity as well as for quality services, for expertise as well as for service delivery. If the field can satisfy these two requirements, it will have moved a long way toward solving the "noteworthy puzzle."

Is there, upon reflection, a single problem involving social work practice today that can be defined in any way but through its systemic complications? A sophisticated view of practice would suggest that there is no purity to clinical definitions of pathological states; there is no unique or master theory that explains behavioral-societal manifestations; there is no classification of persons that is airtight; there are fewer and fewer dependable symptoms, few replicable behaviors, and no useful classifiable etiology of problems.

Apparently there is no single treatment prescription. For a field that has followed the medical model for so long, these are serious charges.

In the linear, psychosocial framework, problems are assessed along the range of psychological to social phenomena, with one emphasis being greater than the other in some cases. Actually, knowledge of psychological phenomena has been more unified, definitive, and compelling, so that in the linear approach, attention to the social part of the framework has been almost peripheral. In comparing knowledge and action possibilities of the psychological and social polarities, it has been no contest; the pivotal construct has remained psychological. No amount of pressure could "put the social back into social casework" because the power of the knowledge of the individual was overwhelming and therefore determined practice techniques. It was impossible to stretch the techniques based upon one half of the concept to cover the other half. The social part of the equation did not have a definitive, unified theory to draw upon, and it contained too many variables, most of them unreachable from the point of view of a practitioner. It is small wonder that when social workers found it impossible to effect real changes in the milieu, or even to comprehend social forces, they fell back to viewing the "case," defined essentially in psychological terms. At least one could do something about one family member's feeling toward another, so why not remain in that locus, especially, for example, when the housing situation was devastating and public assistance budgets were meager?

In a different world it might seem so, but in this present reality where people are highly interdependent with all social institutions and of necessity rely upon social provision, because the decline of primary groups and the rise of urban impersonality have woven each individual into the crazy-quilt fabric of society, it has become apparent that family members' feelings are colored, shaped, and determined by their intimate environmental situations, including culture, class, and ethnicity, as much as by their individual personality development. A systems perspective allows for viewing the family in that context, while the linear view that polarizes psychological and social influences in a case tends to weight the efforts of the practitioner to the psychological side of the line.

So far as service delivery is concerned, the logic of the linear approach would continue to lead practitioners to select and concentrate on those decreasing number of families whose environment is not so impaired as to make them less accessible for psychological treatment. The question we face today is whether this model can survive the demands of quantity service, or even of professional accountability, to cope with the kinds of problems that are pressing in the world—not the kinds that make for neat and tidy and gratifying psychotherapeutic work. A linear view thus raises questions of relevance and viability.

Manpower utilization is one of the major keys to improved quantity and thus to delivery of social services. A systems perspective permits the argument that imaginative use and deployment of manpower teams, as in the model of the Episode of Service,[36] where an array of competencies can be made available to clients, would also enhance the quality of services. In a systems framework, where concepts of input and output and of reciprocity take on meaning, we can cease our unending search for cause and effect. We find in the notion of equifinality that there is more than one way to achieve an outcome in a case because each action taken will rebound upon another which will set in motion yet other movements for change. These actions or tasks may be of long or short duration, or repetitive; since they are not restricted to personality change effected through the highly structured one-to-one psychotherapeutic interview, some tasks may be better carried out by a worker with a master's degree, or by one with a bachelor's degree, or by a member of the group being served. Not only would there be no damage to the helping process to include at some phase the services of a self-help group, but it would appear necessary to take advantage of the experience and skills of such a consumer group.

The framework makes possible imaginative uses of all levels of manpower, each working according to his own ability achieved through a combination of training and experience. The burden of a caseload of sixty-five families would be quite different were that caseload managed by a professional social worker as leader of a social work team. The availability of such a team undoubtedly would loosen the restraints upon an agency's intake policy, and probably would make it more practical for agencies to seek out unserved cases in the community. The availability of social work personnel with diverse skills and energies to apply to the fluid case situation in all of its psychological dimensions inevitably would broaden and enrich the repertoire of service modalities, just as it would extend the impact of the social work practitioner in the community.

What does the systemic framework do to the case as the unit of attention? It simply expands the conceptual and actual boundaries within which the practitioner employs his knowledge and skills. The case might be defined as a person, a family, a hospital ward, a housing complex, a particular neighborhood, a school population, a group with particular problems and needs, or a community with common concerns. Where a large case is involved, like a school, work can be allocated to social work teams in accordance with grades, age levels, or whatever administrative arrangements make sense. The drawing of a systemic boundary rather than a linear one provides for the true psychosocial perception of a case, because it includes the significant inputs into the lives of the individuals involved.

What would a typical case look like as it might be assigned to a graduate social work practitioner and his team? It might be one floor of a large public housing project, a hospital's emergency room, a neighborhood service center, a square city block, a pediatric ward, an outpatient clinic in a psychiatric facility, two cottages in a residential treatment center, or a geographic area in which there were parents with children in foster care. The case then, might be defined geographically, functionally, or according to problem or interest groupings. The responsibility of the practitioner would be to use his team and himself, directly and indirectly as the case demanded, to assess the needs and problems of the individuals involved and to intervene through all available human and physical resources. Where changing visiting hours in a pediatric ward is the task, for instance, this would be a helping (therapeutic?) action affecting all of the families involved. This achieved, if a family does not visit a child, another level of case intervention is required. Where medical information is needed by the parents, or where the disease of certain children has unusual consequences, group meetings of parents might be productive. These actions could be undertaken while each child was in individual, daily contact with members of the team most qualified through skill, experience, or identification to visit with him. Accountability would not be assessed by numbers of interviews held with doctors, nurses, parents, children, but by criteria that would describe well-being, autonomy—or whatever "success" would mean in a particular case.

The systemic framework does not make individual assessments in a case unnecessary; on the contrary, it provides a conceptual structure that insures a true transactional understanding of the person-in-situation. Its most salutary feature is that it provides for multifaceted interventions, determined by the needs of the case and made possible by the opportunity to utilize the available manpower from all levels of education, experience, and expertise.

Far from negating personal contact with individuals, this framework allows for flexible modes of help as needed, so that clients are not fitted into a single methodology. It is true individualization to confront the complexities of a case that the client himself is locked into. It frees the professional head of the team to *think* and use his knowledge about people in society, and it provides for alternatives in the use of rapidly developing helping modalities, because manpower teams can be used in wide-ranging ways.

What does it surrender? It is difficult to assess this, because for social workers, the notions of clinical diagnosis, treatment, and cure, of psychotherapeutic interviewing as modal, of expertise fixed only upon the professional therapist, and of professional status often associated with the medical model may only have been fictions after all. At least they belonged to a different era when change came more slowly, when perceptions of people and the world were more fixed, when helping systems were not so vulnerable to community pressures, and when social work practice was a fairly private affair between selected clients and the profession. If change promises to liberate the field from the moral dilemmas of social control versus help-in-becoming, or self-actualization, from inefficiency and insufficiency versus broad service delivery and full social accountability, the direction that practice takes will reflect values that will have to be debated in the professional and public arena. Our farewell to certainty carries with it the same anxiety that any separation does; we cling to what we know because we know it, because it has served us well, because separation from the known leaves us stranded, and because we have no assurances that the future way will be better. Uncertainty is indeed a weak reason for affiliation; its main service to the social work profession will be to open up new vistas of thought and action, to unbind us from our single-minded commitments of the past, and to give us a better chance of noticing what it is exactly that people are asking of social work practice. It may not be a fair ideological trade, but it has intellectual challenges that will perhaps compensate for the loss of ideology.

The universe of knowledge is vast indeed, and it will always be the problem of teaching and practice to distill what is known and to explain it so that the class or the case is served with as little confusion as possible. Every task in practice will be a cross section of the whole and not a separate slab. Every technique that is used in practice reflects the knowledge base from which it is derived; it ought never be a wild, unfocused attempt to help. Despite the fact that practitioners concentrate upon their skills and techniques, there is a rationale behind their use that a professional knows. It is built into his muscle; it serves as a framework for his understanding of how, when, where, and under what circumstances to intervene. We need to order concepts that will provide the largest possible umbrella of ideas beneath which the individual practitioner will be able to act, selecting techniques that best suit the occasion. One tends to embrace the technique that works; but it may not work for all occasions, so we must not define the field by its techniques. It will have to rethink its humanistic commitment and consider the broadest boundaries of knowledge and skills that society and our intelligence will allow. A resilient practice is adaptive to the world as it is.

How is the world? It is changing very rapidly, discarding old and sometimes beautiful things. It is more open now and is reaching toward a more egalitarian way of life. It is concerned with ecology and growth-enhancing environments that will remain in balance with people. Social work concerns itself with the tensions between people and their environments; the interfaces where transactions take place. The creative task is to make these transactions enhance human dignity and self-esteem, and to free people to make their social networks more serviceable. Despite the complexity of the world and the breakdown of services, people continue to survive, drawing upon their essential social competence, their natural yearning to relate, to know, and to master their lives. Perhaps the best model social work can follow is life itself; thus the most valid context for social work might indeed be found in the ways of the world itself.

Notes

[1] Alvin Toffler, *Future Shock* (New York: Random House, 1970).

[2] Charles Reich, *The Greening of America* (New York: Random House, 1970).

[3] Ivan Illitch, *Deschooling of Society* (New York: Harper and Row, 1971).

[4] Thomas S. Kuhn, *The Structure of Scientific Revolutions* II, No. 2 (2d ed.; Chicago: University of Chicago Press, 1970), 144.

[5] Mary Richmond, *Social Diagnosis* (New York: Russell Sage Foundation, 1917).

[6] Gordon Hamilton, *Theory and Practice of Social Casework* (2d ed.; New York: Columbia University Press, 1951).

[7] Florence Hollis, *Casework: a Psychosocial Therapy* (2d ed.; New York: Random House, 1972).

[8] Jessie Taft, *A Functional Approach to Family Casework* (Philadelphia: University of Pennsylvania Press, 1944).

[9] Virginia Robinson, *A Changing Psychology in Social Casework* (Chapel Hill: University of North Carolina Press, 1930).

[10] Ruth Smalley, *Theory for Social Work Practice* (New York: Columbia University Press, 1967).

[11] Helen Harris Perlman, *Casework: a Problem-solving Process* (Chicago: University of Chicago Press, 1957).

[12] Edwin Thomas, "Behavioral Modification and Casework," in Robert Roberts and Robert Nee, eds., *Theories of Social Casework* (Chicago: University of Chicago Press, 1970), pp. 183–218.

[13] Carel Germain, "Casework and Science: a Historical Encounter," *ibid.*, pp. 28–29.

[14] Gisela Konopka, *Social Group Work: a Helping Process* (Englewood Cliffs, N.J.: Prentice-Hall, Inc., 1963).

[15] Grace Coyle, *Group Experience and Democratic Values* (New York: Women's Press, 1947).

[16] Gertrude Wilson and Gladys Ryland, *Social Group Work Practice* (Boston: Houghton Mifflin Co., 1949).

[17] Robert D. Vinter, "Problems and Processes in Developing Social Work Practice Principles," in Edwin J. Thomas, ed., *Behavioral Science for Social Workers* (New York: Free Press of Glencoe, 1967).

[18] William Schwartz and Serapio Zalba, eds., *The Practice of Group Work* (New York: Columbia University Press, 1971).

[19] George Brager and Harry Specht, *Community Organization: Process and Practice* (New York: Columbia University Press, 1973).

[20] Robert Morris and Robert H. Bienstock, *Feasible Planning for Social Change* (New York: Columbia Univeristy Press, 1966).

[21] Murray F. Ross, *Community Organization Theory and Principles* (New York: Harper & Bros., 1955).

[22] Anthony M. Platt, *The Child Savers: the Invention of Delinquency* (Chicago: University of Chicago Press, 1969).

[23] Michael Harrington, *The Other America* (New York: Macmillan Co., 1962).

[24] Carol H. Meyer, "Individualizing the Multiproblem Family," *Social Casework*, XLIV, No. 5 (1963), 267–72.

[25] E. Y. Harburg and Burton Lane, *Finian's Rainbow.*

[26] Scott Briar and Henry Miller, *Problems and Issues in Social Casework* (New York: Columbia University Press, 1971).

[27] Lydia Rapoport, "Crisis-oriented Short-Term Treatment," *Social Service Review*, XLI, No. 1 (1967), 31–43.

[28] William Reid and Ann W. Shyne, *Brief and Extended Casework* (New York: Columbia University Press, 1969).

[29] Perlman, *op. cit.*

[30] Schwartz and Zalba, *op. cit.*

[31] Carol H. Meyer, *Social Work Practice: a Response to the Urban Crisis* (New York: Free Press, 1970).

[32] Alfred Kadushin, "The Knowledge Base of Social Work," in Alfred J. Kahn, ed., *Issues in American Social Work* (New York: Columbia University Press, 1959), pp. 29–79.

[33] Eugene A. Weinstein, *The Self-Image of the Foster Child* (New York: Russell Sage Foundation, 1960).

[34] National Institute of Mental Health, Center for Studies of Schizophrenia, *Special Report: Schizophrenia* (1971).

[35] Bureau of the Census in Cooperation with the Center for Disease Control, "Report on Polio from Study Conducted September, 1971" (unpublished).

[36] Robert L. Barker and Thomas L. Briggs, *Trends in the Utilization of Social Work Personnel: an Evaluative Research of the Literature* (New York: National Association of Social Workers, 1966).

Norman A. Polansky

❀

BEYOND DESPAIR

No one can be certain about the future, but it is part of our job as professionals to project what needs will be long before they have penetrated the mass consciousness. We must try to imagine a social work appropriate to the last decades of the twentieth century. Otherwise, we shall be, as we have often been, unprepared for what is already upon us and following a trend when we ought to be leading it.

We have to sense the fads, the currents and major social movements, the alterations in our material world which will have impacts on the lives of the people. How can we make our estimates? Experience of the past 100 years tells us how best to predict. We have learned, by now, that it is nearly always foolish to seek forecasts from so-called "practical" men, the men of affairs, for they are too involved in what is to guess what will be. The "men of judgment" have shown relatively little prescience; they have been better architects of their own survival than of ours. At a time when the possible is so readily transformed into the probable, their predictions have been consistently poor.

We do better to watch the gyrations of our artists, writers, and intellectuals. With their antennae nervously and suspiciously testing the drafts, they have provided indicators superior to the placid pronouncements of seemingly more "realistic" contemporaries. What do we in our plodding fashion learn from them?

We learn that a social work for the late twentieth century must reflect the collapse of faith and the death of illusion. This is true not only for our society, but also for ourselves. Without optimism, chary of hope, we must find the means and the will to work. We are skeptical about the future and, indeed, have no guarantee that there will be one.

Until now, social work has ridden on sentiments already present at its birth among the founders of the Charity Organization Society in the 1860s and the Fabian socialists, who came a bit later. Our professional ancestors were not silly rebels wishing on clouds. They were dry-eyed visionaries. Still, they did believe in the perfectibility of man and of his institutions. In casework, they relied on the gentle arts of reasonableness and persuasion to bring clients to rational plans; social action, they thought, consisted in arousing the public to conditions needing change, after which humane legislation would be forthcoming.

It is the mark of how far our generation has fallen from grace that we find reasoning so rudimentary. It requires an effort not to regard an appeal to sweet charity as simply fatuous. So, one safe prediction is that the future of social work will be moved by sentiments less comforting than those with which we began. But, since we shall certainly try our best despite less certainty of ultimate success, we do ourselves honor.

A second prediction has to do with the priority of problems to be confronted in our work. We cannot, here, deal with all that man may be expected to face during the remainder of this century. But one trend has been continuous since the early 1900s. Either the loneliness of the individual soul which has always been man's lot is getting worse, or we are less willing to tolerate loneliness. The evidence is that both are true, and that the amelioration of loneliness, by whatever name we know it, will be a major project for social work during the foreseeable future.

I am aware that some of what follows may seem to be a variant on existentialism, or derived from existential psychoanalysis. In this regard, a quotation from Sartre, writing about man's "fundamental project," is germane:

The being which forms the object of the desire of the for-itself is then an in-itself which would be to itself its own foundation; that is, which would be to its facticity in the same relation as the for-itself is to its motivations. In addition the for-itself, being the negation of the in-itself could not desire the pure and simple return to the in-itself. Here as with Hegel, the negation of the negation can not bring us back to our point of departure. Quite the contrary, what the for-itself demands of the in-itself is precisely the totality detotalized—"In-itself annihilated in for-itself." In other words the for-itself projects *being as for-itself,* a being which is what it is. It is as being which it is not, and which is not what it is, that the for-itself projects being what it is.[1]

While it is nearly impossible for a reasonably literate person not to be more or less derivative of *someone*, I should prefer not to be regarded as deeply influenced by the above. So far as I know, this discussion and its conclusions are founded in standard psychoanalytic ego psychology. Connections to existentialism are coincidental.

Alienation

An off-brown, fetid, psychological smog has descended on the America of our generation. Just as with our polluted air, we cannot quite remember when it began to go bad. There were traces in the atmosphere early in the century, which were felt by the more sensitive among us, but we saw no reason then to join their alarums. It is impossible to put our finger on the point in time when a minor nuisance became a major problem, demanding solution. All we know for sure is that at some time, years ago, things no longer smelled quite right and breathing itself became difficult.

Our social unease has many symptoms: violence and living in fear of violence; disappearance of craftsmanship; casual dishonesty.[2] But the biggest complaint has to do with feelings. More and more, the average man finds himself cowering alone in a malevolent universe that does not offer even the comfort of giving meaning to his suffering. It is customary to say of such a man that he is "alienated."

The concept of alienation has moved from the vocabulary of the professional sociologist into popular journalese. It is one way to describe our social-psychological pollution. However vaguely the term is used, we feel intuitively that it encompasses a major insight into what is wrong with us. This insight dates back at least to the beginning of the century, and much that we are now going through was rather accurately predicted by sociologists of that era, most notably Émile Durkheim.[3] What does alienation mean, more precisely?

Seeman [4] has identified five major meanings of the concept: powerlessness, meaninglessness, normlessness, isolation, and self-estrangement. *Powerlessness*, he says, refers to the person's feeling that he cannot determine the outcomes or satisfactions he seeks by his own efforts. *Meaninglessness* implies doubt whether one can predict the results of what he attempts, the sense that one does not really "know the score." *Normlessness* derives ultimately from Durkheim's notion of anomie; following Merton,[5] it involves the feeling that goals are to be achieved by actions that are *dis*approved by society. In the present context, *isolation* has to do with a refusal to commit oneself to goals and rules of conduct highly valued by one's culture. Finally, there is *self-estrangement*, a notion which Seeman recognizes as a key element in alienation, but which eludes him. We would see it as treating others and oneself as objects to be manipulated rather than valued for themselves.

From Seeman's cogent analysis we might conclude that alienation subsumes five quite disparate and conceptually distinct phenomena. I believe, however, that these attributes are always highly intercorrelated; they are five aspects of the same thing. That is, the processes in the person underlying "alienation" may express themselves in some or all, of these varied ways.

A very wide assortment of the folks who disturb us are thought of as "alienated" from the general community. They include the lower-class criminal and the exploitative developer, the social climber and the social dropout, the mentally ill, and the apathetic, neglectful mother.[6] Many accept Marx's formulation that because of their lack of control of the processes of material production, the poor inevitably constitute a whole alienated class. Battle and Rotter, and Polansky,[7] have independently demonstrated that a sense of powerlessness may affect anyone, but in this generation it is less likely to be found among youngsters who are white and in secure economic circumstances.

Yet, in all the sociological explanations of deviance which invoke the concept of alienation there are vagueness and slippage. A major difficulty is the failure to account for marked individual differences. This was already visible in Merton's influential paper. Why, for example, should one person react to the state of anomie by becoming a hobo while another emulates Al Capone? Among those who know the American poor most intimately, Marx's prediction of an entire class of alienated people is not taken seriously. Like Miller,[8] it is now possible for us to identify in our cities a stabilized lower class with its own life style and its own values—even if these are "alien" to those of the middle class.

There is slippage in theorizing about alienation because an essentially psychological conception is introduced into sociological formulations in an unclear fashion.[9] In this instance, the two levels of discourse do not articulate readily. Hartmann has said that psychoanalysis assumes "average expectable environmental conditions";[10] sociology assumes an average expectable person. Both assumptions are made for convenience in expressing theory, but neither is empirically correct. It seems appropriate for sociologists to describe the social situations which have a high potential for producing alienated people. But to specify how the situations are individually experienced, why some people remain immune while others are affected, requires thorough knowledge of the personality. Let us briefly review, therefore, how phenomena related to alienation appear psychologically.

FUTILITY AND DETACHMENT

A feeling of futility is the aspect of alienation most often cited as a consequence of poverty. The person without money or influence is not only objectively but subjectively powerless. In addition, he usually feels unable to predict the effects of his efforts with any confidence. Therefore, he may see no point in trying to better his lot —he feels futile and apathetic. This is a most sensible analysis, but it has two limitations. Quite a few poor people retain a good deal of zest; moreover, human psychology is not so logical or sensible as this analysis assumes.

Intellectuals often experience futility, but they do so in more impersonal and universal terms: "Man suffers alone and helpless in a universe that has no meaning." To a professional philosopher, this may be only a playful conclusion which will not dull the gusto of his appetite for lunch. But sentiments like these have been known to lead to suicide or to accompany it. When that happens, we must conclude that there were some really charged feelings behind the grandiloquent words.

For the experienced clinician, feelings of futility are immediately associated with the schizoid personality. Along with shyness and a generally odd demeanor, futility is a distinguishing mark of the schizoid. The clinical observations that seem most likely to illuminate the sociological work on alienation are those which have to do with exploring the origins of futility. The investigations revolve around what Fairbairn [11] has called the "schizoid position"; they have been carried forward notably by Guntrip.[12]

We begin by recognizing that although we are accustomed to thinking of schizophrenia as a severe illness, and of the schizoid as a cold, unhappy person, there are schizoid elements in each of us. Rather than categorize, it is more accurate to consider people along a scale which we call the "schizoid spectrum." A person's position on this scale depends on the extent to which schizoid elements dominate in his personality. The elements which we find in the adult personality are of course remnants of the past—in this instance, from a phase of development in early infancy. And the reason we all have such remnants is because each of us has passed through the same developmental crisis, more or less successfully. So, the issue is not whether we have dealt with problems in the schizoid realm but how we have resolved them. What is the developmental phase? What outcomes lead to the detachment and futility we associate with withdrawn personalities?

In the first days of life, the principal preoccupation of the newborn is with survival. From his mother's breast come two essential ingredients: water, without which there is no internal environment; and food, to energize the whole. It is commonplace, mundane, to talk of maternal deprivation or cultural deprivation. To the neonate, the danger in loss of his mother's care is death by starvation or death by desiccation. Here is the primordial dread of emptiness so many patients report, as well as the terror of being alone and unloved.

Yet, the mother on whom we are so dependent for life itself inevitably becomes our target for bad feelings. After all, not even the most attentive mother can be so responsive to her baby's every need that he never experiences neglect. The developmental crisis, consequently, centers around the fate of the bad feelings toward one's mother. One reaction, of course, is to become enraged. "This is the problem of *hate, or love made angry*." [13] This form of hatred of the mother leads to depression.

Anger, however, is not the most primitive reaction to deprivation. An even more basic one is to become hungrier and hungrier, feeling more and more empty, and frightened for one's very survival. This is the reaction which accounts for the otherwise puzzling fact that it is children who have been markedly deprived who cling most desperately to their mothers. When this reaction occurs, it leads to a ravenous desire to possess the mother utterly, to devour her (or the breast). But this would destroy the very object of one's needs. Even more basic than the despair of love made angry is the futility of love made hungry. This is the schizoid problem; it lies beyond depression, beyond despair.

The dilemma of the schizoid position is this: to love is to destroy the very object of the love, the source of supply; not to love is to die alone. Faced with such dismal alternatives, the organism withdraws. He detaches himself from the situation and numbs himself against the feelings it generates. "Whereas the depressed person turns his anger and aggression back against himself and feels guilty, the schizoid person seeks to withdraw from the intolerable situation and to feel nothing." [14] Here, then, in the original despair, and the use of detachment as a defense against it, lie the primordial feelings of futility, with associated feelings of emptiness and nothingness. The depressive reaction is a later one, developmentally speaking; the schizoid reaction is one to which the infant may regress when even depression becomes intolerable. In short, detachment and its accompanying sense of futility are initially defensive reactions dating back to the earliest of all interpersonal problems: hatred of one's mother.

Fairbairn and Guntrip are not the only psychoanalytically oriented writers to refer to the use of detachment as a defense. John Bowlby [15] identified stages the infant goes through following separation from his mother. He labeled the phases "protest" (anger), "despair" (depression), and "detachment" (defense). That detachment is indeed a defense and not a final resolution may be demonstrable in later life. Suppose you have loved a girl but lost her to someone else. Although you no longer think of her, feelings remain. Of this, you become aware when you encounter her. Suddenly, you are flooded by a mixture of anger, guilt, and depression which you would have thought had long since disappeared.

Because we have been discussing this form of psychological "splitting" in relation to the schizoid personality, we have emphasized its symptomatic or pathological quality. But the same maneuver may serve adaptive purposes. Cumming and Henry,[16] for example, have discussed the mutual cutting of ties that goes on when a person becomes old, loses his ability to work, and becomes aware that the time remaining to him is short. They postulate that he and society disengage in a pattern that makes the inevitable more bearable.

Now, let us see how far we have come. We may assume that bad feelings toward the mother are universal. Every infant, without exception, must deal with the primitive mixture of good mother-bad mother feelings which Melanie Klein,[17] for example, postulates as instinctual. It is part of man's fate, man's lot in life, that he begins, therefore, with potential for emphasizing either of two attitudes in regard to these bad feelings: the depressive and the schizoid positions. Viewed from this standpoint, when we describe a man as "alienated" we are saying that schizoid elements have come to predominate in his personality, that he has withdrawn from the people around him and lost interest in how they feel, what they want, and what they believe.[18] And when we say he is alienated from a particular aspect of society, such as the church or the political system, we are saying that he has withdrawn from these institutions. In effect, he has walled off these social structures, has split them off from the mainstream of his conscious functioning.

OUTCOMES OF THE SCHIZOID PROBLEM

Discussions of alienation are typically colored by an unspoken dream. The idea is that this state represents a descent from Eden. It is as if man would be naturally ebullient, loving, goal-directed, and hopeful unless some pathological social process intervened and alienated him. Is this really so? Are the phenomena of alienation so alien? It has been insufficiently emphasized that the Freudian view of man and his chances is infinitely bleaker than the assumption implicit in the writings of Durkheim and Merton. What if we assume that it is normal—by which we mean highly expectable—to live with an undercurrent of depression, withdrawal—or both—and that the best we may hope for is to have fought successfully against being overwhelmed by these feelings?

There are three possible outcomes of the original conflictual feelings toward the mother:

1. Most pathogenic is to have one's hunger not only go unassuaged but to intensify. This mounting hunger and sense of emptiness lead to the urge to devour the loved person, which in turn causes a fear of loving lest one destroy the person he loves. The defense in this instance is detachment, with the apathy, numbing, and avoidance of people we associate with a strongly schizoid core in the personality.

2. Another outcome is that the unmet hunger leads to anger, the anger leads to guilt and is turned against the self—the depressive stance. This position implies that hunger has been fed somewhat, but insufficiently; there is surviving ability, therefore, to form relationships. Unfortunately, those with this pattern find themselves unaccountably growing angry even as they start to love. They form intensely ambivalent attachments, and live with an undercurrent of depression.

3. The outcome that some prefer to regard as "normal" involves actually resolving the bad feelings toward one's mother, or at least markedly abating them. Resolution occurs when the child is sufficiently reassured about being fed when he needs to be; the strength of his drive abates and he passes on to other developmental tasks.

But there is nothing inevitable or natural about resolving bad-mother feelings. Even with a loving and competent mother, digestive disturbance in the infant can throw the process off stride; so may illness in the mother or other family trouble which coincides with a crucial phase of the infant's development. This is why it is so common to find people with markedly schizoid or depressive cores in their personalities. Indeed, we must postulate that some schizoid and depressive remnants are ever present in each of us. They come to the fore during periods of regression, weakness, and the like. Some of us, therefore, are totally alienated, some are alienated in respect to certain social situations or institutions, and any one of us is a likely candidate for despair—or for detachment and futility as a defense against it.

SUPPORTS TO KEEP DEFENSES WORKING

From my formulation thus far, it must appear that I have dealt with the problem of alienation by simply reducing a major set of sociological insights to Freudian ego psychology. The usual next step is to minimize the significance of the phenomena, to demonstrate that in the long run they all go back to childhood neuroses and are to be treated in the same old way. This familiar game has served rigid followers of Freud well over the years, but I do not intend to play it.

The evidence is overwhelming that the social conditions one faces, even long after his basic personality cast is set, have powerful effects on him. Let me point out, on the one hand, that these effects are not so straightforward and simple as the sociologists have assumed. On the other hand, neither are they trivial. Speaking technically, one may say that his interpersonal environment determines whether a man will live along with a relatively benign character neurosis, or break down with an acute, symptomatic, emotional illness. How shall we view the interaction of personality and social situation in relation to the phenomena of alienation?

Of all the many people who do not resolve their bad-mother feelings in infancy, and who therefore emerge with depressive and/or schizoid cores, relatively few seem severely damaged. This is because the process of adaptation to one's inner difficulties does not end with infancy. Later social supports may combine with internal adjustments so that we compensate for initial difficulties.

A man with a markedly depressive core thrives on busyness. He is reassured when people ask him for assistance, because this tells him that he is not so unlovable as his early guilt feelings made him believe. Such a man finds it hard to give up and relax, therefore, even if ordered to do so for medical reasons. Instead, he responds happily to a work situation that is structured and which makes demands on him. He may complain, but he is satisfied, really, as he groans. Just as a woman may collapse after her children have grown up and left her, loose ends expose this sort of man to the despair that lies within. So, instead of "frustrating" him, the effect of rigid structure is to offer such a person a good bit of support.

From our own work in mental hospitals in this country, we know that many schizophrenics need strong external controls to compensate for the looseness of ego boundaries within. Projecting from our democracy to the rest of the world, who knows how many potentially very sick people are being held together by subjection to one or another crazy totalitarian regime? If Stalin could rule Russia so long, then anything is possible.

Other men are confronted with self-imposed isolation. It helps them to feel less subhuman if they appear to be warm and related. But of course they cannot stand too much intimacy. If they can find occupations that throw them into frequent but superficial contact with others, they may be in good balance, especially if these contacts are dictated by the nature of the job. Doctors, waitresses, professors, and prostitutes with such schizoid problems may be comforted by the side benefits of their occupations.

Feelings of futility are less apt to overwhelm us when they are consistently unconfirmed by the group around us. However, when the void within is matched by poor group morale from without, the result is alienation. In short, it seems to take both an anomic social situation and schizoid elements within the personality to produce what is classically regarded as alienation. A state in society in which norms have ceased to bind does not instill a sense of futility in the person. The fault of the social system lies in its failure to help man defend himself against the impulse to detach that he carries around anyway.

Now, a sense that each person is alone is not just a distortion. We are born alone; we die alone. Most of the time, however, we succeed in erecting shields against the starkness of the night. Belonging to a group may help a person to face his ultimate loneliness and to comfort himself through the closeness he attains to others in a like situation. If you live in an impersonal city where no one knows your name and few would even notice if you were to disappear, you are not getting this sort of comforting. Nor does it help to work in a large plant where your replaceability is thrown in your face day after day. It is nice when you want a vacation, but it is not nice when you want to be missed!

We see, therefore, that whether an individual succumbs to the syndrome called "alienation" is really determined by three things. First, there is the outcome of his early childhood. Second, there are all the subsequent life experiences which serve either to confirm or to cushion his initial attitude toward the world. In these experiences, his family, his other primary groups, and the whole society of which he is a part play their roles. And, third, there are his own vigor and determination to fight against being overwhelmed by the dismal devils that lie within his breast.

I have sketched a theoretical model of alienation which resembles in some ways, and departs in others, the one to which we are accustomed. While the formulation may hang together psychologically, further questions emerge: What meaning does this have for the future of social work? What are its implications for our future as an occupation?

The Task before Us

During the next decades, the most pressing task confronting American social work will be the defeat of personal and social isolation. The problems I have sketched extend to all segments of society, affluent and poor. Our job has many facets. So it is fortunate that it is not solely ours. At the level of social change, we shall continue to be involved in freeing minorities and redistributing income. Individually, we shall be treating more and more instances of what I have termed the "apathy-futility syndrome." [19] But all these diverse efforts are connected. Our job is to stem the tide of futility—alienation, if you prefer—that threatens to overwhelm us all.

While this may be a new way of expressing our mission, the mission is not itself new. We have always acted as scavengers for society, picking up where established institutions leave off. We have been urgent that no one should find himself powerless because he felt alone in an indifferent culture. But now we are inundated with loneliness.

As I have said earlier, the loneliness is partly based in reality, in the ultimate fate of each mortal. In my observation this does not frighten people nearly so much as loneliness that is self-imposed. For detachment makes it impossible for a man to take what comfort people can offer each other against the surrounding dark and the cold.

There was a time when our religions, our thoughts about the supernatural, cheered us, but these are no longer so widely accepted. Along with others, therefore, social workers inherit part of the job of helping people confront their realistic aloneness and learn to live with it. This is the approach of all the major religions that do not base themselves in illusion.

I have said that the task before us is worsening and that we are in real danger of being overwhelmed. On what do I base this? I base it in large measure on the fact that some sociologists made predictions about the course of Western society some seventy or eighty years ago, and these have proved surprisingly accurate. Durkheim, for example, said that as the population in communication with each other increased, so would the specialization of occupations. And as the occupations specialized, there would be a multitude of competing sets of norms in place of the old, simpler universals. From this diversity and complexity, he predicted an increasingly normless, lonely society. Was he wrong? Others made dire predictions about the effects of industrialization and urbanization on our country, unless specific measures were taken to ward them off. Were they wrong?

The fact is, therefore, that while mothers may be doing a better and better job of mothering, for all I know, the rest of our institutions are providing less and less to counterbalance the inescapable depressive and schizoid trends that lie within us. Our economic and industrial organizations do not refute the dire fantasies we carry from childhood. The reality is worse.

What we have to do, therefore, is to work at changing both the social institutions and the individuals with whom we deal so that our clients can make use of such human comforting as is available. Much of the loneliness that is self-imposed can be dissolved; and we can erect social barriers against the remaining void.

An End to Romance

The disillusionment which affects so much of our surrounding culture also applies to those of us in social work, of course. We are now fully conscious of our own limitations, for one thing. We know so much more about how to destroy a human personality than how to reverse the damage once it has occurred. Unlike Charles Dickens, we see no reason to idealize the poor in order to want to help them, for they are as varied and as potentially avaricious for material things as are the rich. Neither can we, while seeking his cure, delude ourselves about the selfishness and meanness so visible in the average drug addict or alcoholic.

We have all been reared in the tradition that someday we will all find a way to revert to an aboriginal happiness, man's natural state. Oddly, the idea that the earlier, the natural, is "better" is an illusion sold by old men, recalling their long-spent youths, to gullible juveniles. The Nazi party was a natural expression for many, many Germans, and we have seen this in our own lifetime. I am even of the opinion that cities are potentially far superior places to live than nearly all small towns—if we could make them a little less representative of "doing what comes naturally."

In our own field, we learned long ago that the ideal treatment institution is a far cry from the human family as we usually know it. Rather, it is an artificial environment, deliberately designed and engineered for its treatment task.[20] What I foresee, therefore, is the death of the romantic era in social work. I hate to see it go, because our hearts were young and gay; but I welcome its departure because the end of illusions may free us to get on with our jobs.

Implications

Let me now draw a few implications from what I have presented above, starting with an unsentimental view of some of the problems before us.

ON PARENTING

It seems perfectly obvious that social work as we have known it will either change markedly or disappear as a profession. One aspect of it which certainly will have to change is its emphasis on the family as the unit of discourse, the unit of treatment, and, to a surprising extent, the social unit around which our services are organized. Well, what do we really know about families?

If our goal is to be containment of alienation, we begin by looking to its roots, and its roots are in the sacrosanct mother-child relationship. Let us face it, many couples should not become families, just as some women should not try to mother. As things now stand, we scrutinize prospective parents from head to toe and sideways before making an adoptive placement, but any pair of idiots can bear their own, and we will rush social services into action to make it easier for them to do it again.

In a substantial percentage of families there is a need for supplemental cognitive and emotional feeding of their children. This, not just the work opportunities for women on relief, ought to be the prime purpose of the day care centers we are proposing to set up.[21] When experts on child development meet nowadays to discuss primary prevention they are never able to accept a lower limit on the age when prevention should begin—we are back to conception! But when social workers discuss intervention, we are always gearing up to "offer assistance." The mothers with sense enough to know they need help are not our most severe problem. Is it not time we removed the blinders we put on to preserve our own hostile idealization of our own mothers?

During the past six years I have been studying problems of child neglect in rural homes.[22] It is striking how many neglectful mothers have large families. Already inadequate, often disturbed, they are further discombobulated by the demands of five children under age five! One would think that anything as obvious as a program of birth control would have been vigorously pushed by welfare authorities for years. Instead, social workers have been prattling about parents' rights. How about children's rights? A major reason for childbearing among childish women is that the child is a buffer against loneliness, which, as we know, is often due to infantile hunger and detachment. Surely we can find a pacifier for adult women less destructive to the next generation than the human infant. The alternative is what we have termed "a cycle of infantilization." [23]

ON POVERTY

Provision for all reasonable wants, not to mention needs, is well within our grasp as a society. Yet, we have not even made real progress in eliminating starvation. We live in a country in which, for the past twenty years, there has been a famine, artificially induced. There are two major reasons for our failure to provide well for everybody at this stage in our technology. First, we do not invest work and workmanship with pleasure; so we do not produce to capacity. Second, we do not invest sharing with pleasure; so large segments of the power structure find withholding far preferable to distributing.

We get defensive when our clients are accused of it, but let us take a look at unwillingness to work. The proportion of unemployed and underemployed Americans far exceeds the economists' statistics. We get data on the poor, or at least those who claim to be seeking work. We have no data on all the many well-to-do men and women who do no serious work, never have. Neither do we have figures on the huge group of people in professional, executive, and brokerage positions who do hardly anything. Most of our armed forces and armaments industries are underemployed while overpaid. One of the polarities to which Erikson refers in recounting successive life crises is industry versus inferiority.[24] Obviously, most of these citizens never made a successful resolution of this problem of the primary school years.

More important is the problem in this culture of maldistribution or, better stated, of nondistribution. What is the dynamic behind the private greed so pandemic in America? Hunger can be easily understood; greed needs to be explained. The pressure behind the greed is the emptiness associated with detachment and futility. It is a bottomless pit in the stomach which possessions can assuage, but which cannot really be filled.

In our society, the impact of avarice is further complicated by another feature of the schizoid. Schizoid personalities treat others not as fellows with whom they can empathize, but as things or tools to be manipulated. If such a coldly manipulative attitude is coupled with great intelligence and cunning, as it sometimes is, it can lead to enormous fortunes under our present system of rewards. We then have a Howard Hughes or a J. Paul Getty—not the most admired Americans, but still the richest.

Here is a point, therefore, on which Freudian theory would seem to agree with socialist. Since their greed is ultimately a defense, with roots that are deeply unconscious, there is no reason to believe that those who now own most of the country will be motivated to share it by appeals to reason. They will simply have to be forcibly controlled by some of the more mature egos in the society. As Lyndon Johnson once let slip, the "boys will have to be satisfied with a little less blood." Since the personalities involved are pretty well unchangeable, and since the system permits them to emerge into power, obviously one has to change the system. I see no probability of any easy solution to our economic problems for which the so-called "war on poverty" was really only a face-saving skirmish.

ON INTEGRATION

Our hope was that progress toward civil rights would immediately bring warmth and closeness. But this has not been our experience, and it should not have been predicted. When the races draw closer, the detachment of the blacks is being penetrated. Feelings of futility are then replaced with underlying depression and anger. Only after the anger has been "worked through" on both sides can we hope for something truly approaching integration. Unfortunately, there are all too few whites as well as blacks who have successfully surmounted their depressive and schizoid problems. Therefore, our best hope is to have the expressions of rage take verbal forms until the feelings modulate. Those social workers who preach power and the use of force are unnecessary; they pour oil on a gasoline explosion.

Perhaps these are enough examples to indicate what the "collapse of faith and the death of illusion" might do to some of our cherished assumptions in social work. As a student once remarked to me, "What this field needs is some new clichès." The loss of old distortions could portend an era of greater effectiveness. In any event, we have no choice, for we no longer blindly believe. And abandoning our hope that, because we are virtuous, progress is inevitable is a sad event. No wonder our field is undergoing the depression and futility which recur whenever an adult is subjected, still again, to an identity crisis!

Group Supports

Much that we know about helping people cope with life's emergencies we have learned from scrutinizing the behavior of healthy egos responding to crisis. Knowing what healthy "grief work" is, we can encourage clients to express feelings in order to avoid longer-lasting depressions.[25] Similarly, we can often (not always) learn from the social movements which arise spontaneously. We in social work must be alert to these, for they may be harnessed to help us both in treatment and in prevention.

Now widespread is the fascination with various forms of group living. With roots tracing to the Utopian experiments in our own country in the last century, and to the Israeli *kibbutzim* in this one, various forms of group experience are being sought all over the country. Such groups have a variety of potentials.

First and foremost, as we have noted, there is no realistic escape from man's ultimate loneliness. Anyone who has ever faced death is quite aware of it. The infant seeks to evade this truth by losing himself in his mother, pretending that he and she are as one. When an adult attempts to use the same maneuver it has the effect of driving others from him, either because he is so demanding, or so absorbing, or so obviously indifferent to *their* needs. In short, the infant in his death-motivated greed does not dispel his aloneness; he exacerbates it. An adult, however, has another chance. He can live and let live, recognizing that he is separate and yet drawing what comfort he can from communing with the other person. This is a major function which group living can serve.

Others seek out groups because they offer them the best adaptation they can afford. We are familiar with people who withdraw physically because of their schizoid trends; we forget the others who exploit the protections available in the group to live at an optimal distance from others. In a communal society, in which there is always someone around to talk to "when you feel like it" they can alternate closeness with fleeing. Similarly, they are crippled with respect to forming pair relations, but when these are watered down by total group living, they can take them better. I do not think we have ever had an adequate analysis of how shipboard living in the navy or barracks life in the army feeds the needs of men with strong schizoid cores who find there a balance between fear of closeness and utter loneliness. To many who are now forming communes around the country, the groups are extended families at a level of intensity they prefer to nuclear family life.

The encounter groups, the "touchy-feely" groups now coming into vogue, serve similar functions for a few hours at a time.[26] They offer no magic: when the external support is withdrawn, the brittle tissue of reserve and isolation shows through once again. But their existence signifies a spontaneous effort at coping which we would do well to take under responsible sponsorship.

In other countries, such as China, we are witnessing a state of affairs in which "groupiness" will probably end up as crippling, constricting, and ultimately as valueless as what it was supposed to replace. What we really need, and a democracy can permit, is a multitude of different forms of group life. One of the virtues of non-monopolistic capitalism is that it is possible to fail without being forever defeated. We need a kind of group life in which it is possible to be dropped by, or to drop out of, the group and still find one's way elsewhere. From Israel we already have learned that group living is not for everyone; we also can easily observe that *kibbutz* living could become infinitely tedious and dull, for each *kibbutz* in the last analysis is a kind of peasant village. So, we do not yet know all the answers. However, it seems to me that a field which began, in part, with groups of volunteers living in true social settlements has skills and knowledge to offer to an emerging, freely communal society for part of America.

A Defiance to Live By

As this is being written, there is plentiful evidence of unease within the social work profession. People make statements such as "I'm not sure I believe in social work any more." Although the members of my generation who became social workers took vows of poverty (not of chastity) I had not thought we were a religious order. We do not need people merely to believe; we need them to work.

Still, the statements are indicative of the identity crisis that young workers are passing through. And a not unusual reason for the crisis stems from the sorts of people we have latterly recruited to our work. Some of them expect to be morally superior, financially comfortable, and unpressured—all the while helping their fellow men. There is a second reason for their disillusionment, however, and this is to be taken seriously. It comes out as, "I doubt we are doing that much good." We are in a kind of work in which all of us necessarily waste effort part of the time; but very large segments of the profession do very little good any of the time. I think such jobs should be abolished because I am for life and such make-work amounts to trivializing life. It were better that our field should disappear.

Even a mature and realistic person must stand in some awe at the bleak landscape that remains after the removal of the illusions we have lived by. This is where Freud eventually arrived in his own pursuit of truth. Why should one keep going on with the effort to improve the lot of his fellow men?

There is no stock answer. Each must find his own. Many summer soldiers do not belong with us; they will opt out as they begin to realize the difficulty of our task. Others, alas, will stay the course out of sheer inertia. But some of us will continue simply because we are determined to push things a little closer to what we had in mind when we began. In short, we plan to do what we do because we have chosen to do it. We live with responsibility for that choice, and fully aware that we have no magical knowledge of how men should live. (Our expertise, rather, is in how they should *not!*) We will do our best, but we nourish no fantasy of an imminent paradise on earth.

Perhaps many, like the writer, still believe in God. No doubt our commitment is strengthened thereby, since much that social work stands for is also taught in the Bible. Yet, this does not say that others must believe. Nor is there any guarantee that we will enter Heaven by being social workers on earth.

We are left, at last, with man's defiance in the face of his own weakness and mortality. Shaking our fists at the unavailing skies, we mutter, "Here I take my stand." If, in our offer to help others overcome their isolation we also overcome our own, then we profit along with those we help. For, beyond despair for the infant lies detachment, since he seeks to be completely fused with the one he loves. The mature person, seeking less, can find more. Beyond despair for the adult lies closeness to his fellow man.

Notes

[1] Jean-Paul Sartre, *Existential Psychoanalysis* (Chicago: Henry Regnery Co., 1962), p. 39.

[2] For a thorough, popularized description of what is wrong with America see Charles A. Reich, *The Greening of America* (New York: Bantam Books, 1971).

[3] Émile Durkheim, *Suicide* (New York: Free Press, 1966; orig. French in 1897).

[4] Melvin Seeman, "On the Meaning of Alienation," *American Sociological Review*, XXIV (1959), 783–91.

[5] Robert K. Merton, "Social Structure and Anomie," in Merton, ed., *Social Theory and Social Structure* (Glencoe, Ill.: Free Press, 1949), pp. 125–49.

[6] Maxwell J. Schleifer and James E. Teele, "The Mother of the School Dropout—the Alienated Adult" (Boston: Judge Baker Guidance Center, 1964; mimeographed); Hylan Lewis, "Syndromes of Urban Poverty," in Milton Greenblatt, Paul E. Emery, and Bernard C. Glueck, Jr., eds., *Poverty and Mental Health* (Washington, D.C.: American Psychiatric Association, 1967).

[7] Esther S. Battle and Julian B. Rotter, "Children's Feelings of Personal Control as Related to Social Class and Ethnic Group," *Journal of Personality*, XXXI (1963), 482–90; Norman A. Polansky, "Powerlessness among Rural Appalachian Youth," *Rural Sociology*, XXXIV (1969), 219–22.

[8] Walter B. Miller, "Implications of Urban Lower-Class Culture for Social Work," *Social Service Review*, XXXIII (1959), 219–36.

[9] Subsequent to writing this, I was introduced to the recently translated book by the Danish sociologist, Joachim Israel, *Alienation: from Marx to Modern Sociology* (Boston: Allyn & Bacon, Inc., 1971). Clearly aware of confusions in use of the term, Israel asserts it has had two, "one referring to *sociological processes* and one to *psychological states* (p. 5). However, nowhere in his text is he then able to provide an adequate psychological formulation of the term. Practice, in social work, requires the kind of detailed explication offered here.

[10] Heinz Hartmann, *Ego Psychology and the Problem of Adaptation* (New York: International Universities Press, 1958), p. 46.

[11] W. Ronald D. Fairbairn, *An Object-Relations Theory of the Personality* (New York: Basic Books, Inc., 1952).

[12] Harry Guntrip, *Personality Structure and Human Interaction* (New York: International Universities Press, 1961).

[13] Harry Guntrip, *Schizoid Phenomena, Object Relations and the Self* (New York: International Universities Press, 1969), p. 24.

[14] *Ibid.*, p. 25.

[15] John Bowlby, "Separation Anxiety: a Critical Review of the Literature," *Journal of Child Psychology and Psychiatry*, I (1961), 251–69.

[16] Elaine Cumming and William E. Henry, *Growing Old: the Process of Disengagement* (New York: Basic Books, Inc., 1961).

[17] Melanie Klein *et al.*, *Developments in Psychoanalysis* (London: Hogarth, 1952).

[18] For a more extended treatment see Norman A. Polansky, *Ego Psychology and Communication* (New York: Atherton Press, 1971).

[19] See Norman A. Polansky *et al.*, "Two Modes of Maternal Immaturity and Their Consequences," *Child Welfare*, XLIX (1970), 312–23.

[20] Arthur Blum and Norman Polansky, "Effect of Staff Role on Children's Verbal Accessibility," *Social Work*, VI, No. 1 (1961), 29–37.

[21] Bettye Caldwell and Lucille E. Smith, "Day Care for the Very Young—Prime Opportunity for Primary Prevention," *American Journal of Public Health*, LX (1970), 690–97.

[22] Norman A. Polansky, Christine De Saix, and Shlomo A. Sharlin, "Child Neglect in Appalachia," in *Social Work Practice, 1971* (New York: Columbia University Press, 1971), pp. 33–50.

[23] Shlomo A. Sharlin and Norman A. Polansky, "The Process of Infantilization," *American Journal of Orthopsychiatry*, XLII (1972), 92–102.

[24] Erik H. Erikson, *Identity and the Life Cycle* (New York: International Universities Press, 1959), pp. 82 ff.

[25] See Polansky, *Ego Psychology* . . ., pp. 73 ff.

[26] Jane Howard, *Please Touch* (New York: McGraw-Hill, 1970).

Charles Grosser

A POLEMIC ON ADVOCACY: PAST, PRESENT, AND FUTURE

Past

"The future is not improvised, one can build it only with the materials we have from the past." [1]

Advocacy has had a long tradition in modern social welfare history though its nature has varied with time and circumstance. Despite social welfare's function as a regulator of social stability [2] one might argue that the tradition of *noblesse oblige* carried, at least for some, a bona fide commitment to the unfortunate. Certainly many undertook the cause of particular groups in society, such as children, the mentally retarded, and so on, as a matter of personal moral or ethical conviction. These paladins represented their own views of the needs and the abuses of these constituencies to the community at large. They also, on occasion, undertook to champion the cause of neglected populations in assertive and partisan ways. The social reform efforts conducted by the settlement movement on behalf of the urban poor were precursors of contemporary advocacy.

The settlements were, early on, forced to come to grips with the fact that their neighborhood improvement efforts and subsequent service programs (recreation, education, child care, medical, housing and employment services) did not and could not deal with the problems of the communities they were attempting to serve and restore. The settlement workers faced then, as we do now (and as is likely to be the case in the foreseeable future), the problem of establishing priorities regarding prevention and/or treatment. Settlement experience demonstrated that the best programs were failures when appraised as measures to reduce urban pathologies (unem-

ployment, poverty, inadequate education, poor housing, and insufficient recreation facilities). Confronted with the specter of
this failure, leaders of the settlement movement were pressed to
social reform, activism, lobbying, muckraking, education, and political pressure to attempt to meet the needs of the urban poor.
The issues ranged from child labor to housing to peace, and the
champions who came forward, from Florence Kelley to Jacob Riis
to Jane Addams, are well known.[3]

Though the social settlement worker was not specifically characterized as an "advocate," it is clear that the reformer role which
many such workers embraced was to "plead, defend, or espouse the
cause of another." [4] This position was taken as a matter of conviction by persons who were themselves largely unaffected by the social inequities they sought to correct. These were essentially middle
and upper-class persons using professional and personal skills and
talents, contacts with sources of influence, data they collected and
interpreted—in short, their own resources—to take action on
behalf of others. They were, in the main, reformers in the literal
meaning of the word in that they believed that their efforts could
solve problems by modifying (rather than replacing) existing social
arrangements. There were some exceptions. Florence Kelley and
Vida Scudder were socialists before they were reformers, and others
such as Ernest Poole and William Walling became socialists as a result of their settlement experience.[5] Their view that major social
reordering was necessary to the solution of the problems of the poor
did not preclude their day-to-day efforts to modify existing conditions or to provide services. The experience of the socialist settlement workers demonstrates that a dual perspective is possible, encompassing the conviction that the system is basically flawed and
that social reform is needed. This perspective provides a basis for accepting that systemic changes are necessary while not ruling out the
ability to provide ongoing services.

Their activities and the issues with which they struggled suggest
that there are significant parallels between the experience of the settlement reformers and that of their present-day advocate counter-
parts.

Present

In the varied assertive activities of social workers on behalf of the poor during the 1930s, and in other ways, advocacy continued through the 1960s. However, the last three decades of this period also saw social work devoting the bulk of its energies to the development of rehabilitative techniques and to the professionalization of the field. Through the glass of self-conscious professionalization based on a methodology for the restoration of damaged individuals, an advocacy stance appeared somewhat inappropriate. For advocacy was not compatible with such professional values as clinical objectivity and neutrality. For example, from the professional perspective, partisanship, which advocacy invokes, was and still is viewed by many as overidentification. Overidentification, of course, makes professional practice impossible. Professionalization was accompanied by the bureaucratization of social work auspices, as new agencies were created, grew, and amalgamated. These evolving service institutions which housed practice also inhibited the exercise of advocate options.

The hiatus in partisan social reform which accompanied the professionalization and bureaucratization of social welfare was considerably modified by the reemergence of advocacy in the early 1960s. The events and programs which led to and shaped the antipoverty efforts of the 1960s, and the political and social movements which occurred simultaneously, created the context from which advocacy reemerged. It was a somewhat new advocacy, different in many important ways from its antecedent forms, but nevertheless basically similar.

By the early 1960s most social welfare services were administered by academically credentialed professionals or civil service practitioners, through large public or quasi-public formal organizations which were supported entirely or in large part by public funds. Acknowledgment of the dominance of the public sector resulted, among other things, in emergence of the notion that benefits, having been defined by a legislative or administrative process, were entitlements rather than privileges. Entitlements could not be altered by local discretion or interpretation, nor could they be considered privileges which could be provided as acts of charity—or withheld. Entitlements were considered to be rights which beneficiaries could demand. In practice, however, it was, and still is, apparent that many beneficiaries who met the legal requirements for various services did not receive them. The processes whereby benefits are withheld are many, a few of which are: keeping information regarding eligibility from prospective users; establishing administrative procedures which contradict the language or intent of the enabling laws; discouraging requests for service by bureaucratic harassments and delays; refusing to implement review procedures; and conducting illegal searches and investigations which deprive beneficiaries of certain rights as citizens. Voluntary and public social welfare service systems frequently interact with powerless recipients in an overtly negative manner. These systems all too often respond to internal organizational imperatives and to political pressure from powerful constituencies rather than to the implicit needs and entitlements of potential or actual recipients.

In addition, it has become apparent that various other components of the social welfare complex, such as those which deal with apprehending criminals and administering justice, regulating consumer practices, enforcing housing and health codes, and educating children, also exercise sanctions and dispense benefits in a manner neither neutral nor benign, much less recipient-oriented. Such systems as these, for a variety of reasons, make invidious definitions of lower-class and minority group mores, behaviors, and culture. As a result, they inevitably define variance from convention as pathology or deviance and exercise their administrative sanctions on the basis of such misperceptions. Reflecting this the criminal justice system will characteristically harass more commonly, apprehend more frequently, judge more harshly, and punish more severely those who are different and powerless and whom society has forced into marginal social, economic, and political status.

Awareness that social welfare benefits were withheld and that social institutions operated on dual standards made the need for assertive practice on behalf of the poor evident and legitimate. Supporting this awareness, the much-heralded rediscovery of, and subsequent war on, poverty created a political and bureaucratic climate which permitted, and even unwittingly abetted, activism and partisanship on behalf of those whom an affluent society had left behind. Under these circumstances advocacy was sought as a device to attempt to bring more equity to the distribution of limited social service benefits, and to the administrative practices of regulatory and penal agencies. Social welfare workers in a variety of settings took this partisan stand on behalf of their constituents. Such advocacy practice, particularly prominent in many antipoverty programs and in community organization, was widespread, encompassing casework in voluntary settings [6] and in large public agencies. This prominence was also reflected in the introduction of advocacy as a component in training social work students.[7] In 1968 the Board of Directors of the National Association of Social Workers through its task force on the urban crisis and public welfare problems circulated a statement endorsing advocacy as an integral part of social work practice and committed its resources to support their position:

. . . the professional social worker is ethically bound to take on the advocacy role if he is to fulfill his professional responsibilities. The ensuing obligation to the professional association is to protect the worker and develop a program to advance the continuing education of social workers in their role of advocates.[8]

Distinctions of Present from Past

A number of the ways in which advocacy in the 1960s was singular stemmed from the assertion that social benefits are rights provided as a responsibility of government rather than as assuagements of *noblesse oblige*. This point of view had, of course, been eloquently and ably stated in our own literature in the 1940s and 1950s,[9] however, it was in the 1960s that it was brought into active practice. The transition from statement to action was facilitated by many factors, several of which have been noted. An additional influence of no small consequence was the new working relationships which developed between social welfare workers and attorneys. These new alliances, formulated in the legal services programs of the early comprehensive juvenile delinquency projects, were continued through the various poor man's law programs funded by the Office of Economic Opportunity, special institutes (usually university-based), innovative programs sponsored by legal aid agencies, and voluntary efforts by attorneys in private practice.

The law provided social welfare with a model of advocacy which supplemented its own less assertive role of representation. In addition, by maintaining that benefits are nonstigmatized rights,[10] and by providing strategies whereby eligible beneficiaries could receive their due, lawyers gave impetus to recipients' actions on their own behalf. Client activities were a central part of the controversy which surrounded the Community Action programs mounted under the Economic Opportunity Act of 1964, particularly in the turmoil generated by the stipulation that there be "maximum feasible participation" by program participants. Client movements, most notably agitation for welfare rights, were unique; they distinguished the advocacy of the 1960s from earlier efforts by their inclusion of service recipients.

The alliance between attorneys, social welfare workers, and constituents found a new arena for social welfare advocacy and reform in the courts. Test cases, class actions, court orders, and other formal legal and administrative procedures were utilized to assert such prerogatives of service recipients as eligibility, equal treatment, and protection. Not infrequently the object of this legal advocate action was a public welfare agency or some other branch of municipal or state government. Legal action by beneficiaries against the public department which administered their entitlement was another distinctive feature of social welfare advocacy in the 1960s.

Advocate situations such as these created a new state of affairs in the profession. Social workers engaged in adversary actions against colleagues; placed client interest ahead of professional or agency loyalties; publicly opposed or contradicted a colleague; named a colleague or an agency as a defendant in a legal action; and generally accepted conflict as a means of inducing social change. It is noteworthy that the utility of social conflict has long been recognized,[11] yet when conflict was introduced as part of the advocacy of the 1960s it was viewed askance by most professionals, who saw in it a denial of traditional social work values and roles.[12] As a result of new-found attitudes toward advocacy, staff members of agencies which ignored or altered the rights of their constituents confronted their dilemma in a new way. Heretofore, professional protocol called for attempting to solve such problems through agency channels; failing that, to request the professional association to exercise sanctions and, if no change was realized, to leave the agency's employ.[13] Such a procedure was time-consuming and ultimately left the agency's beneficiaries in the same state that produced the grievance, except that the sympathetic staff member was no longer present. Advocacy suggested that, if necessary, it was a worker's responsibility to support the beneficiary in confrontation with the agency. Perhaps even more significant was the fact that numerous workers actually took such stands,[14] that they no longer believed, as they were once taught, that agency, professional, and constituent interests were always identical. Social workers acting as advocates openly took positions against agency policy, joined constituents in public protest and direct action, offered testimony that contradicted official agency positions at legislative, legal, and administrative hearings, and provided constituents with information which would enable them to deal more effectively with complicated or obscure administrative practices.

Such instances serve to represent, not catalogue, some ways in which advocacy in the 1960s was distinctive. They were not characteristic of all social welfare practitioners during that decade, however,[15] for conventional practice continued and regressive practices developed at the same time that advocacy emerged.

THE MORE THINGS CHANGE
THE MORE THEY REMAIN THE SAME

Genuine social welfare reform at its most militant undertook the modification and improvement of existing social systems and subsystems. With few exceptions, advocates, whether friendly visitors or militant activists, did not seek to institute or argue the need for alternative social systems. In this regard, the more assertive positions taken during the 1960s were similar to those of dedicated reformers in earlier decades. In both instances, social reform was attempted without seeking to confront such issues as the dilemmas of incrementalism, the corruption of social reform for corporate or individual profit, and the imperative of increasing needs and decreasing resources. Such issues were left in abeyance, except as matters for occasional discussion, as reformers sought to modify existing circumstances. Although the benefits realized through such modifications are valid in and of themselves, the issues remain, and we believe that they can no longer be held separate from practice.

It is our view that it is no longer possible to ignore the problems which accrue from choosing between reforming or replacing existing systems. Attempting to deal with this question does not imply that we abandon services and devote ourselves to revolution. However, raising the issue has considerable impact on any estimate one would make of advocacy.

SOME LIMITATIONS OF ADVOCACY

Contemporary advocacy and earlier efforts at social reform brought about changes in service systems and other social institutions which benefited many. In some instances benefits were substantial, affecting large numbers in important ways. In other instances, benefits were less significant in that they affected few or were quickly nullified by changing circumstances. Whether short-lived or skimpy, such successes were as relevant as other efforts made on behalf of people in need.

One must, however, look to some of the dysfunctions of advocacy as a device to improve or modify social arrangements. Titmuss [16] and others argue that basic social welfare problems stem from the unequal distribution of resources—services, income, power, property. Solutions, therefore, must be predicated on redistribution, a strategy which affects the entire community, not just its have-nots. This argument, which is in effect for alternative systems, was ignored by many in the United States in the 1960s. For it was assumed that the gross national product was expanding so rapidly that equity could be achieved by increasing the rate of expansion for the have-nots while not appreciably decreasing it for the haves. Such was the underlying view of the guns-and-butter policies of the Johnson Administration with regard to financing the war on poverty and the war in Southeast Asia. Its lack of efficacy has been demonstrated by the fact that poverty, which was rediscovered in the late 1950s, has not been decreased or eliminated, though it has changed in style.[17] In significant instances, such as minority youth unemployment, purchasing power of the elderly, cost of social necessities—medical care and housing—and the availability of local tax funds for education, sanitation, and welfare, the situation has probably worsened over the past decade.

Advocates who have been successful in bringing about change in any part of the welfare service system have done so within existing resources and structures. As a consequence, as the system strives for institutional homeostasis, it, in effect, withdraws resources and adjusts structures in other areas to accommodate and neutralize the change efforts of the advocate action. What may actually be accomplished is that advocacy for some produces deprivation for others —others who are more anonymous, who are dependent and helpless and are not represented by advocates.

This phenomenon is illustrated by the experience of welfare advocates in the many states which made separate provision for nonrecurrent budget items. These benefits, provided by special grants, were largely ignored by welfare departments. Recipients were not aware that they were entitled to be brought up to a reasonable standard and that there was a schedule to maintain that standard with regard to replacing furniture, kitchen utensils, clothing. Welfare advocates (recipients, lawyers, social workers, welfare department employees) developed a highly successful campaign to get such benefits by asserting their options. In their efforts to hold down costs, local departments of welfare had made no provision to supply all eligible recipients with these entitlements, although they were given to those who demanded them. While in some communities most recipients were in touch with welfare advocates and aware of their entitlements, in others, such contact was rare. In these latter cases eligible recipients continued to be neglected. In New York State the welfare administrators actually used this state of affairs to argue the impropriety of the welfare movement. The movement was accused of making the department unfair by forcing it to make payment to some rather than actually complying with its own rules and providing benefits for all. Though able to achieve increased expenditures for nonrecurrent items, advocacy was unable to change the practice of welfare systems so that such benefits would be categorically distributed. That is to say, in this instance advocacy without structural change amounted to limited service provision which determined by default who should be excluded as well as who should be benefited.

When, largely as a consequence of the activities of welfare advocates, structural changes were finally realized, they were introduced by welfare departments to save money and disarm the movement rather than to benefit clients. For nonrecurrent items, making a flat grant (automatically administered at regular intervals) has always been viewed by welfare personnel as professionally and administratively desirable. However, this conviction was never acted on until advocate pressure substantially increased welfare expenditures. As a result of this pressure, a major functional purpose of the nonrecurrent arrangement was destroyed; that is, to claim that needs were met because provisions had been made to meet them, while avoiding the cost of these services by keeping them from recipients. Advocacy raised the ante by making nonrecurrent entitlements available. And it was then, when the institution of a flat grant would reduce costs and disarm advocates, that it was enacted. As a result, flat grants were introduced by legislatures at a level considerably below the inadequate recommendations of welfare officials. And though in some instances budgets were raised moderately at the same time, these increases were withdrawn after a short period.

When the social-change outcome of this advocate action is reviewed in this light it can be seen as, in fact, regressive. In a peculiar turnabout, welfare advocates who had always championed flat grants as alternatives to the vagaries of nonrecurrent provision were forced to oppose such grants as totally inadequate. This very same phenomenon took place on a national level in connection with the opposition to the Nixon Administration's Family Assistance Plan. Again, a seeming innovation in the direction of guaranteed entitlements was proposed as a regressive, money-saving device.

These examples illustrate that:

1. Though service benefits can be gained for some, advocacy, in effect, allowed the nature of the changes to be determined by the institution under pressure, not by those from whom pressure came.

2. Concessions wrested from reluctant systems were temporary and often were eliminated by subsequent policy and structural changes.

3. In asserting client prerogatives in accordance with the institution's rules, advocates may actually be forced to argue for regressive alternatives in order to keep benefit options open.

All of these limitations notwithstanding, we assert again the viability of advocacy among the scarce strategies available to those who seek reform on behalf of recipients. However, the lesson we draw from this experience is that the social welfare field, and social workers most particularly, must consider new forms of advocacy; specifically, such forms as will raise the issue of alternate social systems to replace those which provide such meager benefits to substantial numbers of recipients.

Future

The legal model of advocacy operates in a context very different from that in which social welfare advocacy has been attempted. Particularly, legal advocacy is predicated on a specific set of norms and values regarding the administration of the law and the judicial process. Quite apart from the class biases of the law as written, applied, and practiced and its limitations as a strategy for social reform and change, the clarity of its context provides legal advocacy with options which advocacy in the community at large does not have. When legal systems themselves are corrupted, as in certain instances in this country or as they were in Greece, Germany, and Czechoslovakia, advocacy in the law is also rendered meaningless.

For advocacy in social welfare—indeed, for social welfare itself to survive—the failings of the social, institutional, and economic context in which it is located must be considered. Without such a perspective, advocacy remains little more than an extension of pluralistic, locality-based politics which functions on behalf of the self-interest of various groups within the community. Such representation is a good basis for organizing and is often successful, but it leaves too much untouched. For those who are excluded to insist that "I get mine," without regard to larger issues, is both appropriate and inevitable. For social workers to act as advocates for these groups on the basis of such imperatives is consistent with the commitments and values of the profession. But for social welfare workers to limit their efforts to such representation is to confine them to the practice of partisan welfare politics in the art of succeeding. Such a narrow view is basically conservative in its lack of ideology and perspective with which to encompass the larger community. It is essentially a mirror counterpart to those who would oppose the extension of social welfare and is flawed, as their efforts are, by opportunism and a lack of concern for other constituencies.

What is being suggested is that our national community has been exploited without regard to the interrelationships of its parts or the consequences of exploitation to the community as a whole. And that social welfare workers, while mindful of that fact and often deeply concerned with it, have done nothing as a profession and precious little as individuals about it. To deal with this fact, we suggest that a new kind of advocacy is required, not an advocacy which will champion a person, a family, or a constituency, but rather an advocacy that will represent the case for an alternative social system, for a bona fide welfare state.

Such advocacy is necessary as an additional strategy; it is not suggested to replace interest group advocacy, or any other intervention which realizes direct benefits; for no welfare strategy can ethically trade recipients' entitlements for ideological goals. Such advocacy will perforce be visionary; it will, in fact, be ideological.

CONSTITUENCIES FOR CHANGE

While there is widespread dissatisfaction with much of our current social system, there is no popular support for alternatives. Quite the opposite. In the early 1970s we see a powerful public opinion opposed to socialized or welfare state solutions to the problems of the nation. The basic issue underlying the advocacy of the future is that of creating constituencies which will press for new social structures.

The Medicaid program offers a case in point. Here is a national social strategy conceived for middle America. As implemented in New York State the program initially provided medical services and related benefits to families of four with an annual income of $6,000, with allowable income increasing with family size. After a year, in a rapidly inflating economy, the state legislature reduced allowable income to $5,000 and subsequently to $4,500. It has been reported that as a result of the subsequent reductions (October 1, 1971), 165,000 enrollees who were not on welfare would become ineligible for Medicaid under the new maximum. Substantial reductions in benefits were also in store for those who remained eligible. These reductions were enacted by a state legislature which saw itself as fulfilling the mandate of an electorate opposed to public spending for social welfare. There was no political equity in supporting Medicaid in the majority of the state's electoral districts. In most of the fifty states, public support of Medicaid was so meager that much more limited programs, or no programs at all, were provided. From a purely political point of view, the failure of Medicaid stems directly from the fact that it has no constituency. That the program was expensive is true. That the unanticipated expense stemmed from the corruption of social legislation for profit through the greed of the medical, paramedical, and related services is also true. But a powerful and articulate constituency has never allowed the expense and corruption of highway construction or military appropriations to interfere with continued appropriations for road building or arms. The irony of the political destruction of Medicaid is that it was voted to satisfy the objections of the very people whom it would benefit. This is but one example of the way in which the real grievances of middle America have been distorted. Such distortion produces a public opinion which supports reduced services, political conservatism, and scapegoating. Medicaid is but one of the many areas in which the public interest has been thwarted or ignored because of the lack of an informed constituency of those affected; education, welfare, housing, urban development, mass transportation, consumer protection, the regulation of public utilities, the use of public lands, options for income guarantees, and insurance against unemployment, injuries, and old age are some others.

One of the redeeming features of the professional politician, and one which is consistent and dependable, is that he will act in the way that will further his return to office (even to voting for peace, socialism, or the legalization of pot). This understanding of political behavior has been well utilized by many political and commercial special interests. What is being argued here—embarrassingly simple, obvious, and "old hat" as it is—is that social welfare workers could engage in such a process as well; that ideological advocacy should become a vehicle for building constituencies which support substantive, alternative social arrangements; that ideological advocacy become a lobby, if you will, for socialism and socialized alternatives to current residualism. Legislators do not need to be "educated"; they will respond to political pressure. Ideological advocacy could be directed to putting political clout behind welfare state reforms through proselytizing the disaffected who stand to benefit from such reforms. Elected officials will consider the interests of a committed constituency and are likely to support social change when such support brings them political benefit. An effort such as this, we suggest, is no longer debatable, for social welfare's ability to humanize existing institutions has all but disappeared. Adding ideological advocacy as a substantial component of social work practice will enable social work to attempt to fulfill its own ethical and value commitments to people.

A Polemic

There is no question but that choosing which specific alternative systems ought be introduced to replace inadequate institutions is a complicated, time-consuming process: a process both political and highly technical; a process which can be debilitating; and one which, by turning people away from long-range goals, can be self-defeating. *How* medical care should be socialized, for example, is not the issue. That medical care *should be* socialized is. After a visible, articulate constituency committed to socialized medicine (or to low-cost housing, guaranteed income, adequate social insurances) has been created, then the process of determining the most effective form which the program ought to take can begin. The argument, of course, is that to debate the social alternatives at this point in history is fruitless. A public opinion supporting socialized services, or socialism, does not need to have a specific model in mind. And if an articulate national constituency committed to redistribution has been formed it will perforce hold accountable the technicians and politicians who will construct the social alternatives.

Further, ideological advocacy could make explicit the fact that social problems are closely related to each other and to the society as a whole. For such explication will acknowledge rather than avoid the inevitability of the structural reform of major social institutions and will embrace rather than ignore the need for basic social change. Ideological advocacy can also commit its adherents to change as an end to be desired, and will confront rather than avoid the argument that the reforms they propose are inopportune or controversial, as indeed they are. This, then, is the nature of the ideological advocacy here proposed: one that acknowledges basic dissatisfaction with major components of our social system and accepts that changes in these components will produce changes in the whole.

The plea that ideological advocacy be undertaken by social welfare workers and institutions is not made as yet another of the many admonitions with which the field and its practitioners are so often burdened. What is being asserted is that the imperatives which will move social work in the direction of seeking structural changes will come from the realization that its present programs and past experience which have attempted to reform existing institutions have failed to eliminate social ills or enhance the quality of life. It is acknowledged that such realizations are not easily come by and that organizing constituencies for change is a difficult task. This is particularly true when practitioners and the institutions they serve may themselves be a part of the structure they seek to replace. Nevertheless, it is being argued that for such advocacy to reach significant constituencies it will have to be endemic to social work practice and to the function of social welfare service agencies and training institutions. Ideological advocacy calls for community actions and the participation of social work and its surrogates in every community debate in which alternative social institutions and systems can be considered. Ideological advocacy needs to be carried to local institutions as a matter of agency policy and job responsibility. To be effective, it will do more than make statements to those with whom we are in agreement. It will seek out middle America in service clubs, political parties, trade unions, school forums, the military, and the like. It will also be incorporated into the fabric of social work practice.

For example, we would argue that such advocacy requires that treatment include, as an integral part of its protocol, helping the client to understand the external components of his troubles and to deal with the institutions that generate pathology. The work of Grier and Cobbs illustrates this point. "It is inconceivable," they write, "that a man could love and value himself and survive as a slave." Such a perspective requires of the clinician that he "helps a man to change his inner life so he can more effectively change his outer world." From such a perspective social casework can recognize behaviors which will protect clients from social abuses in a new way. And from such understanding new treatment will emerge of which a substantial part will be facilitating a self-realizing, political consciousness, and the ability to engage in social action out of this new insight. "In sum, let us enter a plea for clinicians who can distinguish unconscious depression from conscious desperation, paranoia from adaptive wariness, and who can tell the difference between a sick man and a sick nation." [18]

If service agencies can embrace treatment perspectives such as these they will be able to form interest-group lobbies because such action will be implicit in treatment goals, and therefore material resources (money, staff, and supporting services) can be unambiguously allocated to their efforts.

From the perspective of ideological advocacy, training institutions and schools of social work, in particular, could insure, as an intrinsic part of their educational commitment, that all students would understand and be able to deal with malfunctioning social institutions. Though social work schools have made genuflections in the direction of social change over the past decade, the fact is that in the main their curriculum is unchanged. Apart from the creation of programs in organizing, policy, and planning, which enroll a scant 10 percent of their students , schools of social work have made no commitment to creating structural change or seeking alternative systems. As a result advocacy, even interest-group advocacy, among our service-providing colleagues is still an anomaly with which they had no direct experience in their professional training. The strange dichotomy between social action and social work practice which the field struggled to accommodate in the early 1950s persists into the 1970s. As late as 1971 social work students active in school social action programs viewed this activity as totally separate from their training as caseworkers. The struggles of the 1960s to deal with the effects of regressive public policies on individuals seems to have had little effect on social work training. Schools have not given their students an appreciation of the fact that social change is an integral part of social work, and they should. This can only be done by developing a field and class curriculum which teaches the nature of society and how to change it. This can only be done by schools which encourage innovation, creativity, and independence; schools which themselves act as ideological advocates in their own communities.

Schools of social work receive support and sanction from many sources, as do all social welfare institutions. Asserting unpopular minority viewpoints is always difficult, but it is too easy to dismiss dissidence as impractical. Efforts have been made by schools and agencies, and these efforts have been supported by the National Association of Social Workers, the Council on Social Work Education, and various client groups. However, in the face of the increasing difficulty in mounting such efforts as we moved from the 1960s to the 1970s many have despaired and sought refuge in neutrality and technical competence. However, a profession which simply reflects the political climate of the moment and trains to meet job market needs abdicates its title, for such valueless technocracy is not professionalism. As Arnold Kaufman has noted, "the likelihood that a goal will be achieved often depends on whether it is believed to be possible." [19] The thrust of this argument is that the commitments of the profession cannot be set aside on the basis of the difficulty in pursuing them. Such action both insures the impossibility of struggling for alternative systems and removes the independent integrity which makes social work a profession.

The substantial difference between ideological advocacy and its interest-group and reform antecedents is that it will be engaged in by social work as a matter of self-interest; it is not a formulation for service to others. Social work has lost credibility over the last decade. Its disappearing role in the Department of Health, Education, and Welfare and in most federal, state, and municipal agencies which formulate social policy, the lack of continued federal support for training, its marginal status in most universities, all attest to this fact. One need not be a Cassandra to foresee the demise of social work as we know it within the next several decades. Only if a new national community is created that assures humanism, individual integrity, respect for difference, and the opportunity for self-realization is there a future for a profession committed to such values. For such a national community to evolve it must reflect new values and take on new forms; it must turn to socialism. For such a direction to emerge there must be a popular constituency which demands and supports such a society. For this to occur there must be cadres working to create such a political climate. There is no assurance that this will occur inevitably from the conflicts inherent in our present society, either by way of Charles Reich or Karl Marx.

Again, the particular shape which a socialized United States should assume is not at issue. A national commitment to change is formed from the experience of the present and the past. The experience from which ideological advocacy can draw to proselytize for an equitable society exists. Determining the nature of that society will have to await a national commitment to change.

It is evident that many groups in contemporary America find it necessary to seek structural alternatives in order to find self-realization. It is also understood that the outcome of their collective efforts cannot be predicted. There are no guarantees of success. Nevertheless, for social work to play a role in defining its future, for it to survive, it will, perforce, become one of the groups engaging in this process.

Notes

[1] Émile Durkheim, *Education and Society*, tr. Sherwood Fox (New York: Free Press, 1956), p. 145.

[2] Richard Cloward and Frances Piven, *Regulating the Poor: the Functions of Public Welfare* (New York: Pantheon Books, 1971).

[3] See Robert Bremner, *From the Depths* (New York: New York University Press, 1956), pp. 60–66, 201–203; Allen F. Davis, *Spearheads for Reform* (New York: Oxford University Press, 1967).

[4] Webster's Collegiate Dictionary, 5th ed., 1942.

[5] Davis, *op. cit.*, pp. 111–12, 242.

[6] See Berta Fantl, "Preventive Intervention," *Social Work*, VII, No. 3 (1962), 41–47; Daniel Langdon, *Family Advocacy* (New York: Family Service Association of America, 1971); *Family Service Highlights*, Vol. XXXI, No. 5 (1970), special issue on advocacy; Scott Briar, "The Current Crisis in Casework," in *Social Work Practice, 1967* (New York: Columbia University Press, 1967), pp. 19–33.

[7] David Wineman and Adrienne James, "The Advocacy Challenge to Schools of Social Work," *Social Work*, XIV, No. 2 (1969), 23–32.

[8] "The Social Worker as Advocate: Champion of Social Victims," *Social Work*, XIV, No. 2 (1969), 16–22.

[9] See for example, A. Delafield Smith, *The Right to Life* (Chapel Hill: University of North Carolina Press, 1955); Nora L. Itzin, "Right to Life, Subsistence, and the Social Services," *Social Work*, III, No. 4 (1958), 3–11, Bertha Reynolds, *Social Work and Social Living* (New York: Citadel Press, 1951).

[10] See Charles A. Reich, "The New Property," *Yale Law Journal*, LXXIII (1964), 733–87, and "Midnight Welfare Searches and the Social Security Act," *ibid.*, LXXII, No. 7 (1963), 1347–60; Jean Cahn and Edgar Cahn, "The War on Poverty: a Civilian Perspective," *ibid.*, LXXIII (1964), 1317–52.

[11] See, for example, Robert Gessner, ed., *Eduard C. Lindeman, the Democratic Man* (New York: Beacon Press, 1956), for reference to conflict, its necessity, and its use in Lindeman's writings in the 1920s and 1930s.

[12] Alan Keith-Lucas, "Ethics in Social Work," in *Encyclopedia of Social Work* (16th ed.; New York: National Association of Social Workers, 1971), pp. 324–28.

[13] National Association of Social Workers, Code of Ethics (1946).

[14] A most notable example from the many which could be cited is that of Benny Parish, an Alameda (Calif.) Department of Social Welfare worker who, by his refusal to participate in unannounced early morning visits of welfare families, precipitated a series of legal actions which re-

sulted in the elimination of "midnight raids." Benny Parish *vs.* the Civil Service Commission of the County of Alameda, State of California *et al.*, 1 Civil No. 22, 556, District Court of Appeal, State of California, First Appellate District.

[15] For a more detailed discussion see, Charles Grosser, *Community Organization: Enabling to Advocacy* (New York: Praeger, 1973). For the intransigence of civil service practitioners in the face of constituent pressure see Frances Fox Piven, "Militant Civil Servants," *Trans-Action*, VII, No. 1 (1969), 24–28, 55.

[16] Richard Titmuss, *Commitment to Welfare* (New York: Pantheon Books, 1968), Part 3, pp. 113–206.

[17] See Joseph Kershaw, *Government against Poverty* (Chicago: Markham Publishing Co., 1970), especially Chap. 8.

[18] William Grier and Price Cobbs, *Black Rage* (New York: Bantam Books, 1968), pp. 144, 151, 132.

[19] Arnold Kaufman, *The Radical Liberal* (New York: Atherton Press, 1968), p. 37.

Sheila B. Kamerman, Ralph Dolgoff,
George Getzel, and Judith Nelsen

❦

KNOWLEDGE FOR PRACTICE:
SOCIAL SCIENCE IN SOCIAL WORK

In contrast to the basic sciences, professions do not seek knowledge for its own sake. For the professions the function of knowledge is to develop an effective practice oriented toward specific purposes and goals. Consequently, a changing practice must constantly translate knowledge into action; it must dictate and define the boundaries of relevant knowledge and stimulate the search for new knowledge. Part of what makes a given profession distinctive is the nature of the action or practice evolving from placing knowledge within a particular frame of reference.

The crucial process thus becomes a dialogue between theoretician and practitioner—between knowledge and action—with each in turn both stimulating and responding to the demands of the other. This is true for all professions, not just for social work. For example, the last decade has seen the emergence of courses in poverty law and public interest and consumer law in the leading law schools around the country. Departments of community psychiatry have been established in several medical schools. These developments have not occurred spontaneously but in response to new tasks and new practice demands on the fields of law and medicine.

Similarly, in social work the experiences of the 1960s led to the emergence of new kinds of tasks, the need for new forms of practice, and therefore a search for new knowledge. The rapid expansion and diversification of social welfare programs generally increased the demands for competent planners and administrators, as well as for more differentially responsive practitioners at all levels. Newly emerging community action programs required both substantive knowledge and skills other than what were needed in the traditional community organization settings of earlier years. Finally, renewed concern with the attainment of broad goals of social justice and social reform impelled a sharp expansion of the parameters of social work practice to include the techniques of planning, policy development and analysis, and programming. The need for new technologies and new kinds of substantive expertise in order to achieve these wider objectives was readily apparent. At the same time, practitioners whose clients were individuals, families, and small groups were pressed to assess broader social conditions before initiating interventions and to master or devise practice models of broader applicability and effectiveness than those available in the past.

Are there no limits to the knowledge relevant for social work? Are not some tasks better performed by other professions? Social work practice encompasses some skills that may also be employed by other professions, such as urban planning, public administration, psychology, teaching, politics, and even business, and thus draws upon some of their knowledge. However, the purposes for which these skills are used become crucial. It is the shaping of these purposes by specific values that makes social work practice unique.[1]

From time to time social workers have discussed their purpose and defined it. We view social work practice as an art that combines professionally mastered knowledge and chosen values with the individual attributes and style of the practitioner. Those who would contribute to the development and enhancement of practice must consider how to build that core of professional knowledge and to guide practitioners in its use. The knowledge that can be commanded and the values that the individual social work practitioner brings to any situation determine both the task and the methods of intervention that can be employed. At the same time, however, as the individual practitioner encounters new and different situations, or as practitioners as a group have similar experiences, there is a constant need for more knowledge. The acquisition of new knowledge performs two functions: it increases the professional skills of the individual worker in task identification and definition as well as in the selection of options for intervention; simultaneously, it adds to the interventive range of the profession as a whole.

Thus it is essential that all social workers begin with some common core of knowledge sufficiently eclectic to keep before them a wide range of task definitions and intervention possibilities. This common core would include knowledge of human behavior as it relates to individuals, families, groups, organizations, communities, and society; knowledge of the social work profession and the organizational context in which practice occurs; knowledge of the social environment, including the decision-making milieu; knowledge of social welfare programs, policies, and issues; and knowledge of the value premises and principles of practice, including a skill and intervention repertoire. It should be substantial, yet cannot be comprehensive.

In addition, each individual social worker will find it necessary to search for more specialized knowledge to meet the demands of his particular and changing practice. As social workers begin to intervene on several levels, increasing attention must be paid to related disciplines that can enhance skills at each level. Commitment to good practice requires both core and particular knowledge, and effective intervention implies a recognition of what particular knowledge is most relevant. The problem for most social work practitioners is a tendency to define tasks solely from the context of knowledge already possessed. Instead, the nature of the task should be the critical factor in determining what is most relevant and what additional new knowledge is needed. This implies the need for: (*a*) a continuing educational process; and (*b*) the socialization and training of the practitioner so that he becomes a lifelong learner, a practitioner-scholar, constantly searching for new knowledge to improve practice and identifying new tasks that require different or more specialized knowledge.

Historically, except for brief interludes in the early part of this century and again in the 1930s when the profession emphasized social reform, social work's primary concern has been with helping people in difficulty, supporting people's socialization and development, and assisting people to receive the rights and services that were their due. Given these goals, the profession's early use of social science knowledge was circumscribed.[2] As Kadushin and others have pointed out, the rediscovery of the social sciences in the 1950s did not involve a major reorientation of the focus of social work. The personality, clinical, and therapeutic orientation remained dominant, and social science material was used, according to Kadushin, "primarily to enhance a more comprehensive understanding of personality development and behavior rather than to reemphasize social action." [3]

Kadushin identifies, in addition to Freudian psychoanalytic theory, the concept of culture and subculture from anthropology, and small-group theory, group dynamics, role, social stratification, reference group theory, and organization theory from sociology, as being the major components of "borrowed" knowledge for social work. He points out that the well-known Stein and Cloward social science reader [4] includes only such material as would provide a deeper understanding of human behavior. Thus, in addition to the earlier mentioned areas, it includes some discussion of the family, deviant behavior, and values. However, a review of major works dealing with social work knowledge and related social science content clearly indicates the limited range of social science incorporated by social work in the past. Close examination of Kogan, Maas, and the first edition of the *Encyclopedia of Social Work* [5] provides no evidence of a broader utilization from the social sciences than we have already indicated.

As no practitioner can hope to know everything, an essential issue becomes how to develop criteria for appropriate selectivity and utilization of the vast amount of social science knowledge available. Which knowledge will enable him to assess the situation, circumstances, and needs involved; to determine, design, and carry out appropriate interventions; to evaluate results; and to prevent, whenever possible, recurrence of difficulty?

Using as our guide the principle that the task should delineate the search for knowledge, we offer the following examples and specify the social science knowledge that would be relevant:

A social worker notices that the hospital where he is employed is increasingly used by Puerto Ricans. What social science knowledge could be helpful to the worker? Included would be the family and kinship patterns in their culture, Puerto Rican attitudes toward illness and medical care; knowledge about the organization of service delivery systems;

and how to effect change in formal organizations such as a hospital so that service delivery patterns can be more responsive to changing community needs.

The social work consultant to a federation of senior citizen clubs is asked to help obtain reductions in public transportation fares, already available to senior citizens in a neighboring city. Social science knowledge that could assist this worker would include knowledge about the political process, about the community power structure, and about the special needs of the aged which would be met by increased mobility.

Administrative officials in a suburban high school approach the school's social worker for help in handling racial unrest. The worker needs to know the cultural and racial backgrounds of the groups involved, small-group theory, and theories of conflict and conflict resolution on both the small-group and the community level.

The parents of a young schizophrenic patient sabotage his attempts at increased independence and will not participate in treatment. The social worker in this situation may need to know about families as social systems and family communication, in order to select an appropriate method of intervention.

A large corporation building a factory in a suburban community expects to employ large numbers of women. Anticipating a need for day care facilities, the company hires a social worker to develop and administer such a program. Social science knowledge which could be helpful includes knowledge about programming for early childhood development, differential use of manpower, and some familiarity with cost-effectiveness approaches to program development.

These examples merely illustrate possible approaches to the selection of relevant social science knowledge. Clearly, as the scope of social work broadens, social workers are required to call on resources beyond and outside their traditional knowledge base. Economics, political science, macrosociology, and communications theory, in addition to new developments in those social and behavioral sciences previously utilized by social work, such as psychology, psychiatry, social psychology, anthropology, and microsociology, are becoming increasingly important. Yet, while the case is readily made, it is apparent that the borrowing and adapting have not kept up with the demands of practice.

We take the position that in two important respects the situation now is quite unlike that in 1945–70. First, the fields to be assessed and the scope of the borrowing must be much wider because of the developments in the range of social work practice. Second, there is less basis for orthodoxy. More perspectives and theories are in legitimate contention in many of the relevant fields. Thus, we would not expect all social work schools or agencies to be alike in their definition of the "common core" for practitioners. We would especially expect diversity as the autonomous practitioner in his search for expertise tests, adapts, and borrows to meet the demands of changing modes of professional practice.

To clarify what exists and to guide the search for what is relevant and useful among the social sciences, we offer an overview. We have found it functional to organize the material along two dimensions: first, the level of intervention for practice; and second, specific social science fields. Each is an artificial distinction utilized only as an aid in the arrangement of the material presented. There are two levels of intervention: micropractice, involving individuals, families, small groups, agencies, and communities; and macropractice, at the city, state, regional, federal, or any large-system level. Specific social science clusters have been assigned to the level of intervention where they are most essential, recognizing, however, that some social science knowledge is relevant at every level. It is often the interfaces of the social sciences that are most relevant for social work, as, for example, political sociology, family sociology, and political economics, each of which includes components from two fields. For each level of practice we will review the social science knowledge that has been borrowed by social work in the past; what is currently being used; and, finally, what is available and not now being used by social work but which would improve practice.

Social Science Knowledge for Micropractice

Micropractice constitutes direct work with individuals, families, groups, and communities. The social science knowledge base for such practice is continuously expanding and diversified. Increasingly, knowledge from psychology, sociology, social psychology, anthropology, general systems theory, linguistics, and communications theory is central for action on the microlevel.

One task for social work is to seek some order or integration of this range and variety of knowledge. General systems theory has been seized by some as an organizing framework, as at an earlier time Lewin's field theory seemed to offer such possibilities.[6] Clearly, the continuing development of such a framework is necessary for the evaluation of future contributions as well as for the transferability and "learnability" of knowledge.

It is further recognized that micropractice must be based on a keen awareness of broader social, political, and economic currents, as these affect the atmosphere in which services are delivered, the resources available for social work activity, and, most importantly, the lives of people who may or may not be clients. However, in the belief that effective practitioners will also seek clusters of knowledge from the social sciences, this presentation has been organized to reflect that clustering.

Social work has borrowed heavily from the psychoanalytic movements; the influx of Freudian thought beginning in the 1920s and Rank's influence in the 1930s are well known. In addition, field theories, such as those of Lewin and Murray, apparently influenced Hamilton to formulate the "person-in-situation" concept.[7] This reemphasis on the continuing influence of environment was also furthered by the impact of sociologists such as Émile Durkheim, Robert Merton, and Talcott Parsons during the 1940s. During the last twenty years, the development of ego psychology in the writings of Anna Freud, Ernst Kris, Heinz Hartmann, Rudolph Loewenstein, Erik Erikson, and others has brought a wealth of theoretical and research material that social work practitioners are still tapping. The contributions of sociology to theories of small-group development and community are also clear. Over the last thirty years, the work of Kurt Lewin, Ronald Lippit, and others, as well as the rediscovery of the contributions of Georg Simmel and Charles H. Cooley,[8] have enriched the understanding of the nature of small groups. Similarly, the early classical studies of community by Robert and Helen Lynd,

John Dollard, and W. Lloyd Warner have been followed by useful studies by Polsby on power relationships in a large city [9] and Gans's work on the urban neighborhood and suburbia.[10]

What borrowed knowledge is currently utilized in social work practice with microsystems, and what are potential directions for future borrowing? First, any understanding of the individual, family, and small group must assume an awareness of how the social structure encourages or constrains human fulfillment.

Social scientists have increasingly realized the essential interrelatedness of personality, family, and social factors. Social workers practicing with microsystems have borrowed knowledge from sociology and social psychology in the areas of role theory,[11] social class, ethnic, and cultural influences, and the impact of racism; [12] functioning of the nuclear family and extended kinship systems; [13] and others. Especially important for practice with small groups is work done on group composition, group development, and variations of groups in different organizational environments characteristic of social work settings.[14] Anthropological studies have been used to amplify understanding of cultural influences on personality, family, and group functioning.[15] Although influences of historical times have rarely been made explicit, these form an important dimension which social work practitioners would do well to note.[16]

Any understanding of personality dynamics usually begins with modified Freudian or Rankian theories. Concepts generally retained in the neo-Freudian approach are the topographical and structural theories, infantile sexuality, the etiology and dynamics of neuroses, and the Oedipal conflict, with perhaps some notions about cultural and cognitive influence on the latter.[17] The emphasis by the ego psychologists on the importance, attributes, and potential strengths of "ego" have of course been welcomed by social workers, who attempt to utilize existing coping capacities in their clients rather than to promote regression. Ruth Smalley claims that in this development Freudian theory reflected the "more optimistic view of man" which Rank and the functional school of social casework had already embraced.[18] Also meaningful for dealing with diverse social work caseloads have been additional contributions by theorists building on or supplementing Freud's works. Anna Freud and Erikson [19] led in the expansion of the consideration of human development throughout the life cycle, especially including normal adolescence, adulthood, and old age. Mahler, and Arlow and Brenner,[20] among others, clarified understanding of the psychoses, whereas Freud's works had been more descriptive than dynamic. Accumulating theory from ego psychologists and others and numerous research studies on early child development have demonstrated the vast importance of the first two years of life for ego development, personality formation, and potential for pathological resolution.[21] For example, Piaget, who independently of the Freudian tradition has clarified cognitive development from infancy through adolescence, suggests what sorts of environmental stimulation and response young children need in order to learn to think normally.[22] It should also be noted that social workers still read post-Freudian personality theorists such as Adler, Jung, and especially Karen Horney, who has become particularly popular now that the role of women in our society is being examined more closely; but the tendency of these authors to emphasize their differences from the mainstream has made them more stimulating than comprehensively useful in many instances.

General systems theory, one means of conceptualizing the mutual interrelatedness of individuals-families-social groups-communities-societies, has recently been borrowed as an organizing schema for use in social work. Its greatest value for micropractice is the forced recognition that "systems" (such as school, employment, medical care, or one's own agency) have a continued impact on clients and vice versa, making such trends as advocacy [23] and the broadening of assessment skills for practitioners [24] eminently sensible. When the idea is accepted that any dynamic entity can be viewed as an open system, with properties such as negative entropy, equifinality, and especially homeostasis, systems theory also becomes applicable to a specific understanding of individuals, families, small groups, and communities.

Thus, to start with personality, Freudian structural theory is easily translated into systems terms. "Ego" is the homeostatic device for finding balance between demands of the individual (id, superego) and the requirements of reality. This perspective has been developed by several authors, most notably Menninger; Nelsen has noted the usefulness of systems theory as a teaching tool in this regard.[25] The ego psychologists' emphases on coping and mastery match the assertion that open systems tend toward negative entropy. Equifinality is the idea that a given end state may be reached in a number of different ways.[26] Certainly this is compatible with social work's understanding of the complexity of personality dynamics. Also, the family as a system has become an increasingly popular notion, both within social work and in related fields.[27] Especially useful is the now widespread notion that a family maintains its own balance, resisting efforts at change in ways that differ from the individual (intrapsychic) resistances of its members. Finally, existing conceptions of small groups translate readily into systems terms.[28] A systems approach to communities, groups, and organizations may be found, for example, in the works of Lippitt, Sanders, and Katz and Kahn.[29] The value of systems translations varies as they contribute new insights, but use of a common terminology could at the least facilitate dialogue between practitioners and other social scientists.

Crisis theory and the crisis intervention modes of treatment which have been devised for individuals and families are examples of both the complexity of knowledge borrowing and the possible utility of systems translations. As Rapoport points out, concepts of crisis were probably first developed in social-psychological studies of populations exposed to extreme stress, but the origins of the theory or "framework" as it now stands can be traced in ego psychology, stress theory, learning theories, studies of family life, social role theory, and the public health model of practice. Her definition of crisis as "an upset in the steady state" [30] obviously fits the systems conceptualization whether applied to individual personality functioning or to families. While newer crisis terminology has not enjoyed wide usage in small-group work, there are similarities between this and the more traditional conceptions, such as group cohesiveness and group conflict.[31] Appropriate for the times, community organization analyses have also begun to deal with the issue of conflict and controversy.[32] Social work has contributed to the pulling together of crisis intervention material, particularly in integrating knowledge about healthy coping with understanding of specific developmental and situation crises to suggest appropriate intervention techniques.

Related to the crisis work is "brief treatment" for individuals and families, based within social work on some of the long-used skills of social work, knowledge borrowed from proponents of short-term work within the psychoanalytic movement,[33] and research, the most extensive on this topic within social work having been done by Reid and Shyne.[34]

At the boundaries of systems, defining their interpenetration, is communication.[35] New understanding of human communication based on developing theories and research could prove immensely useful for social work micropractice. The contributions are in three main areas. First, from linguistics, paralinguistics, and kinesics come recognition of how different language structures determine modes of thinking and the importance of nonlexical vocalization and nonverbal accompaniments in human communication.[36] Greater social work knowledge of this material could increase sensitivity and lessen cultural or idiosyncratic misunderstanding of clients. Second, important research studies, including those by Minuchin and Malone,[37] trace difficulties encountered by children who do not learn communication skills such as vocabulary covering different levels of abstraction and designations for feelings. The idea of these theorists that it is the therapist's job to teach communication skills at the individual and family levels [38] has rarely been consciously applied within social work. However, the socialization model of practice, in which social workers aim to teach "new behaviors, attitudes and skills," is akin to this approach. McBroom traces the origins of the model to "sociology, social psychology, and anthropology, and . . . the current work in all behavioral science on systems and communication theory." [39]

A third emphasis of communications theorists has been on finding inadequate or distorted communication skills behind behavior that others would trace to intrapsychic pathology. Ruesch, writing in the 1950s about patients' blocks in perceiving both intrapsychic and interpersonal communications, seems at times to echo Freudian notions of unconscious defenses and transference,[40] but other theorists more definitely discover new insights. Especially challenging have been applications of the general concept that human communications serve to define or control relationships. According to this notion, the language of the psychoanalytic movement is severely limited in that it applies strictly to the individual.[41] Communications terminology allows explicit recognition that a phobia, for example, may have less to do with an individual's intrapsychic conflicts than with his marital relationship, in which the symptom allows him to use the phobia as a control without having to assume responsibility for doing so.[42] Satir has extensively considered relationship aspects as well as other complexities of family communication,[43] and from Bateson, Jackson, Haley, and Weakland comes the double-bind theory of schizophrenia, according to which schizophrenic communication is adaptive to intrafamilial relationship messages although not to coping with the world at large.[44] Haley makes abundantly clear how varieties of schizophrenic symptomatology are in fact different ways of attempting relationship messages without assuming responsibility for the attempts.[45]

While some of these theorists, especially Satir, also write of "teaching communication," they place a good deal of emphasis on how practitioners can use such communication techniques as a therapeutic double bind to break clients' or families' dysfunctional communication patterns.[46] Haley and Jackson have written extensively on the process of communication in treatment. They suggest, for example, that change occurs not due to insight, but because the therapist refuses in various ways to validate his client's presenting behavior while paradoxically encouraging the client to feel that he is in charge of what transpires in their relationship.[47] The similarities of this approach to transactional theories must be noted, although the latter trace their underpinnings somewhat differently, for example, in the works of Harry Stack Sullivan.[48] Several of the communications theorists proscribe the use of personality theory, with the justification that understanding communication patterns is sufficient for pinpointing difficulties and for treatment.[49] Although most social workers would not go this far, they should find much that is meaningful and challenging in the communications work. For instance, it is apparent that the influence of the therapist as a validating person is greater in a dyad than in a family, group, or community where other potential validating agents are present. The problem of how to produce change may be particularly great with families, where members have had years together to perfect their devices for neutralizing disruptive influences, such as social workers. Communications techniques could doubtless be used in client or community groups.[50] Of course, the use of some devices to produce change can raise value issues. However, as a practitioner or as a human being, one cannot *not* communicate [51]—therefore a better understanding of communications processes seems essential for responsible social work practice.

Another group of theorists who have not cared to look inside the person are the behaviorists. They have had an increasing impact on social work practice in the last decade. Basically, behaviorists see behavior as related to environment. Skinner's work on "operant conditioning" has been central in extending the early theoretical contributions of Pavlov's "reflex learning theory" to nonreflexive behavior.[52] Behavior is seen as governed by subsequent positive or negative reinforcement. Reinforcement may range from food to approval to threat of disapproval. Out of the "new" behaviorists' theoretical formulations, the behavior modification approach has gained a stronger foothold, generally as a treatment modality.

Social work, in its search for an enhanced repertoire of interventive possibilities to deal with difficult problems such as juvenile delinquency, drug addiction, and mental illness, has been drawn to behavior-modification techniques based on operant conditioning and related formulations. The works of Thomas, Vinter and others have sought to integrate behavior-modification techniques into practical frameworks for social work practice in work with individuals and groups.[53] More recently, social workers and psychologists have sought to make these techniques applicable in "open," natural settings, as opposed to the laboratory and protected situations more characteristic of social agencies. Behaviorist approaches in social work are often combined with social system concepts to fit the complex service environment in social work.[54]

The appeal of behavior modification is its emphasis on present environment as crucial to the frequency of behavior, which lends a more optimistic outlook for the change of human personality. Outcomes translated in behavior terms allow for scientific measurement of the effectiveness of treatment activity. Controversy often surrounds the introduction of behavior modification. Critics deplore the reduction of holistic personality formulations, "circumscribed" bits of behavior. The issues of social control and the centrality of the therapist in behavior modification are also raised. Behaviorists counter that all of these objections apply equally to traditional formulations.

The use of behavioristic approaches may often constitute an eclectic orientation in which behavior modification plays a major part. Because many practitioners in other clinical professions are attracted to and use behavior techniques, it is clear that they will remain an important influence in social work practice.

Another major influence in psychological thinking that touches social work practice broadly can be defined as "humanistic" or "growth" psychology. A strong existential element characterizes many of these formulations. The focus is on the "here and now" and the struggle of individuals to overcome obstacles in self-development. An extreme position taken by some is that a complete process orientation is necessary for understanding human behavior and the world. The claim is made that to structure conceptual knowledge is actually to distort the reality, and thus knowledge as organized conceptualizations has only limited value. This is obviously in marked contrast to the traditional, analytic, retrospective proclivity.

Among these diverse formulations are the works of Rogers, Frankl, Maslow, and Perls.[55] In Rogers's personalistic orientation, the treatment process focuses the skill of the practitioner to support "freedom," "creativity," "diversity of experience," and "faith in human potential." Frankl, as a result of experiences in a Nazi concentration camp, suggests that human beings can and do defy their early rearing by giving meaning to life through strong experiences, such as suffering, or the love of others or of God. For Frankl, a sense of meaninglessness in life represents psychological failure. Maslow's personality formulation suggests a hierarchy of needs and progressive movement toward self-actualization as part of the human potential. Perls and his followers have had a strong influence in providing a holistic view of human experience through their *Gestalt* approach. Emphasis is upon expanding awareness of man and his immediate environment in order to support self-actualization.

The use of groups as a modality is characteristic of *Gestalt* psychology,[56] *T*-group training,[57] and encounter groups [58] arising out of these growth psychologies. A discernible gray area for social work practitioners has evolved because of the development of the so-called "self-help" groups, which are not readily open to, or are even antagonistic toward, the professionals' quest for systematic analysis. These groups, however, have mounting impact in areas of public concern, such as drug addiction, the role of women, and the general alienation and isolation faced by many individuals in contemporary society.

As in the past, of course, social workers planning interventions in microsystems do not borrow uniformly from the social sciences. Some practitioners adhere strictly to a chosen theory, be it Freudian or behaviorist, while others foreswear all theory to follow more mystic or existential leanings. The vast majority seem to borrow widely, according to what is meaningful for their practice—an eclecticism which at least helps get the job done—while social scientists themselves are far from agreement as to which knowledge is most useful. Social workers may even have a special facility at defining "useful for what," as well as for innovating when theory leaves gaps in understanding necessary to practice. The potential of social work not only for borrowing knowledge from the social sciences, but also for lending to them, has scarcely been realized.

Social Science Knowledge for Macropractice

Options for social work practice at the macrolevel have expanded substantially in recent years. Planning, policy analysis and development, and programming at the federal, state, local, and large-system level offer new opportunities in middle-management positions for the well-trained professional, and schools of social work are more and more revising their curricula to respond to the demands of such practice.

The organizational context in which macropractice occurs, as well as the functions and goals of such practice, involves a greater recognition of the interrelationship of the economic, political, and social systems in society, and the awareness that social problems, programs, and issues rarely occur in isolation but are almost inevitably intertwined with political and economic factors. According to a recent report on the behavioral and social sciences, "almost all such [social] problems are found in a political and economic context, which means that legitimate power and material resources must be brought to bear before a solution can occur." [59] Social policy is never formulated without some explicit consideration of its economic and political consequences as well as of its social objectives; furthermore, although economic policy is often made without consideration of social consequences, these are almost always present.

For practitioners to understand the problems facing them, to define these problems appropriately, to develop solutions for them, and to prevent their recurrence requires familiarity with this knowledge. Without this, competent and effective practice is impossible. The issue becomes what parts of the enormous range of knowledge in the social sciences is most applicable for macropractice.

The behavioral and social science knowledge that has been utilized in the past has been limited to the needs and demands of micropractice. New trends in practice highlight new needs and indicate new directions for social work to take in its search for knowledge. As macropractice is in its emergent phase now, updating social science utilization becomes particularly crucial.

Three traditional social sciences are particularly relevant for macropractice: economics, political science, and sociology. In addition, the emerging management and decision sciences may also contribute to such practice. This does not imply that these have no relevance for micropractice. On the contrary, sociology has been heavily utilized, as already indicated. Also, some concepts of political science have been used in work with communities. Although economics describes and accounts for the conditions under which all people live, thus far social work has utilized that knowledge very little, at any level. It is not implied that useful knowledge for macropractice is not available in those social sciences which have already been discussed. Communications theory, for example, can be an important aid in understanding organizational change and decision-making.

Human ecology, another emerging social science, has relevance for all levels of social work practice since it involves the interrelationship of man and his environment.[60] Integral to the ecological view is that everything is connected to everything else and that every choice has a cost. These "laws of ecology" have implications for social work practice, making human ecology potentially fruitful for further study.

The term "policy science," or "policy sciences," has come into greater use in recent years. Regardless of whether one thinks there is such a fully evolved science, the concept seems viable in so far as it identifies a cluster of social sciences (economics, political science, sociology, and management and decision sciences) which are essential for policy analysis and development. Clustered aspects of these social sciences provide an analytic tool for social work practice at several levels. Ultimately, however, it is understood that policy decisions remain normative decisions and are made in the context of political and other influences.

SOCIOLOGY

Sociology has historically been a prime source of knowledge for social work practice. For example, in the late nineteenth century Social Darwinist theories reflected notions of society and man that strongly influenced strident social policies toward the poor and the mentally handicapped. The early part of the twentieth century featured the "discovery" of poverty, and sociological analysis focused heavily on "social problems."

In more recent times, sociological theory has been a corrective factor in favor of environmental influences on behavior for a social work profession heavily enamored of psychoanalytic understanding of human problems. Sociology, thus, has yielded valuable knowledge for social workers in small-group and family theory, normative behavior, and the nature of social conditions and problems.[61]

With the social work profession's growing contribution to social planning and policy, sociology becomes a source of knowledge of the nature of large-scale societal organization and processes. For example, serious questions addressed to social planners would be: How does one measure the impact of different social welfare programs?

How can one predict the potential consequences of social policy en-
actments? What standards are reflective of the health of a whole society?

Potential sociological contributions to social work practice will be
viewed here by defined areas of academic sociology in relation to
interventions at several levels of social structure, ranging from the
interface of primary groups and organizations to the total societal
level.

Of particular value to social work practice at the interface where
individuals and primary groups come in contact with the social institutions in society is organizational theory. Social work has only
recently begun to explore in depth the potential contribution of organizational theories for improved practice. More and more practitioners are working in highly complex organizations. In recent
years, social work practitioners have grown sensitive to the effect of
the organizational environment on their practice and on the delivery
of services.[62]

Of special interest in this area is the work of Litwak, Meyer, and
their colleagues at the University of Michigan. They have recently
attempted to reformulate and extend the theory of the relationship
between primary groups and bureaucratic structures. The question
then becomes: how do primary groups and bureaucracies coexist
and influence each other? In recent years, Max Weber's traditional
monocratic view of bureaucracy has been extended by the structur-
alists who have combined it with notions of informal structure from
the human relations school of thought. The perspective of traditional bureaucratic theory does not account for the variation among
formal organizations or for the impact of primary groups on them.
Based on the approach of Litwak and others, new theoretical constructs are available to explain the linkages between primary groups
and bureaucracies, thus facilitating the development of more effective service delivery and accountability.[63]

Along these lines is the concept of ad-hocracy as developed in the
writing of Bennis. Ad-hocracy is a reflection of the attempt to modify and negotiate the rigidities of formal organizations through the
use of problem-focused task forces of differential duration based on
organization and service needs.[64] Blau and Scott, who also have in-
vestigated the organization as an environment for service, have made

an important contribution by differentiating organizations by examination of the beneficiaries and the consequent structural implications.[65] Thompson has sought to look at the structure and requirements of organizational units and their interrelationships with goals.[66] Etzioni has looked at power relationships as they affect compliant structures for the goal-achievement function of organizations.[67]

As with other professions, there has been a rapid bureaucratization of social work, intensely rationalizing the context of professional practice. This process has heightened conflicts between professional and organizational norms, a feature of the organizational context which impinges on the practice of many professions.[68]

Socialization theory is another area of sociological inquiry of value to practitioners. Socialization theories have previously been used by social workers to understand child rearing and family interaction and have now been expanded to include studies on adult socialization. Out of this new knowledge, insights have been gained as to how social situations can be made to offer opportunities which support adult change.[69] Furthermore, studies of professionalization and career patterns have offered additional insights on the forces which impinge on professionals and modify and change their behavior. Social planners and policy-makers must give consideration to socialization not only as it affects those whom they wish to serve, but also as it relates to the selection, training, and adaptability of personnel at different levels in the delivery of human services.

The last twenty years have been characterized by social work's increased and more complex collaboration with a variety of professionals—physicians, urban planners, economists, psychologists, systems analysts, and others. This circumstance has encouraged renewed interest in the character of professionals in general and of social workers in particular, especially because of the necessity of cooperative efforts. Close interrelationships with other professions have forced social workers to scrutinize the position that social work occupies in relation to them and to clarify the nature of recruitment, training, knowledge, and professional norms. These factors play a substantial role in the prestige of the profession and the manner in which social work practice will be carried out.

A long-time concern of the social work profession has been its interest in defining its unique function and its claim for professional status. Sociologists who have examined social work activities in particular and professions in general have raised questions about the nature of social work as a profession. Blau and Scott, for example, note that often the organizational activities of social workers detract from a service orientation. Etzioni states that social workers are semiprofessionals. However, the traditional notions about professions have undergone critical review, and one can anticipate much change in this aspect of the sociology of professions.[70]

Knowledge about theories of change is also of great importance to social workers who wish to become involved in organizational and system reform or political activity. Social change varies from society to society, and there are social systems in which change is more controlled than has been possible in the United States.[71] Nonetheless, within the United States social changes occur along a continuum from incremental and discrete changes to more comprehensive change. This approach to change and planning has been spelled out in the work of Dahl, Lindblom, and others who have made contributions to political science and planning theory.[72] If social changes are to be effected, social workers will need knowledge of those changes and the conditions under which they can be made, and they must be able to select under what circumstances one strategy —incremental or comprehensive—is best chosen. In order to bring about change, social work practitioners also need information about political decision systems, levels of coordination, and regionalization, especially the sort which takes power away from people. A central area of sociological thought is the determination of social change as a result of "natural" social process and social engineering. The tracing of patterns of change on a societal level has been extended by sociologists,[73] most recently in attempts to develop social indicators of the "health" of an entire society.[74]

Contemporary organizations after which social welfare organizations are modeling themselves are calling on large bodies of knowledge to facilitate their operations, continuity, and effectiveness. Organizations are moving into the acquisition and packaging of ideas, problem-solving methods, and coordination. Wilensky has presented a review of the potential organizational barriers to efficient utilization of information.[75] The contribution of information theory, cybernetics, and feedback as a requisite for the life of productive social systems has been developed by Wiener, Etzioni, and Simon.[76] A further extension of the search for organizational intelligence has been forwarded through the use of large-scale sampling in social research. This includes opinion polling and demographic surveys of social conditions and groups.

In recent years sociology has opened up new research possibilities through the use of various techniques and concepts. For example, multivariate analysis, when linked with sociological theory, suggests that social events originate through the interaction of many variables. Computers have allowed additional developments, such as simulations and mathematical analysis of recurrent behavior. Game theory has also afforded new opportunities for the study of potential consequences of actions of practitioners on the micro- and macrolevels. This clearly is an area for future study by social workers, especially as society becomes more complicated and centralization of information and decision-making takes on added importance in organizational systems.[77]

Educational and medical sociology can have a major impact on social work and social welfare services in that insights and information are afforded about the organization of services and the interplay of professionalism, interinstitutional forces, and consumer needs. Social workers have a special need to understand these factors as they affect in multiple fashion the behavior and life chances of individuals, groups, and communities.[78] Also, social policy and planning for social welfare require an intimate knowledge of the interorganizational effects and possibilities.[79]

An often overlooked area of sociological knowledge is that of social stratification formulations. These formulations can enable social workers to understand and estimate different life styles on the microlevel and the macrolevel and can lead to greater understanding of class, status, equality and inequality, and social power potentials that go beyond individual personal attributes.[80]

In the 1960s, social workers' forays into the inner city in order to identify the unmet needs of the poor necessitated a better understanding of the densely populated urban scene. Often overlooked are the changing character and unique aspects of social conditions in rural areas, a factor that can heighten understanding of the urban environment through knowledge of behavior patterns of new arrivals from rural environments.

Emerging political forms, political participation, changing power relationships, voting, decision-making, lobbying, and centers of power are all being studied by sociologists, and an understanding of these factors is crucial for practitioners interested in successful policy or planning interventions.[81] It is important to ascertain how political mechanisms are or are not used to resolve or not to resolve social issues. This knowledge, an important insight from the literature of political sociology, is based upon a choice of two fundamental theories—power distribution and change.

If a social worker wishes to become involved in social planning or social policy, then it is necessary to frame a conscious choice of perspectives about the distribution of power and decision-making. A traditional view of decision-making suggests that there is a power elite which influences all decisions of importance. The work of Mills, Hunter, and the Lynds [82] supports this view. This power elite is interlocked in order to control access to the decision-making process and also to control the ultimate decisions. In recent times, another perspective has been introduced which suggests a "pluralist" power distribution and decision-making process. Dahl, Polsby, Meyerson and Banfield, and Long [83] have documented the pluralist position. According to this view, political power alters with the content of the issue, and power thus shifts from place to place and influential to influential upon the basis of the issues raised, the peculiar political context, and the leadership and other resources available at any one time and place.

Sociologists have offered information which can help social workers to understand two fundamental issues in this society. First, there has been intensive exploration of the existence and pervasiveness of racism and its impact on minority groups and society at large.[84] Sociologists have also examined interracial and intergroup relations in detail. A second related issue is the pluralist nature of the national community and to what degree the differences among people can be understood, protected, and fostered for human betterment. These two issues—racism and pluralism—constantly confront social workers, and it is hoped that the knowledge provided on these subjects by sociological studies can support social work's attention to planning and policy-making to enhance diversification and individual rights to varied life styles.[85]

The study of conflict has presented alternative perspectives for social workers. Coser, Boulding, and Sherif [86] suggest that conflict has both positive and negative attributes and is necessary for the very solidarity of society. Social workers can make use of conflict theory for a wide range of interventions extending from the positive use of confrontation for group formation to the creation of planning for varied interests.

With the heightened emphasis on organizational theory and planning at higher levels of government, the utilization of community theory takes on new forms. Warren, as well as other sociologists, has been interested in the community as a lateral societal structure intersected by the vertical impact of strong organizational interests such as government at higher levels and national agencies, both public and private.[87]

From this brief, selective survey of sociology it is clear that this discipline will continue to provide a rich conceptual lode for emerging frameworks of macro-social work practice. As social work moves into more sophisticated areas of macropractice, such as planning and policy development, specialists in these areas will have to develop both an appreciation of, and a familiarity with, relevant sociological theories and will need to formulate individually functional principles of selectivity.

ECONOMICS

Historically, social work has evinced only limited interest in economics, except as it related to the financing of social welfare programs or the development of income-maintenance programs. Even though economics defines the purview of social planning and policy, and every mention of these domains includes economics, references to the uses of economics are almost nonexistent in the social work literature of the early 1960s.[88] Eveline Burns, however, strongly emphasizes the interrelationship between economics and social work,

and all her writings continue to be particularly relevant for social
work.

Cohen was among the few social workers who recognized the importance of economic and political factors, and he urged social
workers to look at the new dynamic concepts emerging from economics and political science as well as from sociology, social psychology, and cultural anthropology.[89] Feldman explored the impact
of economics on family life in relation to the need for budgeting.[90]
Kahn has discussed social work practice within a broader context,
making some mention of the interrelationship of economic and social factors.[91] A review of *Abstracts for Social Workers* issued by
NASW since 1965 reveals a similar pattern. In these years, economics was listed among "relevant fields of knowledge" in only four
out of twenty-eight issues. In the first year, only two articles were
listed on economics, while there were sixteen on psychiatry and
medicine, fourteen on psychology and social psychology, and
twenty on sociology. There are few subsequent references to articles
by economists and addressed to social welfare programs. Although
the current edition of the *Encyclopedia of Social Work* does include
some references to economics and economic planning, the section
on the social science foundations of social planning and community
organization has not one reference to economics.[92]

The experiences of the 1960s clearly indicate the centrality of
economics and politics to social work. A rapid increase in economic
growth coupled with the development of new technologies, urbanization, changing political constituencies, and the influence of the
civil rights movement provided a framework for a substantial
growth in the number and range of social welfare programs. The rediscovery of poverty, the involvement of social workers in antipoverty programs, and the subsequent recognition of the limitations and
failures of these programs led to a reevaluation of the strategies employed.[93] New efforts were made to clarify the meaning of poverty
and the implications of differential definitions for planning, policy,
and programming.[94] An obvious consequence of these programs was
the recognition that a service strategy for selected groups could not
by itself eradicate poverty even if these programs were established

on a much larger scale. It has become equally apparent, however, that an income strategy by itself may not be sufficient either.

Because social problems occur in economic and political contexts, the economist's concept of interlocking systems can provide a helpful framework by means of which social work can view social, economic, and political problems. Macroeconomics, in having as its major policy goals economic growth, full employment, price stability, balance of trade, and the reduction of income inequality, demonstrates the interrelationship of these objectives. This interrelationship has implications for how social workers should approach major social goals, since the achievement of these goals can often reveal inherent conflicts, divergent values, and inevitable trade-offs. For example, as has recently been seen in this country, when price stability is the primary goal, unemployment rises; emphasis on achieving a balance of trade may affect the economies of other countries, leading to negative consequences for this country's economic growth; growing concern with the general welfare of the country raises questions about the goal of economic growth.

In recent years, a large group of economists has turned to econometrics and formal mathematical models, although others have begun to look at social problems in a humanistic perspective. At the same time, social workers are beginning to turn toward economics for a different perspective on their areas of concern, for supportive substantive knowledge, and for new techniques.

One of social work's major concerns is the problem of poverty and its ramifications. As Rein points out:

Particularly with the problem of poverty and the distribution of income . . . economics and public finance seemed to provide more relevant ideas and substantive knowledge. It also presented a way of thinking about the consequences of programs and about the allocation of scarce resources among competing claimants. Economics emphasizes finding and perfecting the right methodology to deal with social and economic problems. It proceeded on the assumption that what was needed was a good tool, which could then presumably be applied to any problem.[95]

Social work's current interest in the problems of definition and measurement of poverty, as well as in strategies for intervention, draws heavily on the work of various economists and clearly indicates the need for some familiarity with the field.[96] There is a growing recognition that poverty is a problem of relative inequality rather than one of absolute standards; [97] that there is a distinction between income poverty[98] and poverty viewed in a social sense; [99] that strategies for the elimination of poverty include not only more income but also a combination of income policy, social utilities, case services, and institutional change; [100] and that income-maintenance programs cannot be effective without consideration of manpower policy and employment programs.[101] Miller and Roby view poverty as social as well as economic inequality.[102] Rein, discusses six types of "intervention strategies" to achieve six goals of poverty reduction: social decency; equality; mobility; social stability; social inclusion; and economic stability and growth.[103] He also says that "poverty is not only a lack of income but a lack of the goods and services necessary to support a desired level of well-being." [104] Included here are general social services, medical services, and housing.

How poverty is defined has important consequences for social policy, Defining it in terms of the absence of minimum provision tends to result in more traditional programs than defining it as a problem of inequality. For example, one economist comments that defining poverty as a problem of subsistence was an important factor in developing a service strategy during the 1960s. He notes that *"a strategy of service . . . stems from and is deeply embedded in a posture derived from the 'subsistence-based' type definition that we use.* Having defined poverty as the gap between consensually determined needs and available resources, we try to fill the gap by providing services." [105] Employing the same concept but applying it to an income strategy implies the development of some form of income-maintenance program, in this case related to how minimum provision is defined. The range of literature on these programs is enormous.[106] Of equal importance to social work is not only which among several negative income tax proposals is preferable, but also whether a negative income tax proposal or a children's allowance, for example, should be the policy of choice.[107] Here again, since it is often the economist's values that prevail, it is important for the social work practitioner to recognize that economists place primary emphasis on the value of "efficiency." [108] Thus, in deciding between a universal or a selective program the latter is often preferred because it addresses a circumscribed population and will be less costly in dollar terms, although emphasis on "efficiency" may ignore potential social costs.

Viewing poverty in terms of inequality leads to different kinds or combinations of policies. It may involve the issue of amenities; the appropriate mix of income, housing, health, education, and employment, referred to earlier; or the more narrow concept of income inequality. The concept of inequality suggests the need for redistribution, a central goal of social policy, and raises questions of how best to achieve this.

In recent years, economists have approached the issue of redistribution from different vantage points. Lampman employs the concept of "transfers." According to him, the government alters the relative economic positions of people by means of taxes and expenditures, through one of three different types of transfers: taxes; transfer payments (public assistance, subsidies, or negative income taxes); or transfers in kind (education). In suggesting that double-entry bookkeeping should be a required course for all those concerned with social welfare policy, Lampman underlines the fact that all transfers should be viewed in terms of who benefits and who pays.[109]

Pechman focuses on the reduction of income inequality as a major objective of federal income tax policy.[110] He points out, however, that gross inequities in this system limit the effectiveness of this instrument for achieving its stated goal. Illustrative of some of these inequities is the fact that certain categories of people—the aged over the young, homeowners over nonhomeowners, business owners over wage earners—receive preferential treatment. Furthermore, the regressive nature of the payroll tax imposes a dual tax burden on those with low and moderate incomes. The principle of minimum taxable income does not apply here as it does with the income tax, further exacerbating an inequitable burden. Finally, state and local sales and property taxes create other inequities.

Another illustration of the use of economics in social work prac-

tice is the utilization of analytic strategies such as programming-
planning-budgeting systems (PPBS), cost/benefit, and cost-effectiveness analyses. The growing involvement of social work practitioners
in middle-management positions in government has demanded of
these workers more familiarity with the various tools and techniques
of decision-making. The application of PPBS by the Department of
Health, Education, and Welfare, as well as by various other levels of
government,[111] the recent employment of management experts by
the New York City Department of Social Services,[112] and the use of
the Rand Corporation as consultant for urban policy and program
development highlight the expanding application of such techniques
to social welfare programs and the need for practitioners in these
areas to enlarge their expertise.

According to Zeckhauser and Schaefer:

An economist approaches a decision by asking "What do we want and
what can we get?" Generally we want more than we can get. . . . Because our capabilities are limited, choices must be made among our
competing desires. Methods for making these choices—"the allocation
of scarce resources among competing ends" are the stuff of
economics. . . .[113]

PPBS, cost/benefit analysis, and cost-effectiveness studies are illustrative of normative economic methods and techniques for dealing with public policy decisions and problems of choice. Although
none of these can substitute for the good judgment, values, and political wisdom of the decision-maker, all can be aids or tools for improving decision-making. Much has been written about these techniques,[114] their application to specific problems and programs,[115]
and their limitations,[116] that has utility for social planners and policy
analysts.

As the major concern of social work is helping those most in need
of help, particular cognizance should be taken of the point Titmuss
makes that much social welfare policy that is designed in theory to
help the poor often helps the middle class more.[117] An interesting
cost/benefit study was done by Hansen and Weisbrod with regard
to public higher education in California.[118] Looking at the assumption that higher education contributes to equality of opportunity,
the study concludes that the structure and financing of public

higher education in California heightens rather than narrows inequalities in economic opportunity. As the most selective institutions involve the highest educational expenditures (and thus the greatest subsidies) and tend to select the highest-income students, low-income families, through the taxes they pay, in effect are helping to subsidize the education of students from high-income families. The authors make certain policy recommendations that have distinct implications for social welfare planners. One such recommendation is that public subsidies should be available to provide alternate routes —apprenticeships and on-the-job training—to greater earning power.

In discussing the importance of these approaches it is not implied that social work practitioners should become heavily involved personally in doing cost/benefit studies, although some may find the pursuit both interesting and valuable and social work policy-makers will need a degree of sophistication if they are to use these studies to advantage. This approach does tend to enlarge the perspective beyond the conventional view of who benefits and who pays. For example, in looking for who benefits from the Medicaid program we might find not only the recipients, but also physicians, pharmacists, proprietary hospitals, pharmaceutical companies, shippers, and makers of prostheses.

Rivlin, in her examination of the contributions that systematic analysis has made to decision-making in social welfare programs, emphasizes the need to test new methods for organizing and delivering social services as well as new ways to make services more accountable to the consumer.[119] Essential for this is the development of measures of effectiveness or performance. Considering current concern as to whether the public or private sector can provide more effective and efficient services, an interesting study could be done comparing proprietary, industry-related, voluntary, and public day care programs in terms of costs and benefits. A limitation in these approaches, as applied to social welfare programs generally, is that of quantifying benefits for both quality care and consumer satisfaction. In addition, there is the problem of identifying the parameters for benefits and costs and measuring the distributional effects in dollar terms.

Cross-cultural studies of economic planning and policy provide a third illustration of knowledge that can enhance social work practice. This content can be especially helpful in efforts to integrate social and economic planning. For example, Shonfield's description of planning in Sweden, with its blurring of the lines between the public and private sectors, its large free zones where planning is not controlled by the government, and its heavy emphasis on a wide range of social welfare programs, provides an interesting model for study.[120] Titmuss's work, with its pervasive focus on the interrelationship of social and economic factors and his conceptual organization of social welfare into three categories (social, fiscal, and occupational welfare), is particularly valuable for its insights in viewing social policy and the social consequences of economic policy. Myrdal, with his emphasis on the place of values in planning and policy and on human resources as an economic value, offers a different approach to planning, with particular relevance and interest for social workers.[121]

The whole field of comparative studies in social planning and policy is extremely important. Studies on comparative policy and programs, on the relationship between the public and private sector in different countries, and on different patterns of organizing and delivering social services are an enormous potential source for new knowledge and improved practice.

As social workers become more actively involved in macropractice, the management and decision sciences at the interface of economics and political science may provide another conceptual framework and technology.[122] However, these will have more relevance for social work in the future than at present. Dror rates these nascent social sciences as the best developed and most important of the interdisciplinary fields. They draw on economics, mathematics, engineering, and business administration for their component sciences, which include operations research, systems management, and cybernetics. Their relationship to the analytic ideologies of the economists is readily apparent, and their relevance for social work is bounded as is economics since they tend to stress rationality, efficiency, and the use of quantitative models. However, considering the burgeoning use of simulation models to attack a wide range of urban as well as world-wide problems, utilization of such approaches appears likely to increase. Its multidiscipline orientation and focus on action make it potentially exciting as a problem-solving approach.

POLITICAL SCIENCE

Myrdal points out that the problems of planning and policy choices have two dimensions: "One is the rational policy choice that derives from value premises and the knowledge of facts acquired by the use of these premises. . . . The other dimension concerns the political development that determines what policy choices will actually be made." [123] Thus, another area essential for macropractice is political science.

An inevitable question for social work practitioners and for all citizens thinking about social problems concerns the balance and distribution of political power, the process and structure of political decision-making, and the purposes for which they are used. There are social implications for all these decisions, and the organization of the decision-making process in and of itself affects people's lives.

How much money is spent, what kind of projects it is spent for, and who receives and pays for the benefits are decisions usually made by politicians operating in particular political climates. Thus, to comprehend the way social welfare policies are made and changed we must understand the ways that political trends and forces interact with people, events, and societies.[124]

Social workers are constantly involved in the politics of service in their own organizations as well as in the governmental bureaucracies which are impinging more and more on social welfare. Most social work practice occurs either in public agencies or in publicly financed programs; major social welfare programs *are* governmental programs by their very definition; decisions regarding these programs and choices between alternative programs and goals are all made within a political framework and the limits of political feasibility. Thus, knowledge of the allocation and distribution of political power, or political variables, processes, structures, and ideologies— the material of political science—becomes crucial for social work practice.

The various tendencies in this society which foster the centralization of decision-making have been heightened in the past decade. Simultaneously, people have experienced mounting frustration with the unresponsiveness and rigidity of the government and evince an expanding desire to be involved in the decisions which influence their own lives. Major questions for social workers arise from these developments. How can the government and the services provided by the government be made more responsive to the people served? Under what circumstances can local citizens be more involved in the decision-making process and what are the consequences of this? The Black Power movement, growing out of the civil rights activities of the early 1960s, has been followed by the activation of Chicanos, Puerto Ricans, white ethnics, American Indians, the aged, women, and counterculture youth. How can conflict between these contending groups, most of which are only now emerging from political apathy and a sense of powerlessness, be equitably resolved? How can social workers evaluate conflict between the poor and lower-middle-class groups in urban areas as each makes claims and counterclaims on limited social resources of housing, education, medical care, legal services, job training, income security, and various social amenities?

Political decisions today are taking place in an era of social disorganization. Change in the political arena is accompanied by the mobility of people from rural to urban scenes; concurrently, major alterations of the traditional power configurations have occurred. For example, several large cities have elected black mayors as a consequence of the exodus of white populations to the suburbs. Following a similar pattern, college students have been elected to office in some university towns as a result of the enfranchisement of eighteen-year-old voters. Local influences and special interests cannot be entirely controlled by central government because of conflicts between constituent groups as well as between serious constitutional issues. Illustrations of the latter which are of concern to social workers include questions of civil and legal rights, of privacy, the "right to education," the "right to treatment."

For social planners, policy analysts, programmers, and administrators to facilitate and implement effective intervention they need to have knowledge of legislative and other decision-making processes,[125] to be familiar with the performance and influence patterns of special-interest groups,[126] and to understand the structure and processes of government.[127] Traditionally, political science offers the necessary information. Equally important is the growing interest in the characteristics of policy-making, the forces which influence its direction, and the content of such policy.[128]

Despite the obvious connections between political science and social work practice at all levels, social work literature has been markedly sparse in its utilization of that knowledge.[129] Only in the areas of community organization, discussions of the antipoverty programs of the 1960s, the shifting locus of political power, and expanded citizen participation is seen an application of political science concepts and approaches.[130] However, there has been little inclusion of political science in works on social policy and planning.[131]

The traditional emphasis of political science has been on the processes by which public policies are made,[132] although recently some political scientists have shifted the focus of their work toward concern with the content of rather than the processes by which public policy develops.[133] Both approaches have relevance for social work. A clearer understanding of how social welfare policies are formed, which interest groups are concerned with what issues and objectives—in other words, the politics of planning and policy development—would be of great value to social work.[134] For example, comprehensive day care legislation may be supported by working mothers, women's liberation groups, proprietary day care facility owners, work-fare supporters, educators, and real estate owners. Obviously, the members of a diverse "lobby" will hold different concepts of the nature of the programs, standards for care, and the importance of administrative controls; this affects the nature of the legislation developed and the decisions made.

Current concern with the content of policy—policy outcomes rather than inputs—is equally important both to social planners and to political scientists.[135] Schoettle points out that policy-making must be viewed within the context of the political system, which includes all actions related to the authoritative allocation of values for society.[136] Viewing policy-making in this way highlights the political aspects of the social system, especially the structures and processes which generate and allocate power.

The usefulness of this concept of "system" becomes reinforced in various other areas treated by political science. Lines are more and more frequently blurred between political and economic systems, between the public and the private sector, and between the various sciences that combine to make up what is sometimes termed the "policy" sciences.[137] This heightens awareness of the importance of certain clusters of the social sciences—political science, economics, and such aspects of sociology as organizational theory and planned change—that are particularly relevant for specific levels of macro-social work practice. For example, the analytic strategies of the economists are employed by political scientists and discussed by them as decision-making models.[138] As Schick comments, "uniting the emergent changes in policies and budgeting is one of the popular metaphors of our time, the central metaphor of the old politics and budgeting was *process*, the key metaphor of the new politics and budgeting is systems." [139]

On the other hand, Lindblom rejects the economist's tendency to emphasize the rationality of decision-making and the development of formal planning models and develops the concept of incremental planning, with its emphasis on small changes implemented within a framework of political feasibility.[140] Whether or not political realities make this limited change inevitable, or whether major social change is possible, is a natural concern of social work, as it leads to decisions about levels and types of intervention. Questions arise as to whether social work practice can deal with symptoms only, applying a Band-aid approach to social problems, or whether institutional change can be addressed and, if so, how.

Further intertwining of the economic and political systems also occurs at the operational level. Regulatory bodies on a state and federal level become "untouchable" by citizens; organizations are formed purportedly for the public good but are created under legislation which makes them essentially unaccountable to the public. Seidman discusses the problems of the regulatory agencies and their confusion regarding function. He says: "Many researchers have isolated and confirmed the regulatory commission syndrome. The symptoms of this geriatric malady are disorientation and growing inability to distinguish between the public interest and interests of those subject to regulation." [141]

Current social work interest in the need for establishing standards for quality services and monitoring both services and the extent to which they reach those in need clearly indicates the need to review other governmental regulatory agencies in order to see how effective they have been. The inherent conflict that would arise between one public agency and another whose operations it was monitoring portends problems in developing similar systems in the field of social welfare. (Several reports of Ralph Nader's study group reflect this dilemma without ever resolving it.[142] As the need for defining and maintaining standards is ever present, the issue is where and how they can be done most effectively—inside or outside government.) The growth of consumer organizations and pressure groups may serve as a limited counterbalance, but funding problems and the restrictions of tax policy inhibit the extent to which pressure can be exerted. The loosening boundaries between the public and private sectors highlight the need for developing improved mechanisms for accountability. Currently, most social welfare services are public in nature. Furthermore, the voluntary sector is largely supported by public funds either directly, in the form of government grants or services purchased from the agencies by the public sector, or indirectly, through the tax-deductible nature of private philanthropic contributions.

Finally, there is also helpful knowledge which can be gained from other countries, through an understanding of the relationships between different political ideologies and types of policy-making structures. Comparative information is useful in offering contrasting and alternate approaches to the structure and allocation of political power. There is also a need for information which explores political events in relation to economic expansion or contraction.

Politics is the ultimate enactment of societal values. Serious issues confront social work. Are social services to be politically weighed during the next decade on the basis of the market as the measure of value? Regardless of the answer, planning and policy formulation in social work will depend on political knowledge and skill.

Toward the Future

Social work and the social sciences share an optimism about the world based on the assumptions that human behavior and the organization of human action are understandable and that it is possible to intervene and alter the course of human events. However, social work, when it selects social science knowledge, must inevitably be selective from the perspective of the professional's values, goals, and tasks. As has been pointed out by Stein and Cloward, social work and social science have different purposes:

In viewing social science material . . . the practitioner should be careful to retain his perspective as a practitioner, rather than to regard himself as a social scientist. He does not have to be a social scientist in order to be a good practitioner and his ultimate function as a practitioner is quite distinct from that of the social scientist. The heart of the distinction lies in the difference between the function of an academic discipline and the function of a professional discipline. The underlying function of the academic discipline, as of all sciences, is to acquire and disseminate knowledge, even if it is knowledge for its own sake. The task for developing means for applying the knowledge in practice belongs to the professional disciplines. The objective of the professions is to help people through social planning and through preventive and direct services, with the acquisition of knowledge being subordinated to this end.[143]

The parameters of our search are delineated by the requirement of social work practice that knowledge provide the ability to deliver services, maintain organizations, and effect change.

Social science knowledge can help social workers choose frames of reference and concepts for understanding society and social problems and for designing interventions. However, it is necessary to guard against the dangers in the uncritical application of knowledge. The acceptance of one social theory to the exclusion of others may result in narrowing the range for intervention, as was experienced in the 1960s when there was an overemphasis on defining social problems within a framework of a so-called "opportunity theory" of individual deviance and, concomitantly, the development of a service strategy to solve them.[144] Subsequently discovered was the enormous complexity of political, economic, and other factors not sufficiently amenable to the narrow range of interventions suggested by that theory.

The specific needs of people may alter over time, but there can be no doubt of the continued need for social welfare programs. Social workers will constantly need new knowledge if they are to help design future services and to intervene successfully in micro- and macrosystems. Within the past decade there has been a spectacular advance in knowledge in the social sciences, resulting in new knowledge focused on conflict theory, game theory, systems theory, mathematical models of social processes, and computer simulations —to mention just a few aspects. The generation of new information will no doubt continue at a rapid pace, creating a need for social work to explore systematically and constantly the frontiers of knowledge which can contribute to improved practice.

It is clear that at a given moment social work education can only prepare quality graduates with specific knowledge, attitudes, and skills. It must remain the responsibility of employing agencies and professional associations, as well as the schools, to provide for continuing education through in-service training, institutes, workshops, and seminars. Having discovered the relevant and useful new knowledge, there must also be a systematic means for the dissemination of that knowledge. Books, journals, and abstracts must reflect new developments in the social sciences and their applications to social work practice. Professionally trained people will be needed to translate this knowledge into usable forms for practice and communicate it to practitioners at every level. Ultimately, it must be the responsibility of the individual social worker to be a lifelong learner, and this can only occur where there is a foundation of wisely designed professional education.

For a profession which has moved beyond the valid but limited role of service to individuals, families, groups, and communities, there is important knowledge from the social sciences that can be used to understand larger systems, including societies. We need to know more about the processes of social innovation and change at every level, about influencing public attitudes, political bodies, and bureaucratic organizations. We need to know how to design services that are responsive to the changing needs and wants of the people being served and develop methods to ensure accountability both to these people and to the public interest generally. Social work knowledge cannot be static. Only through a continuing awareness of the needs and demands of practice and a continuing educational process can the profession become more effective in servicing people directly and in influencing the arrangements through which services are to be provided for ever-changing populations in an ever-changing society.

Notes

[1] See Harriett M. Bartlett (with the assistance of Beatrice N. Saunders), *The Common Base of Social Work Practice* (New York: National Association of Social Workers, 1970).

[2] National Science Foundation, Report of the Special Commission on the Social Sciences of the National Science Board, *Knowledge into Action: Improving the Nation's Use of the Social Sciences* (Washington, D.C.: U.S. Government Printing Office, 1969), pp. 44–49.

[3] Alfred Kadushin, "The Knowledge Base of Social Work," in Alfred J. Kahn, ed., *Issues in American Social Work* (New York: Columbia University Press, 1959), p. 64.

[4] Herman D. Stein and Richard A. Cloward, eds., *Social Perspectives on Behavior* (Glencoe, Ill.: Free Press, 1958).

[5] Leonard S. Kogan, ed., *Social Science Theory and Social Work Research* (New York: National Association of Social Workers, 1960); Henry S. Maas, ed., *Five Fields of Social Service* (New York: National Association of Social Workers, 1966); Henry S. Maas, ed., *Research in the Social Services: a Five-Year Review* (New York: National Association of Social Workers, 1971); Harry L. Lurie, ed., *Encyclopedia of Social Work* (1st ed.: New York: National Association of Social Workers, 1965). In contrast to social work, a recent article by urban planners thoroughly surveys relevant social science content. See Lawrence D. Mann, "Social Science Advances and Planning Applications: 1900–1965," *Journal of the American Institute of Planners* XXXVIII (1972), 346–58.

[6] Kurt Lewin, in *Field Theory in Social Science, Selected Theoretical Papers*, Dorwin Cartwright, ed., (New York: Harper and Brothers, 1951).

[7] Gordon Hamilton, "The Underlying Philosophy of Social Casework Today," in *Proceedings, National Conference of Social Work*, 1941 (New York: Columbia University Press, 1941), pp. 237–53.

8 See A. Paul Hare, Edgar T. Borgatta, and Robert F. Bales, eds., *Small Groups: Studies in Social Interaction* (New York: Alfred Knopf, 1965).

9 Nelson Polsby, *Community Power and Political Theory*, Yale Studies in Political Science (New Haven, Conn.: Yale University Press, 1963).

10 Herbert Gans, *The Levittowners* (New York: Pantheon Books, 1967); Herbert Gans, *The Urban Villagers* (Glencoe, Ill.: Free Press, 1965).

11 For a review see Herbert Strean, "Role Theory, Role Models, and Casework: Review of the Literature and Practice Applications," *Social Work*, XII, No. 2 (1967), 77–88; Victoria Olds, "Role Theory and Casework: a Review of the Literature," *Social Casework*, XLIII, No. 1 (1962), 3–7; Edwin Thomas, ed., *Behavioral Science for Social Workers* (New York: Free Press, 1967), Part II.

12 See, for example, Mirra Komarovsky and Jane Phillips, *Blue Collar Marriage* (New York: Random House, 1964); Frank Riessman, Jerome Cohen, and Arthur Pearl, eds., *Mental Health of the Poor* (Glencoe, Ill.: Free Press, 1964); Elliot Liebow, *Tally's Corner* (Boston: Little, Brown and Co., 1967); Andrew Billingsley, *Black Families in White America* (Englewood Cliffs, N.J.: Prentice Hall, Inc., 1968); Marcel Goldschmid, *Black Americans and White Racism* (New York: Holt, Rinehart, and Winston, 1970); Stein and Cloward, *op. cit.*; Oscar Lewis, *La Vida* (New York: Random House, 1965); Oscar Lewis, *Children of Sanchez* (New York: Alfred Knopf, 1961).

13 See, for example, Hope Leichter and William Mitchell, *Kinship and Casework* (New York: Russell Sage Foundation, 1967); Norman Bell and Ezra Vogel, eds., *A Modern Introduction to the Family* (New York: Free Press, 1968); Stein and Cloward, *op. cit.*; James Framo, "Systematic Research on Family Dynamics," in Ivan Boszormenyi-Nagy and James Framo, eds., *Intensive Family Therapy* (New York: Harper and Row, 1965), pp. 407–62.

14 James K. Whittaker, "Models of Group Development: Implications for Social Group Work Practice," *Social Service Review*, XLIV, No. 3 (1970), 308–22; William Schwartz, "Neighborhood Centers," in Maas, *Five Fields of Social Service*, pp. 144–84; William Schwartz, "Neighborhood Centers and Group Work," in Maas, ed., *Research in the Social Services: A Five-Year Review*, pp. 130–91; Margaret Hartford, *Groups in Social Work* (New York: Columbia University Press, 1972).

15 See, for example, Clyde Kluckhohn and Henry Murray, eds., *Personality in Nature, Society, and Culture* (New York: Alfred Knopf, 1953); Bell and Vogel, *op. cit.*; Erik Erikson, *Childhood and Society* (New York: W. W. Norton and Co., 1950); and many of the compilations listed in footnote 12.

16 See Erikson, *op. cit.*, pp. 23–47.

17 Theodore Lidz, *The Person* (New York: Basic Books, 1968), pp. 189–234.

18 Ruth Smalley, "Social Casework:the Functional Approach," in Robert Morris *et al.*, eds., *Encyclopedia of Social Work* (2d ed.; New York: National Association of Social Workers, 1971), pp. 1195–97.

19 Anna Freud, *The Ego and the Mechanisms of Defense* (New York: International Universities Press, 1966), especially pp. 137–72; Anna Freud, "Adolescence," in Ruth Eissler *et al.*, eds., *The Psychoanalytic Study of the Child* (New York: International Universities Press, 1958), XIII, 255–78; Erikson, *op. cit.*; Erik Erikson, *Identity, Youth, and Crisis* (New York: W. W. Norton and Co., 1968).

20 Margaret Mahler, *On Human Symbiosis and the Vicissitudes of Individuation* (New York: International Universities Press, 1968); Jacob Arlow and Charles Brenner, *Psychoanalytic Concepts and the Structural Theory* (New York: International Universities Press, 1964).

21 Among many others Mahler, *op. cit.*; Erikson, *Childhood and Society;* John Bowlby, *Maternal Care and Mental Health* (New York: Schocken Books, Inc., 1966); David Fanshel, "Child Welfare," in Maas, ed., *Five Fields of Social Service;* Alfred Kadushin, "Child Welfare," in Maas, ed., *Research in the Social Services*, pp. 13–69; Freda Rebelsky and Lynn Dorman, eds., *Child Development and Behavior* (New York: Alfred Knopf, 1970); Philip Lichtenberg and Dolores Norton, *Cognitive and Mental Development in the First Five Years of Life* (Rockville, Md.: National Institute of Mental Health, 1970); Morris Haimowitz and Natalie Haimowitz, eds., *Human Development* (New York: Thomas Y. Crowell Co., 1960); René Spitz, *The First Year of Life* (New York: International Universities Press, 1965).

22 Jean Piaget, *The Language and Thought of the Child* (New York: Harcourt Brace and Co., 1926); Jean Piaget and Barbel Inhelder, *The Growth of Logical Thinking from Childhood to Adolescence* (New York: Basic Books, 1958); John Flavell, *The Developmental Psychology of Jean Piaget* (Princeton, N.J.: Van Nostrand, 1963); Jean Piaget and Barbel Inhelder, *The Psychology of the Child* (New York: Basic Books, 1969).

23 See, for example, *Ad Hoc* Committee on Advocacy, "The Social Worker as Advocate: Champion of Social Victims," *Social Work*, XIV, No. 2 (1969), 16–22.

24 Carol H. Meyer, *Social Work Practice: a Response to the Urban Crisis* (New York: Free Press, 1970), pp. 123–44.

25 Karl Menninger, *The Vital Balance* (New York: Viking Press, 1963), especially pp. 76–124; Judith Nelsen, "Uses of Systems Theory in Casework I and II: a Proposal," *Journal of Education for Social Work*, VIII, No. 3 (1972), 60–64.

26 Walter Buckley, *Sociology and Modern Systems Theory* (Englewood Cliffs, N.J.: Prentice-Hall, Inc., 1967), p. 60.

27 See, for example, Frances Scherz, "Theory and Practice of Family Therapy," in Robert Roberts and Robert Nee, eds., *Theories of Social Casework* (Chicago: University of Chicago Press, 1970), pp. 219–64; Framo, *op. cit.*

28 See Theodore Mills, *The Sociology of Small Groups* (Englewood Cliffs, N.J.: Prentice-Hall, Inc., 1967); and for application, William Schwartz, "The Social Worker in the Group," *The Social Welfare Forum, 1961* (New York: Columbia University Press, 1961), pp. 159–72; Lawrence Schulman, *A Casebook of Social Work with Groups* (New York: Council on Social Work Education, 1968.

29 Ronald Lippitt, Jeanne Watson, and Bruce Westley, *The Dynamics of Planned Change: a Comparative Study of Principles and Techniques* (New York: Harcourt Brace and Co., 1958); Irwin Sanders, *The Community: an Introduction to a Social System* (New York: Ronald Press, 1966); Daniel Katz and Robert L. Kahn, *The Social Psychology of Organizations* (New York: John Wiley and Sons, Inc., 1966).

30 Lydia Rapoport, "Crisis Intervention as a Mode of Brief Treatment," in Roberts and Nee, *op. cit.*, pp. 268–76.

31 Helen Northen, *Social Work with Groups* (New York: Columbia University Press, 1969), pp. 40–48.

32 Irwin Epstein, "Professional Role Orientations and Conflict Strategies," *Social Work*, XV, No. 4 (1970), 87–92; Harry Specht, "Disruptive Tactics," *Social Work*, XIV, No. 2 (1969), 5–15; Martin Rein and Robert Morris, "Goals, Structures, and Strategies for Community Change," in Mayer Zald, ed., *Social Welfare Institutions* (New York: John Wiley and Sons, Inc., 1965), pp. 367–82.

33 See Rapoport, *op. cit.*, pp. 265–312; Howard J. Parad, ed., *Crisis Intervention* (New York: Family Service Association of America, 1965).

34 William Reid and Ann W. Shyne, *Brief and Extended Casework* (New York: Columbia University Press, 1969).

35 See Buckley, *op. cit.*, pp. 49 ff.

36 See, for example, Ray L. Birdwhistell, "An Approach to Communications," *Family Process*, I (1962), 194–201; Charles Osgood and Thomas Sebeck, eds., *Psycholinguistics: a Survey of Theory and Research Problems* (Bloomington, Ind.: Indiana University Press, 1965); Albert Sheflen, "Explaining Communicative Behavior: Three Points of View," in Nathan Ackerman, Frances Beatman, and Sanford Sherman, eds., *Expanding Theory and Practice in Family Therapy* (New York: Family Service Association of America, 1967), pp. 93–98; Israel Zwerling, "Nonverbal Communication: Analyzing Body Movements," *ibid.*, pp. 83–88.

37 Salvador Minuchin *et al.*, *Families of the Slums* (New York: Basic

Books, 1967), pp. 192–216; Charles Malone, "Developmental Deviations Considered in the Light of Environmental Forces," in Eleanor Pavenstedt, ed., *The Drifters* (Boston: Little, Brown and Co., 1967), pp. 125–62.

38 Minuchin *et al.*, *op. cit.*, pp. 244–97.

39 Elizabeth McBroom, "Socialization and Social Casework," in Roberts and Nee, *op. cit.*, pp. 315–16, and 324–25.

40 Jurgen Ruesch, "The Therapeutic Process from the Point of View of Communication Theory," *American Journal of Orthopsychiatry*, XXII (1952), 690–701.

41 Don D. Jackson, "Psychoanalytic Education in the Communication Processes" in Don D. Jackson, ed., *Therapy, Communication, and Change* (Palo Alto, Calif.: Science and Behavior Books, 1968), pp. 97–114.

42 William F. Fry, "The Marital Context of an Anxiety Syndrome," *ibid.*, pp. 41–48.

43 Virginia Satir, *Conjoint Family Therapy* (Palo Alto, Calif.: Science and Behavior Books, 1967).

44 Gregory Bateson *et al.*, "Toward a Theory of Schizophrenia," in Don D. Jackson, ed., *Communication, Family, and Marriage* (Palo Alto, Calif.: Science and Behavior Books, 1968), pp. 31–54.

45 Jay Haley, *Strategies of Psychotherapy* (New York: Grune and Stratton, 1963), pp. 88–92.

46 See general selections from the two Jackson volumes, *op. cit.*

47 Don D. Jackson and Jay Haley, "Transference Revisited," in Jackson, *Therapy, Communication, and Change*, pp. 115–28; Haley, *op. cit.*, pp. 72–85.

48 See Robert Carson, *Interaction Concepts of Personality* (Chicago: Aldine Publishing Co., 1969), especially pp. 23–56; Eric Berne, *Transactional Analysis in Psychotherapy* (New York: Grove Press, 1961); Thomas A. Harris, *I'm O.K. You're O.K.* (New York: Harper and Row, 1967).

49 Christian Beels and Andrew Ferber, "Family Therapy: a View," *Family Process*, VIII (1969), 280–318.

50 See, for example, Eugene Litwak, "Policy Implications in Communications Theory with Emphasis on Group Factors," in Thomas, *op. cit.*, pp. 105–17.

51 Satir, *op. cit.*, p. 78.

52 B. F. Skinner, *Science and Human Behavior* (New York: Macmillan, 1953).

53 See Edwin J. Thomas, "Behavioral Modification and Casework," in Roberts and Nee, *op. cit.*, pp. 181–218; Edwin J. Thomas, "Selected Sociobehavioral Techniques and Principles: an Approach to Interpersonal Helping," *Social Work*, XIII, No. 1 (1968), 12–26; Robert Vinter, ed., *Readings in Group Work Practice* (Ann Arbor, Mich.: Campus

Publications, 1967); Robert Vinter and Rosemary Sarri, "Malperformance in the Public School: a Group Work Approach," *Social Work*, X, No. 1 (1965), 3–13.

[54] Ronald G. Tharp and Ralph J. Wetzel, *Behavior and Modification in the Natural Environment* (New York: Academic Press, 1969); Eileen D. Gambrill, Edwin J. Thomas, and Robert Carter, "Procedure for Sociobehavioral Practice in Open Settings," *Social Work*, XVI, No. 1 (1971), 51–62.

[55] Carl Rogers, *On Becoming a Person* (Boston: Houghton Mifflin Co., 1961); Victor Frankl, *Psychotherapy and Existentialism: Selected Papers on Logotherapy* (New York: Simon and Schuster, 1957); Victor Frankl, *Man's Search for Meaning: an Introduction to Logotherapy* (New York: Simon and Schuster, 1963); Abraham Maslow, *Toward a Psychology of Being* (New York: Van Nostrand Reinhold Co., 1962); Frederick Perls, Ralph Hefferline, and Paul Goodman, *Gestalt Therapy* (New York: Julian Press, 1951).

[56] Frederick Perls, *Gestalt Therapy Verbatim* (Lafayette, Calif.: Real People Press, 1969).

[57] Bradford Gibb and Kenneth Benne, eds., *T-Group Theory and Laboratory Method* (New York: John Wiley and Sons, Inc., 1964).

[58] Carl Rogers, *On Encounter Groups* (New York: Harper and Row, 1970).

[59] National Academy of Sciences and Social Science Research Council, *The Behavioral and Social Sciences: Outlook and Needs* (Englewood Cliffs, N.J.: Prentice-Hall, Inc., 1969), p. 92.

[60] For further discussions of the field of human ecology see Geoffrey Vickers, "Ecology, Planning and the American Dream," in Leonard J. Duhl, ed., *The Urban Condition* (New York: Basic Books, 1963), pp. 374–96; F. Fraser Darling, "A Wider Environment of Ecology and Conservation," *Daedalus*, XCVI (1967), 1003–19; F. Fraser Darling and Raymond F. Dasman, "The Ecosystems View of Human Society," *Realitas*, No. 2591 (1972), pp. 19–26; Barry Commoner, *The Closing Circle* (New York: Alfred Knopf, 1971); Margaret Sprout and Harold Sprout, *The Ecological Perspective on Human Affairs* (Princeton, N.J.: Princeton University Press, 1965).

[61] See Scott Briar, "Social Casework and Social Group Work: Historical and Social Science Foundations," in the *Encyclopedia of Social Work* (2d ed.; 1971), pp. 1237–45; Brian J. Heraud, *Sociology and Social Work* (Oxford, England: Pergamon Press, 1970); Henry J. Meyer *et al.*, "Social Work and Social Welfare," in Paul F. Lazarsfeld, William H. Sewell, and Harold L. Wilensky, eds., *The Uses of Sociology* (New York: Basic Books, 1967).

[62] See Zald, *op. cit.*

[63] Eugene Litwak, "Models of Bureaucracy That Permit Conflict,"

American Journal of Sociology, XXVI (1961), 177–84; Eugene Litwak and Henry J. Meyer, "A Balance Theory of Coordination between Bureaucratic Organizations and Community Primary Groups," *Administrative Science Quarterly*, XI (1966), 33–58.

[64] Warren Bennis, "Beyond Bureaucracy," *Trans-action*, II, No. 5 (1965), 31–35.

[65] Peter M. Blau and W. Richard Scott, *Formal Organizations: a Comparative Approach* (San Francisco: Chandler Publishing Co., 1962).

[66] James D. Thompson, *Organizations in Action* (New York: McGraw-Hill, 1967).

[67] Amitai Etzioni, *A Comparative Analysis of Complex Organizations: on Power, Involvement, and Their Correlates* (Glencoe, Ill.: Free Press, 1961); Amitai Etzioni, *Modern Organizations* (Englewood Cliffs, N.J.: Prentice-Hall, Inc., 1964).

[68] Irwin Epstein, "Organizational Careers, Professionalization and Social-Worker Radicalism," *Social Service Review*, XLIV (1970), 123–31; Andrew Billingsley, "Bureaucratic and Professional Orientation Patterns in Social Casework," *Social Service Review*, IX (1964), 400–407.

[69] Orville G. Brim, Jr., and Stanton Wheeler, *Socialization After Childhood* (New York: John Wiley and Sons, Inc., 1966).

[70] Blau and Scott, *op. cit.*; Amitai Etzioni, *The Semi-Professions and Their Organization* (New York: Free Press, 1969); Donald Feldstein, "Do We Need Professions in Our Society?" *Social Work*, XVI, No. 4 (1971) 5–11; Wilbert E. Moore, *The Professions: Roles and Rules* (New York: Russell Sage Foundation, 1970); Howard M. Vollmer and Donald L. Mills, eds., *Professionalization* (Englewood Cliffs, N.J.: Prentice-Hall, Inc., 1966).

[71] Andrew Shonfield, *Modern Capitalism: the Changing Balance of Public and Private Power* (London: Oxford University Press, 1965).

[72] Robert A. Dahl and Charles E. Lindblom, *Politics, Economics, and Welfare* (New York: Harper and Co., 1953); Charles E. Lindblom, *The Intelligence of Democracy* (New York: Free Press, 1965).

[73] See Wilbert E. Moore, *Social Change* (Englewood Cliffs, N.J.: Prentice-Hall, Inc., 1963).

[74] See Raymond A. Bauer, ed., *Social Indicators* (Cambridge, Mass.: Massachusetts Institute of Technology Press, 1966); Eleanor B. Sheldon and Wilbert E. Moore, eds., *Indicators of Social Change: Concepts and Measurements* (New York: Russell Sage Foundation, 1968).

[75] Harold Wilensky, *Organizational Intelligence* (New York: Basic Books, 1967).

[76] Norbert Wiener, *Human Use of Human Beings* (New York: Doubleday and Co., 1954); Amitai Etzioni, *The Active Society* (New York: Free Press, 1968); Herbert A. Simon, *The New Science of Management Decisions* (New York: Harper and Row, 1960).

[77] Robert Boguslaw, *The New Utopians: a Study of System Design and Social Change* (Englewood Cliffs, N.J.: Prentice-Hall, Inc., 1965).

[78] See James S. Coleman, *Equality of Education* (Washington, D.C.: U.S. Department of Health, Education, and Welfare, Office of Education, 1966); David Rogers, *110 Livingston Street* (New York: Random House, 1968); John Kosa, Aaron Antonsky, and Irving Zola, *Poverty and Health: a Sociological Analysis* (Cambridge, Mass.: Harvard University Press, 1969); William Ryan, ed., *Distress in the City: Essays on the Design and Administration of Urban Mental Health Sciences* (Cleveland: Case Western Reserve University Press, 1969).

[79] Roland L. Warren, "The Interorganizational Field as a Focus for Investigation," *Administrative Science Quarterly*, XII (1967–68), 396–419.

[80] See Gerhard E. Lenski, *Power and Privilege: a Theory of Social Stratification* (New York: McGraw-Hill, 1966); Thomas E. Lasswell, *Class and Stratum* (New York: Houghton Mifflin Co., 1965); S. M. Miller and Pamela Roby, *The Future of Inequality* (New York: Basic Books, 1970).

[81] See Talcott Parsons, *Politics and Social Structure* (New York: Free Press, 1969); Eric A. Nordlinger, ed., *Politics and Society: Studies in Comparative Political Sociology* (Englewood Cliffs, N.J.: Prentice-Hall, Inc., 1970); Morris Janowitz *Political Conflict: Essays in Political Sociology* (Chicago: Quadrangle Books, 1970); David Easton and Jack Dennis (with the assistance of Sylvia Easton), *Children in the Political System: Origins of Political Legitimacy* (New York: McGraw-Hill, 1969).

[82] C. Wright Mills, *The Power Elite* (New York: Oxford University Press, 1956); Floyd Hunter, *Community Power Structure: a Study of Decision-Making* (Chapel Hill, N.C.: University of North Carolina Press, 1953); Robert S. Lynd and Helen M. Lynd, *Middletown* (New York: Harcourt Brace and Co., 1929).

[83] Robert C. Dahl, *Who Governs?* (New Haven: Yale University Press, 1961); Polsby, *op. cit.*; Charles E. Lindblom, *The Intelligence of Democracy* (New York: Free Press, 1968); Martin Meyerson and Edward Banfield, *Politics, Planning and the Public Interest* (Glencoe, Ill.: Free Press, 1955); Norton E. Long, "The Local Community as an Ecology of Games," *American Journal of Sociology*, LXIV (1958), 251–61.

[84] See *Report of the National Advisory Commission on Civil Disorders* (New York: Bantam Books, 1968).

[85] See Roland L. Warren, ed., *Politics and the Ghetto* (New York: Atherton Press, 1969).

[86] Lewis Coser, *The Functions of Social Conflict* (New York: Free Press, 1956); Kenneth Boulding, *Conflict and Defense: a General Theory* (New York: Harper and Bros., 1962); Muzafer Sherif, *Intergroup Relations and Leadership: the Robber's Cave Experiment* (Norman, Okla.: University of Oklahoma Press, Institute of Group Relations, 1961).

142 Knowledge for Practice

[87] Roland L. Warren, *The Community in America* (Chicago: Rand McNally, 1966).

[88] References to economics are not found in any of the following: Stein and Cloward, *op. cit.*; Kadushin, *op. cit.*; Kogan, *op. cit.*; Robert Morris, "Social Planning," in Maas, *Five Fields of Social Service;* Maas, *Research in the Social Services.* Roland L. Warren, "Application of Social Science Knowledge to the Community Organization Field," *Journal of Education for Social Work*, III, No. 1 (1967), 60–72, stresses the contribution of sociology to community organization exclusively.

[89] Nathan E. Cohen, "Reversing the Process of Social Disorganization," in Kahn, ed., *Issues in American Social Work*, pp. 138–58.

[90] Frances Feldman, *The Family in the Money World* (New York: Family Service Association of America, 1957).

[91] Alfred J. Kahn, "The Societal Context of Social Work Practice," *Social Work*, X, No. 4 (1965), 145–55.

[92] Jack Rothman and Irwin Epstein, "Social Planning and Community Organization: Social Science Foundations," in *Encyclopedia of Social Work*, pp. 1351–60.

[93] See Alfred J. Kahn, *Studies in Social Policy and Planning* (New York: Russell Sage Foundation, 1969), pp. 10–67. Of the numerous books written on the antipoverty programs of the 1960s, perhaps the best is Sar Levitan, *The Great Society's Poor Law* (Baltimore: John Hopkins Press, 1969). A more recent effort, including an attempt at employing a cost/benefit analysis for these programs, is Joseph Kershaw, *Government against Poverty* (Washington, D.C.: Brookings Institution, 1970).

[94] See Martin Rein, *Social Policy: Issues of Choice and Change* (New York: Random House, 1970); Robert Lampman, *Ends and Means of Reducing Income Poverty* (Chicago: Markham Publishing Co., 1971), pp. 8–43; Kershaw, *op. cit.*, Chap. I.

[95] Rein, *op. cit.*, Introduction, p. x.

[96] In addition to Rein, *op. cit.*, see such collections as Margaret S. Gordon, ed., *Poverty in America* (San Francisco: Chandler Publishing, 1965); Leo Fishman, ed., *Poverty and Affluence* (New Haven, Conn.: Yale University Press, 1966); Leonard H. Goodman, ed., *Economic Progress and Social Welfare* (New York: Columbia University Press, 1966).

[97] Victor R. Fuchs, "Redefining Poverty and Redistributing Income," *The Public Interest*, No. 8 (1967), pp. 88–95; Robert J. Lampman, "Income Distribution and Poverty," in Gordon, *op. cit.*, pp. 102–14.

[98] Lampman, *op. cit.*

[99] See Richard Titmuss, *Commitment to Welfare* (New York: Pantheon Books, 1968), pp. 153–65.

[100] Alfred J. Kahn, *Theory and Practice of Social Planning* (New York: Russell Sage Foundation, 1969); p. 182; Rein, *op. cit.*; Miller and Roby, *op. cit.*

[101] *Poverty Amid Plenty*, report of the President's Commission on Income Maintenance Programs (Washington, D.C.: U.S. Government Printing Office, 1969), Chap. 6, especially pp. 65–68.

[102] Miller and Roby, *op. cit.*

[103] Rein, *op. cit.*, pp. 224–29.

[104] *Ibid.*, p. 425.

[105] Oscar A. Ornati, "The Spatial Distribution of Urban Poverty," in Warner Bloomberg, Jr., and Henry Schmandt, eds., *Power, Poverty and Urban Policy*, Urban Affairs Annual Review (Beverly Hills, Calif.: Sage Publishers, 1968), II, 69 (italics added).

[106] For example, see Alfred J. Kahn, *Studies in Social Policy and Planning*, pp. 105–56; Otto Eckstein, ed., *Studies in the Economics of Income Maintenance* (Washington, D.C.: Brookings Institution, 1967). The best work on negative income taxes is Christopher Green, *Negative Taxes and the Poverty Problem* (Washington, D.C.: Brookings Institution, 1967). See also Helen O. Nicol, "Guaranteed Income Maintenance: Another Look at the Debate," *Welfare in Review*, V, No. 4 (1967), 1–13; Robert Theobald, ed., *The Guaranteed Income* (New York: Doubleday, 1966); Milton Friedman, *Capitalism and Freedom* (Chicago: University of Chicago Press, 1962), pp. 190–95.

[107] For a discussion of children's allowances, see Eveline M. Burns, ed., *Children's Allowances and the Economic Welfare of Children* (New York: Citizens Committee for Children, 1968); Alvin L. Schorr, *Poor Kids* (New York: Basic Books, 1966).

[108] For a simple and concise definition of the economist's concept of "efficiency" see Aaron Wildavsky, "The Political Economy of Efficiency," in Austin Ranney, ed., *Political Science and Public Policy* (Chicago: Markham Publishing Co., 1968), p. 56.

[109] Robert Lampman, "Transfer and Redistribution as Social Process," in Shirley Jenkins, ed., *Social Security in International Perspective* (New York: Columbia University Press, 1969), p. 49.

[110] Joseph Pechman, *Federal Tax Policy* (Washington, D.C.: Brookings Institution, 1971); Joseph Pechman, "The Rich, the Poor, and the Taxes They Pay," *The Public Interest*, No. 17 (1969), pp. 21–43.

[111] William Gorham, "Notes of a Practitioner," *The Public Interest*, No. 8 (1967), pp. 4–8; Elizabeth B. Drew, "HEW Grapples with PPBS," *ibid.*, pp. 9–29; Alice M. Rivlin, *The Planning, Programming, Budgeting Systems in the Department of Health, Education, and Welfare: Some Lessons from Experience* (Washington, D.C.: Brookings Institution, 1969; reprint).

[112] "City's New View of Welfare: a Job for Businessmen," *New York Times*, February 1, 1972.

[113] Richard Zeckhauser and Elmer Schaefer, "Public Policy and Normative Economic Theory," in Raymond A. Bauer and Kenneth J. Gergen, eds., *The Study of Policy Formation* (New York: Free Press, 1968),

p. 27; Harry J. Johnson, "Economics and Public Policy: I," *The Public Interest*, No. 12 (1968), p. 71.

[114] Perhaps the two best books are David Novick, ed., *Program Budgeting* (Cambridge, Mass.: Harvard University Press, 1965); Harley H. Himricks, and Graeme M. Taylor, *Program Budgeting and Benefit Cost Analysis* (Pacific Palisades, Calif.: Goodyear Publishing Co., 1969). See also Kahn, *Theory and Practice of Social Planning*, pp. 240–61.

[115] Samuel B. Chase, Jr., ed., *Problems in Public Expenditure Analysis* (Washington, D.C.: Brookings Institution, 1968); Robert Dorfman, ed., *Measuring Benefits of Government Investments* (Washington, D.C.: Brookings Institution, 1965); Kershaw, *op. cit.*; Abraham S. Levine, "Cost Benefit Analysis and Social Welfare," *Welfare in Review*, IV, No. 7 (1966), 1–9; Edward E. Schwartz, ed., *Planning, Programming, Budgeting Systems (PPBS) and Social Welfare* (Chicago: University of Chicago Press, 1970).

[116] Ida Hoos, *Systems Analysis in Social Policy: a Critical Review* (London: Institute on Public Affairs, 1969); G. H. Peters, *Cost/Benefit Analysis and Public Expenditures* (London: Institute of Economic Affairs, 1968); Aaron Wildavsky, *The Politics of the Budgetary Process* (Boston: Little, Brown and Co., 1964); Aaron Wildavsky, "The Political Economy of Efficiency," in Ranney, *op. cit.*, pp. 55–82.

[117] Titmuss, *op. cit.*, pp. 188–99.

[118] W. Lee Hansen and Burton A. Weisbrod, *Benefits, Costs, and Finance of Public Higher Education* (Chicago: Markham Publishing Co., 1969).

[119] Alice M. Rivlin, *Systematic Thinking for Social Action* (Washington, D.C.: Brookings Institution, 1971).

[120] Shonfield, *op. cit.*

[121] Gunnar Myrdal, *The Challenge of World Poverty* (New York: Pantheon Books, 1970).

[122] See Yehezkel Dror, *Public Policy Making Reexamined* (Scranton, Pa.: Chandler Publishing Co., 1968), pp. 236–324; Yehezkel Dror, *Ventures in Policy Sciences* (Amsterdam, the Netherlands: Elsevier Publishing Co., 1971); Harold Lasswell, *A Pre-View of Policy Sciences* (Amsterdam, the Netherlands: Elsevier Publishing Co., 1971).

[123] Myrdal, *op. cit.*, p. 438.

[124] Daniel Hirshfield, "Social Policy and Political Trends," in *Encyclopedia of Social Work* (2d ed.; 1971), p. 1414.

[125] See Frederic N. Cleaveland and associates, *Congress and Urban Problems* (Washington, D.C.: Brookings Institution, 1969). On decision-making through the federal budgetary process, see Aaron Wildavsky, *The Politics of the Budgetary Process*.

[126] Illustrative is Meyerson and Banfield, *op. cit.*

[127] Alan Altshuler, *The Politics of the Federal Bureaucracy* (New York: Dodd, 1968); Cleaveland *op. cit.*; Dahl, *op. cit.*; Harold Seidman,

Politics, Position and Power (New York: Oxford University Press, 1970).

128 For excellent discussions of this see Dror, *op. cit.*; Ranney, *op. cit.*; Ira Sharkansky, *Policy Analysis in Political Science* (Chicago: Markham Publishing Co., 1970).

129 See the earlier discussion of the social work literature with reference to economics. The pattern is remarkably similar. Since 1965 only one issue of *Abstracts for Social Workers* has included a reference to political science as a relevant field of knowledge, and very few articles relate to political science. Jack Rothman and Irwin Epstein, "Social Planning and Community Organization: Social Science Foundations," in *Encyclopedia of Social Work* (2d ed.; 1971), p. 1359, include one paragraph referring to the relevance of political science for community organization.

130 George A. Brager and Harry Specht, "Mobilizing the Poor for Social Action," in *The Social Welfare Forum, 1965* (New York: Columbia University Press, 1965), pp. 197–210; George A. Brager, "Institutional Change: Perimeters of the Possible," *Social Work*, XII, No. 1 (1967), 59–69; George A. Brager, "Advocacy and Political Behavior," *Social Work*, XIII, No. 2 (1968), 5–15; Jack Rothman, "Community Organization Practice," in Maas, ed., *Research in the Social Services: a Five-Year Review*, pp. 70–107; Polsby, *op. cit.*; Alan Altshuler, *Community Control: The Black Demand for Participation in Large American Cities* (New York: Pegasus Western Publishing Co., 1970); Warren, "Application of Social Science Knowledge to the Community Organization Field." The political scientists tend to support pluralist theories of power in contrast to sociologists' support of elitist theories, as in Hunter, *op. cit.*, and Mills, *op. cit.*

131 For some discussion of the political science concept of "incremental" planning applied to the antipoverty program see Kahn, *Studies in Social Policy and Planning*, pp. 64–67. For works of political scientists dealing with areas of interest to social workers see Frances Fox Piven, "The Great Society as Political Strategy," *Columbia University Forum*, XIII, No. 2 (1970), 17–22; Frances Fox Piven and Richard A. Cloward, *Regulating the Poor: the Functions of Public Welfare* (New York: Pantheon Books, 1971); John C. Donovan, *The Politics of Poverty* (New York: Pegasus, 1967); Gilbert Y. Steiner, *The State of Welfare* (Washington, D.C.: Brookings Institution, 1971); *Social Insecurity: the Politics of Welfare* (Chicago: Rand McNally, 1966).

132 David Truman, *The Governmental Process: Political Interests and Public Opinion* (New York: Knopf, 1951); Wildavsky, *The Politics of the Budgetary Process;* Meyerson and Banfield, *op. cit.*

133 For some discussion of this changed focus, see Austin Ranney, "The Study of Policy Content: a Framework for Choice," in Ranney, ed., *op. cit.*, pp. 3–21.

134 Piven and Cloward, *op. cit.*, is an illustration of this approach.

[135] For discussion of this current trend see Allan Schick, "Systems Process and Systems Budgeting," *Public Administration Review*, XXIX, No. 2 (1969), 138–39; Ranney, "The Study of Policy Content," pp. 3–21; Lewis A. Froman, Jr., "The Categorization of Policy Contents," pp. 41–54; Robert H. Salisbury, "The Analysis of Public Policy: A Search for Theories and Roles," pp. 151–78 all in Ranney, ed., *op. cit.*

[136] Enid Curtis Bok Schoettle, "The State of the Art in Policy Studies," in Bauer and Gergen, *op. cit.*, pp. 149–79, especially pp. 168 ff; Easton, *A Systems Analysis of Political Life* (New York: John Wiley and Sons, Inc., 1965).

[137] Don K. Price, *The Scientific Estate* (Cambridge, Mass.: Harvard University Press, 1967).

[138] Wildavsky, "The Political Economy of Efficiency: Cost-Benefit Analysis, Systems Analysis and Program Budgeting," in Ranney, ed., *op. cit.*, pp. 55–82.

[139] Schick, *op. cit.*, p. 138.

[140] Lindblom, *op. cit.*; Kahn, *Theory and Practice of Social Planning*, pp. 331–40. Schoettle, *op. cit.*, uses incrementalism as her frame of reference for policy-making.

[141] Seidman, *op. cit.*, p. 224.

[142] The investigatory reports of Ralph Nader and his associates reflect this emergent development. See, as examples, James S. Turner, *The Chemical Feast* (New York: Grossman Publishers, 1970); Claire Townsend, *Old Age: the Last Segregation* (New York: Grossman Publishers, 1971).

[143] Stein and Cloward, *op. cit.*, p. xviii.

[144] For a discussion of opportunity theory see Richard A. Cloward and Lloyd E. Ohlin, *Delinquency and Opportunity* (New York: Free Press, 1960).

Willard C. Richan

✿

THE SOCIAL WORK PROFESSION AND ORGANIZED SOCIAL WELFARE

A chronic obsession of social workers has been their professional status. The attempt to answer the question, "Is social work a profession?" has represented an expenditure of great energy with no visible progress toward finding an answer. One of the sources of difficulty in this search has been the tendency to frame the question in the wrong terms. Characteristically, we have borrowed some prevailing list of descriptive attributes of professions and then sought to apply these to the field of social work.[1] Unavoidably, the answer must come out as either "yes" or "no" or "partly." One must then ask, "So what?"

Eliot Friedson suggests that such a laundry list approach to professionalism is rather unproductive. A more useful line of inquiry, he says, is the institutional context in which the professional activity goes on:

The most critical of such underexamined elements are organizational in character, dealing with the organization of practice and the division of labor. . . . [Such factors] may . . . minimize the importance to behavior of the personal qualities of intelligence, ethicality and trained skill imputed to professionals by most definitions.[2]

Such an approach directs one to issues which have a clear bearing on the nature of professional activity and the constraints upon it. This seems particularly relevant for social work because of its predominantly bureaucratic context. In recent years, this relationship has been the subject of much attention in the literature.[3] For the most part, the focus has been on social workers within an organizational context. But a complementary and potentially fruitful subject of study is the social work profession as a corporate entity in its relation to social welfare as an institutional complex. These two levels of analysis are closely related, for the behavior of the individual social worker within an organization will be influenced by the posture his profession assumes at large; and that posture, in turn, will be modified as the constituency of professional employees find a particular stance more or less consistent with the demands of the work setting.

The social work profession developed initially in response to the manpower needs of the social services, a case of upgrading of bureaucratic functionaries to serve organizational ends. And down to the present time the central determinant of the profession's evolution has been organized social welfare. Not surprisingly, social work shares many characteristics with other professions in which professionals are salaried members of organizations.[4]

The domination of social work by social welfare helps to account for the belated and weak development of enforceable ethical canons and licensure, normal means by which professions regulate their members. It is also directly related to the persistent tendency toward fragmentation of the field. But it is particularly in the realm of professional education that social work shows the influence of the social services.

Initially, social work education went on under the aegis of social agencies. Even as schools moved inside universities, the training resembled apprenticeship training more than it did the kind of education associated with the established professions.[5] The tendency to treat field work training (socialization in agencies, by agency personnel, to agency norms) as the heart of the professional education experience has continued to recent times. And faculties of many social work schools have been composed primarily of erstwhile social work practitioners who brought their agency orientation directly into their teaching without any intervening exposure to advanced academic preparation.

The early professional associations in social work also reflected this influence of organized social welfare. Thus, one finds certain groups of social workers organizing around the special fields in which they were employed: the American Association of Medical Social Workers (1918); the American Association of School Social Workers (1919); and the American Association of Psychiatric Social Workers (1926).[6] And if there were any doubts about where social workers' first loyalty lay, these were eliminated by the obligation to "identify with the agency." Social workers have dual loyalty to the agency and the professional community, wrote Lydia Rapoport in a widely quoted statement, "with the primary tie being to the agency." [7]

It is little wonder, then, that empirical investigations have found that professional social workers' organizational commitments supersede those to both the profession and the clientele.[8] Likewise, the organized professional community has tended to follow the lead of the social services. Indeed, spokesmen for the profession have often seemed to do little more than echo the views of the welfare establishment in their policy pronouncements. Some government officials have paused only long enough to change hats before making public statements in behalf of the National Association of Social Workers (NASW) or the Council on Social Work Education (CSWE), essentially reiterating the views they had expressed in their official capacity.

Some observers agree that there is dominance in the relationship but assert that it is the profession, not the service establishment, which has done the dominating. They cite the fact that social agency board members have been moved further and further away from direct involvement in the control over agency operations; [9] that Congress has found itself unable to control the spending on welfare programs.[10] But what they really seem to be talking about is dominance by cadres of professionals (not all of them social workers, incidentally) within specific service systems whose primary orientation is to their institutions' and their own self-interest. They fit John Kenneth Galbraith's term, "technostructure," the professional-managerial class within an organization which in fact runs the show.[11] In the trade-offs between these in-house elites and their sponsors, the broad social values and commitments of the social work profession can have rather low priority.

Another point where the profession may seem to have dominated social welfare is in the National Conference on Social Welfare (NCSW), the meeting place since 1874 of administrators, practitioners, and volunteers in the field. As Ruth Williams has observed, "the history of the Conference . . . is the history of social welfare in the United States." [12] And to be sure, social workers have had a major role in shaping this organization. From 1917 until 1956 this dominance was recognized in the title, the National Conference of Social Work. At the point that the name was changed to the National Conference on Social Welfare, it was said that:

The new name . . . reflects the sweep of the membership's interests, aims and concerns which extend beyond the immediate province of social work. The profession, which at times has struggled to assure its right to *"eminent domain,"* is now enjoying the rewards that come from sharing a common domain with countless others.[13]

But the specific role played by the profession in the Conference is less important than the general impotence of the Conference itself. This was demonstrated graphically in a series of confrontations in the late 1960s. As militant activists were to discover, to take over the Conference was to take over very little of real consequence for social welfare.[14]

Flexner Revisited

If the early social workers were aware of their subservience to organized social welfare, they did not show it. While preoccupied with the need for educational credentials, they showed little interest in professional autonomy per se. The history of Abraham Flexner's famous speech to the 1915 National Conference on Charities and Correction serves as a case in point. It is generally agreed that Flexner's judgment that social work could not be considered a profession signaled a major drive by social workers to remedy the situation. His audience focused on his remarks regarding the lack of a distinctive and communicable technology.[15] But Flexner also spoke about professional autonomy: In a full-fledged profession, he said,

The agent—physician, engineer or preacher—exercises a very large discretion as to what he shall do. He is not under orders; though he be cooperating with others, though the work be team work, rather than individual work, his responsibility is no less complete and no less personal.[16]

Among six criteria for professions, Flexner's first item was that they "involve essentially intellectual operations *with large individual responsibility*." [17] This was the major basis, in fact, on which he excluded pharmacists and trained nurses from his list of professions. Of the latter's relationship to the physician, Flexner declared: "The trained nurse plays into his hands; carries out his orders; summons him like a sentinel in fresh emergencies; subordinates loyally her intelligence to his theory, to his policy." [18] It is ironic that social workers have treated as the ultimate in professionalism, psychiatric and medical social work, two fields in which the worker has characteristically been ancillary to the physician.

The most serious and sustained attempt to redefine professional social work's relationship to organized social welfare has been the private practice movement. In their more polemical moments social workers have reduced this thrust to little more than a matter of status aspirations. The more serious criticism has centered on desertion of social work's broad social commitment and accountability.[19] But in recent years the private entrepreneurial model has been viewed by some as a way of making social workers more and not less responsive to human need, more and not less socially accountable in a broad sense. The argument is that domination of social workers by social welfare systems which are attuned to their own self-interest distorts and defeats both the service impulse and the ability to act on it effectively.[20]

The fact that the proponents of private practice in social work have appeared at various times to be aligned with both clinical and reform orientations suggests that this movement's true importance lies elsewhere than in the ideological realm. The underlying issue is one of professional autonomy, a problem which is of equal concern to all social workers.

In the 1940s social caseworkers became increasingly divided over the issue of "diagnostic" versus "functional" social work. Important in this struggle was conflict over the relative importance of the agency's function as a determinant of the worker's role. But in retrospect, both factions appear to have placed major emphasis on the agency's mission, so that the differences were in fact only relative.[21]

The Process of Institutional Integration

One might anticipate inherent strains between a professional community seeking desperately to achieve social acceptance in its own right and a complex of bureaucratic institutions. The fights over professional versus lay control of public education come readily to mind. But the early history of the relationship between social work and social welfare is notably free of serious conflict.

One factor which may help to explain this apparent anomaly is the looseness which characterized both social work and social welfare. Early in this century, for example, it was still relatively easy for a handful of dedicated individuals to launch a settlement house program. This allowed dissident elements in social welfare to break off from the main body without disturbing it unduly. Similarly, social work was a relatively amorphous collectivity with an equally amorphous mission.[22] But increasingly there was integration on both sides.

At the 1957 Annual Forum of the National Conference on Social Welfare, sociologist Lloyd Ohlin described the trend toward institutional integration in America and its behavioral counterpart, conformity.[23] He spoke to a major concern among social workers about the loss of creativity and personal freedom in an increasingly bureaucratic environment. Ohlin saw a steady trend toward organizational integration in two ways:

In the first place it is proceeding through the development of increasingly large organizations with greater potentiality for monopoly control over particular areas of interest. Secondly, integration is proceeding by much closer coordination and sharing of control between different organizations.[24]

In the field of social welfare, the trend of which Ohlin spoke had greatly accelerated in the years following the Second World War, as the federal government extended its hegemony. Not only were publicly administered programs vastly expanded, but the government also penetrated the voluntary sector through rules governing tax exemption, purchase-of-service contracts, and grants for special projects. The large-scale entry of government into the health care field of the 1950s and 1960 further accelerated the push toward integration. Within private philanthropy also there was a steady movement toward consolidation.

Ohlin noted a similar trend in social work:

The social work profession also shows evidence of this movement toward integration. The struggle toward federation on the part of social welfare associations in the National Association of Social Workers provides recent evidence of the increasing coordination and integration of welfare services. The Council on Social Work Education plays a significant integrating role in the clarification of minimum standards for the achievement of a professional social work education.[25]

NASW, established in 1955, brought together the professional associations of social workers under one roof. Step by step, a unified organization was welded out of the disparate antecedent bodies. Equally important was the increasing control over practice exerted by NASW. What began as essentially a symbolic system of regulation in 1960, the Academy of Certified Social Workers, a decade later established tangible criteria for entry including a test of competence.[26] The Code of Ethics, adopted in 1960 as a set of broad and ambiguous principles, had this item added to it in 1967:

I will not discriminate because of race, color, religion, age, sex, or national ancestry, and in my job capacity will work to prevent and eliminate such discrimination in rendering service, in work assignments, and in employment practices.[27]

By casting this obligation in negative terms and using specific behavioral criteria, NASW acquired a more enforceable mandate than had existed before. A position statement on advocacy, adopted in 1968, was an explicit attempt to commit NASW to a tangible and binding interpretation of the vague language of the Code.[28]

A major stride in professional integration occurred in 1969 with the extension of NASW membership eligibility (and potential professional regulation) to the vast majority of social work personnel who had previously been excluded because they lacked a master's degree.[29]

What happened in NASW was paralleled in social work education. The Council on Social Work Education was formed in 1952.[30] At first a struggling organization with barely enough resources to stay alive, CSWE eventually became the acknowledged standard-setting body for social work education. In the 1960s a proliferation of new schools of social work, which were more vulnerable to pressure than the older, established institutions, helped to fix firmly the position of the Council and the reality of its regulatory powers.[31] Eventually, NASW, which contributes substantially to the Council's financial support, sought to increase its own influence in CSWE, a step which would further integrate the social work professional community.

In his 1957 paper, Ohlin suggested that the press toward professional integration served primarily as a functional alternative to bureaucratic mechanisms of control in service organizations. Agencies could afford to allow their employees to innovate—a necessary adaptive device in periods of rapid change—if professional values provided an internalized system to assure conformity to organizational ends.[32] And in the context of the 1950s, social work professional standards and policies appeared indeed to be highly compatible with social welfare's interests, a means of assuring a loyal and predictable work force, in keeping with Ohlin's thesis. The increasing institutional integration in the respective systems, bureaucratic and professional, was complementary and mutually reinforcing.

What could not be foreseen at that point was the wrenching turmoil of the 1960s, which would drastically alter the direction of both systems and precipitate a crisis in their relationship. Under these circumstances, this same internal integration would sharpen the differences between the social work profession and organized social welfare.

A Crisis within the Profession

The Administration of President John F. Kennedy recognized what had been missed by its predecessor: the potent political base and potential trouble represented by the rising aspirations of blacks and other minorities locked in America's ghettos. In fairly traditional fashion, whatever the rhetoric, the federal government embarked on a program of cooptation of this newly significant force in American political life. The field of social welfare was a natural conduit for the federal largess with which the energies of the ghetto were to be harnessed.

But as the Kennedy and then the Johnson Administration poured funds into programs oriented to increasing educational and employment opportunities, the target populations and the conduits themselves went through a process of transformation. The innocent phrase in the war on poverty, "maximum feasible participation of the poor," became a battle cry in a war on the establishment. Mobilization for Youth, the pioneering antidelinquency and antipoverty program on New York's Lower East Side, epitomized the shift from relatively paternalistic if innovative notions of uplift for the disadvantaged to an alignment of the service staff with the clientele against welfare and other service systems.[33] The shift from service by "outsiders" to staff-client coalitions occurred in some form or other in dozens of community action agencies across the country.

Thus the federal government helped to stimulate rising expectations in the nation's ghettos as well as to channel them along basically political lines. In time, new organizations outside the social agency framework—the National Welfare Rights Organization being the most prominent—would rise up to pose a more formidable challenge to established elements in social welfare.[34]

Pervading the growing movement of social change were a deep-seated rejection and a mistrust of established social welfare institutions. Many social workers became caught up in this mood. Direct confrontations with welfare agencies and organizations tended to radicalize significant elements in the social work community, particularly among young and minority workers.

This general unrest found organized expression in such groups as the National Association of Black Social Workers and a militant amalgam of students and young social welfare employees called Social Welfare Workers Movement. Both of these organizations emerged in the midst of the aforementioned confrontations at successive Annual Forums of NCSW.[35] Both movements posed a direct threat to the ability of NASW to recruit and hold onto these elements, and forced it to move in new directions.

It was inevitable that the schools of social work would feel the full impact of the revolt of the late 1960s. But even before this, major changes were taking place in social work education. After years of domination by clinically oriented faculty members with close ties to the social agencies from which they had come, schools of social work had begun to stir out of their intellectual isolation in the late 1950s and early 1960s. The proliferating doctoral programs were socializing aspiring young social work educators to the norms of scientific inquiry. A new breed of faculty members challenged old shibboleths and sacred principles, just as a new breed of students would challenge the basic assumptions of social work education in the years to come. The infusion of federal funds allowed social work schools to experiment with new forms of field work training, thus helping to break the tight grip of the traditional agencies on the schools.

As the decade of the 1960s unfolded, school after school found itself in the throes of internal conflict which sometimes saw younger faculty members aligned with students against their older colleagues. The alliance of new elements often combined intellectual and reform interests—the challenge to pretentious and doctrinaire theories of practice supporting the challenge to the social welfare establishment. The large-scale recruitment of black and other minority students and faculty to schools intensified this trend.[36]

The Professional Institutions Respond

Growing tensions within NASW erupted at the Association's 1969 Delegate Assembly (biennial conclave). The immediate precipitating event was a severe financial crisis, but this forced to the surface a basic malaise in the organization.[37] The previous year, two NASW-sponsored meetings, close on the heels of the assassination of Martin Luther King, Jr., had provided an official forum in which dissident elements challenged the Association's leadership.[38] It was at the Delegate Assembly that bread-and-butter issues of organizational survival came together with questions of the Association's purpose. Specifically, if NASW were to continue at all, it must lure back into the fold those constituencies which were threatening to abandon it as irrelevant and ineffectual.

One major consequence of the crisis was a change in the historic relationship between NASW and organized social welfare. At the Delegate Assembly in 1971, NASW laid the foundation for setting standards for social service programs and organizations. In the past, the Association's use of direct leverage on agencies had been limited to matters of personnel practices as they affected NASW members. The new step would potentially make it possible to take direct action against agencies which trampled on clients' rights.[39]

Even more to the point was development of a system for rating prisons and jails as to their treatment of inmates and protection of their civil rights. These ratings would be circulated to social workers.[40] Unlike policy statements dealing with broad social issues, these measures are potentially coercive—a direct departure from social work's traditional practice of walking on eggshells when it comes to dealing with social welfare institutions.

These official actions by the delegates took place amid growing signs of a generally tougher attitude of the Association toward social welfare institutions. A few months before, new procedures were set forth by NASW for adjudicating workers' complaints against social agencies for interfering with their right to act in behalf of their clients (as advocates). And the Association acted in an uncharacteristically vigorous manner in pursuing cases involving allegedly shoddy personnel practices.

NASW, like other professional institutions, altered its direction in response to forces which were pressing in on it. The steps were basically accommodations, attempts to make the necessary adjustments without seriously disrupting the Association's relationships. But, like other institutions, NASW had turned a corner in the process. It would not be possible simply to go back, once the pressure of the moment subsided.

In a similar way, the schools of social work and CSWE found themselves moving in a new direction. The new message which was being preached more and more was that the social worker's duty to those in need took precedence over duty to agency. And techniques of institutional change became increasingly prominent in curricula.[41]

But perhaps as important as changes in substantive content was the approach to knowledge itself. Historically, social work teachers had carried the norms of the agency over into the classroom. Students became, in effect, clients whose needs were to be diagnosed and treated.[42] In such an atmosphere, students' behavior, including their questioning of dogma, became defined as clinical data. This form of socialization was admirably suited to the need of the social services for compliant staff who would be inclined to question their own attitudes rather than the orientation of the agency itself. But, especially as students learned the value of corporate action in raising educational and political issues, it was no longer possible to maintain such clinical norms in the educational process.

As CSWE sought to deal with the new mood in the schools, it moved in two ways. One was to emphasize affirmative action by schools to recruit minority students and faculty members. The other was to come down hard in its curriculum policies on the side of academic norms of scientific skepticism and openness.[43]

Like NASW, the schools and their Council were seeking to accommodate to pressures in order to survive, responding to dissidents in their ranks and to outside pressures. But in ratifying the new directions, they were doing more than engaging in symbolic gestures. The new thrust, once codified, became a new *status quo*. Particularly because of the ideological emphasis in social work, and specifically because of the heavily ideological flavor of the crisis, the new orientation could not easily be undone.

And herein lies a basic source of strain between the social work profession and the social services. After the brief flirtation with reform in the 1960s the society moved sharply to the right. Predictably, welfare organizations were swept along with such a swing. But such sudden changes are not so easy for professional institutions, which tend to define things in moral terms. Having told social work students to question dogma, social work educators cannot suddenly say they did not mean it. Having set up elaborate machinery for obligating social workers to act as advocates and protecting their right to do so, the National Association of Social Workers cannot rescind the action without risking the loss of its credibility.

Dilemmas of Professionalism

As the social work profession considers its options, the picture is complicated by two major problems. One is a dramatic inversion of what was previously a severe shortage of social work manpower. The manpower crisis has now become a job crisis. The other is threatened withdrawal from the main body of the profession by dissident elements; a major threat now comes from a kind of backlash among clinicians who have felt that their interests were neglected as the professional leadership chased the will-o'-the-wisp of "relevance."

As for the job squeeze, public welfare operations, having previously sought to expand their cadres of social work professionals, are turning to other disciplines, such as vocational rehabilitation and management science. Changes in birth control and abortion practices are sharply reducing the personnel demand in the most highly professionalized sector of child welfare work, the field of adoptions. A brief shift away from casework services by the Community Service Society of New York and tight limits on public family services may portend the end of an enterprise which for many years was virtually synonymous with social work professionalism. And funds for innovative and experimental programs which absorbed many social workers in the past have been drying up, particularly in the area of community action.[44] All this goes on while an expanding social work education system continues to turn out social workers.

Having lost its claim to certain traditional social service functions and having been sharply curtailed in others, might the social work profession simply atrophy, or evolve into a minor element in the professional spectrum? Given the realities of individual and corporate self-interest, this seems highly unlikely. Social work education is now a major industry, on which the careers of a sizable and articulate professional constituency depend directly. The ability of this group to protect its interests was demonstrated in one successful effort to fight off drastic reductions in federal financing of social work education, despite a strong mood of retrenchment in Congress and the Administration.[45] The Council on Social Work Education's expansion of its domain to cover undergraduate social work education, previously a fragmented jumble, offered more dramatic illustration of the power of the organized community of social work educators—again being challenged as this book goes to press.

The most likely consequence of the disparity between an expanding supply of social workers and a shrinking demand in traditional agencies is that professionals will find new arenas where they are "essential." Conversely, institutions which heretofore have made little or no use of social work expertise will find uses for it. The pertinent question, then, is not whether social workers as individuals will find a market for their talents but whether the social work profession as an institution will be able to define how those talents are to be utilized.

The other complicating factor, professional disintegration, is in many ways the more formidable. There are now appearing in many cities societies of clinical social workers. In 1971 they formed the American Federation of Societies for Clinical Social Work. Among other things it called for licensing of workers. While they have made it a point to maintain their identity as social workers, the societies of clinical social workers have also made it a point to organize outside NASW.[46]

In one sense, NASW's very success at professional integration— for instance, in the demands it makes on its members—has contributed to this kind of fragmentation; for the old, loose language, which allowed potential conflict to be hazed over, is being supplanted by more specific expectations and directions. Meanwhile, such constituencies as that represented by the National Association of Black Social Workers have their own momentum and their own logic. They show every sign of continuing as distinct entities.

It was almost with an air of plaintiveness that the Executive Director of NASW wrote to the membership in October, 1971, about the need for professional unity:

Probably the most persistent obstacle to social work unity that we note from the national office vantage point is the dichotomy of clinical practice versus social action. NASW has made much headway in the last year in combating this destructive polarization, but old experiences and attitudes die hard.[47]

He went on to enumerate the many ways in which the Association was seeking to develop social work practice. But underlying the "practice-versus-action" split are far more basic issues: the concept of "service"; the way in which those in need of service are perceived and the relationship of the professionals to them. The traditional clinical approach tended to emphasize pathology and the need to modify the behavior of the people experiencing trouble. A newer orientation, whether on the direct-service or planning level, begins with the presumption that clients are essentially adequate, rights-bearing individuals who are beset by problems largely generated by the environment.[48] To deal with such conflicting views of the targets of social work services, it is not enough to list the achievements of NASW in the "practice" arena.

This issue of professional cohesion is paramount, if social work is to deal with its other problems.[49] A potential basis for unity appears to be the quest for professional autonomy. This is an issue which is vitally important to various elements in the professional community, perhaps for different reasons. It has been a central problem throughout the history of social work, and autonomy for the individual practitioner, vis-à-vis the service bureaucracy, hinges directly on the relationship of the profession, as a corporate entity, to the services as an institutional complex.

Alternative Paths to Professional Autonomy

In theory, at least, the social work profession has a number of options open to it as it ponders the problem of professional autonomy.

1. Disengagement. One alternative is to cease to be an employee profession, at least in the fields with which social work has commonly been identified. The private practitioners by implication if not in actuality represent such an approach. But as a general position for the profession as a whole, this would fly in the face of the current trend toward increasing bureaucratization of established and

traditionally entrepreneurial professions. What is perhaps more realistic is selective disengagement from traditional welfare systems and
entry into new kinds of institutional arrangements; needless to say,
the problems inherent in employee status would remain. Turner
projected such a movement in his landmark paper in 1968:

Social work is handicapped by being wedded to the concept of welfare.
Welfare, historically, has too often meant protective caretaking of the
non-able-bodied. The concepts of caretaking and rehabilitation are too
limited in definition, as it becomes clearer that it is not just people who
are deprived, ill, and unskilled, but that our communities, our social,
economic, and political structures are also sick, dysfunctional, deprived,
in need of crisis intervention, and in need of rehabilitation. If social
work is to be more responsive to the human crisis it must operate from
a concept sufficiently broad to embrace the range of front-line institutional functions that are required to produce and to maintain a socially
productive man in a humanized society.[50]

Turner saw social workers moving into such fields as housing,
employment, education, and health. While social work has been involved in aspects of all these fields, he projected a more initiatory or
institutional, as opposed to a residual, role.[51]

2. Alignment with new elements outside the service system.
A second approach is to seek out alliances with recipients of social service and other dissident elements. This is at least implicit in the new
NASW stand on advocacy and the active wooing of persons indigenous to the client community by some schools of social work.

This is an exciting notion, and for brief periods in local situations
it has offered an alternative to organizational control. For example,
welfare rights groups and staff members in welfare agencies have
come together on a common cause. But there are obvious reasons
why this is insufficient as the primary means of assuring worker autonomy from agency domination. Organized alliances of this kind
have an evanescent quality. Whatever power they may be able to
bring together temporarily is easily eroded without some sort of institutional support.

What does seem to be a realistic prospect is the alliance of clientele with social workers who have sufficient support from their professional community to withstand the inevitable pressure from the
organization. An example of the latter is the legal defense fund

which NASW has established for members who suffer retaliation for engaging in professional action.[52] Again, it turns on a unified professional community.

3. Realignment of social work and social welfare. Finally, there appears to be the opportunity for social work to enter directly into a new kind of working relationship with organized social welfare. This does not preclude, and in fact can be complemented by, selective disengagement and forging of new alliances.

Although the social work profession is likely to continue to expand its horizons in many directions, it shows no signs of withdrawing its interest from areas with which it has traditionally been identified. Even if the demand for social work manpower were to evaporate in some of the fields alluded to earlier, the profession appears to have as big an investment as ever. Rather than abandoning public welfare, for example, NASW is proposing new legislation and becoming generally more aggressive in behalf of the professional employees and their clients.[53]

The logic of such a continuing involvement seems clear. To abandon this sector of our institutional life would raise serious questions about the profession's social commitment, for in so doing social workers would be abandoning countless human beings who will continue to be subject to social welfare systems, willy-nilly. As for relying wholly on coalitions with the client group, this seems at best a romantic and tenuous basis of operation. Rather, what is needed is a shift toward a more equitable relationship between partners instead of the traditional dominance—subservience patterns. For their part, social welfare institutions need social work, both for its expertise and for the linkage it can provide to other elements in the institutional environment.

In the light of current manpower and funding trends this may seem to be the worst time, in effect, to renegotiate the contract. Is not organized social welfare calling the tune, with social work forced to play accordingly? I suggested earlier that although the manpower market in the social services is going through some major adjustments which are having devastating effects, it would not simply dry up. The long-term trend in the demand for social services in this country is up, not down.[54] Social workers can deal with the present crisis successfully if they will come together as an organized entity and make certain that the profession shares in the redefinition of the social service enterprise. That is, they must not simply muddle through the crisis but make positive use of it.[55]

Thus, the issues of professional autonomy and professional cohesion are closely related. To achieve the former, the organized social work profession must demonstrate the latter; that is, its ability to speak for the social work community. And both of these depend, in turn, on effective control over social work practice and the social work education process.

The first of these, regulation of practice, requires that the social work profession determine who is allowed to practice and under what conditions. This means licensure or an equivalent mechanism. It also means enforceable expectations to which social workers can be held accountable. Without such an internal system of regulation, the profession cannot hope to make a persuasive case for lessening bureaucratic control by social service institutions. It thus is in the interests of all social workers, the activists no less than the clinicians, to move in this direction. I am aware of the risks involved in such a development; they are necessary risks. One effect would be that the clinicians and the activists would have to come to terms with one another instead of drifting off in their respective orbits.

Effective control over professional education would seem to be a necessary condition if social work is to achieve the other aims set forth above. I have referred to the growing role of the Council on Social Work Education in regulating all aspects of social work education. A final step in this process is the integration of the educational enterprise with other aspects of professional organization. Ultimately, this means the merger of the National Association of Social Workers and the Council on Social Work Education.

Again, dangers loom in the course I have projected. History is replete with examples of professional irresponsibility and self-seeking. And, in fact, those established professions which have exerted precisely the kind of control I am suggesting are among the worst offenders. But it should be remembered that they come out of a different tradition, that of the medieval guilds. I submit that the commitments of social workers have been and are different. The problem for social workers is not that they have willfully dehumanized but that too often they have been used by institutions whose societal function was to dehumanize, whatever their stated mission. By providing a countervailing force, the social work professional community can free social workers to live up to those high aims which still attract legions of dedicated young people into the field. In short, it can allow them to behave professionally.

Notes

[1] The most celebrated attempt was that of Abraham Flexner at the 1915 National Conference on Charities and Correction. He drew upon his studies of medical education and his background as an educator. See Abraham Flexner, "Is Social Work a Profession?" in *Proceedings of the National Conference on Charities and Correction* (Chicago: Hildmann Printing Company, 1915), pp. 576–90. In more recent years, sociological definitions, also cast in descriptive terms, have been the major source. See Ernest Greenwood, "Attributes of a Profession," *Social Work*, II, No. 2 (1957), 45–55.

[2] Eliot Friedson, "Dominant Professions, Bureaucracy, and Client Services," in William R. Rosengren and Mark Lefton, eds., *Organizations and Clients; Essays in the Sociology of Service* (Columbus, Ohio: Charles E. Merrill, 1970), p. 75.

[3] See, for example, Andrew Billingsley, "Bureaucratic and Professional Orientation Patterns in Social Casework," *Social Service Review*, XXXVIII (1964), 400–407; Peter M. Blau and W. Richard Scott, *Formal Organizations: a Comparative Approach* (London: Routledge and Kegan Paul, 1963); Lloyd E. Ohlin, Herman Piven, and Donnell M. Pappenfort, "Major Dilemmas of the Social Worker in Probation and Parole," in Herman D. Stein and Richard A. Cloward, eds., *Social Perspectives on Behavior* (Glencoe, Ill.: Free Press, 1958), pp. 251–62; and Nina Toren, "Semi-Professionalism and Social Work: a Theoretical Perspective," in Amitai Etzioni, ed., *The Semi-Professions and Their Organization* (New York: Free Press, 1969), pp. 141–95.

[4] See Etzioni, *op. cit.*

[5] See Roy Lubove, *The Professional Altruist: the Emergence of Social Work as a Career, 1880–1930* (Cambridge, Mass.: Harvard University Press, 1965), pp. 137–56.

[6] *Ibid.*, pp. 223 f.

[7] Lydia Rapoport, "In Defense of Social Work," *Social Service Review*, XXXIV (1960), 71.

8 See Billingsley, *op. cit.;* also Herman Piven, "Professionalism and Organizational Structure: Training and Agency Variables in Relation to Practitioner Orientation and Practice" (unpublished doctoral dissertation, Columbia University, 1961).

The research by Blau and Scott did find differences between professional and nonprofessional personnel. But since the comparisons were within the same setting, the relative importance of organizational factors could not be determined. See W. Richard Scott, "Professional Employees in a Bureaucratic Structure: Social Work," in Etzioni, *op. cit.,* p. 91. See also Blau and Scott, *op. cit.*

9 See Lubove, *op. cit.,* Chap. 6.

10 See Gilbert Y. Steiner, *Social Insecurity: the Politics of Welfare* (Chicago: Rand McNally Co., 1966).

11 John Kenneth Galbraith, *The New Industrial State* (Boston: Houghton Mifflin Co., 1967), p. 71.

12 Ruth M. Williams, "Conferences in Social Welfare," in Russell H. Kurtz, ed., *Social Work Year Book 1960* (New York: National Association of Social Workers, 1960), p. 201.

13 Elinor P. Zaki, "Foreword," in *Social Welfare Forum, 1957* (New York: Columbia University Press, 1957), pp. vii–viii.

14 For accounts of the turbulent events of the Annual Forums of 1968 and 1969 see reports and commentaries in *The Social Welfare Forum, 1968* (New York: Columbia University Press, 1968), pp. 156–63, and *The Social Welfare Forum, 1969* (1969), pp. 178–95; William Borders, "Welfare Militants Disrupt Meeting to Press Reforms," New York *Times,* May 26, 1969, p. 1, col. 6.

15 See Frank J. Bruno, *Trends in Social Work as Reflected in the Proceedings of the National Conference on Social Welfare, 1874–1946* (New York: Columbia University Press, 1948), p. 141; Nathan E. Cohen, *Social Work in the American Tradition* (New York: Holt, Rinehart and Winston, 1958), p. 120.

16 Flexner, *op. cit.,* p. 578.   17 *Ibid.,* p. 581; italics added.

18 *Ibid.,* p. 583.

19 See, for example, Sherman Merle, "Some Arguments against Private Practice," *Social Work,* VII, No. 1 (1962), 12–17.

20 See Irving Piliavin, "Restructuring the Provision of Social Services," *Social Work,* XIII, No. 1 (1968), 34–41; Arnold M. Levin, "Financing Social Work Services through Prepaid Social Insurance," in Willard C. Richan, ed., *Human Services and Social Work Responsibility* (New York: National Association of Social Workers, 1969), pp. 321–30.

21 See Cora Kasius, ed., *A Comparison of Diagnostic and Functional Casework Concepts* (New York: Family Service Association of America, 1950). For a discussion of the work setting as an influence on worker role see Helen Harris Perlman, *Social Casework: a Problem-solving Process* (Chicago: University of Chicago Press, 1957), Chap. 4.

[22] See Flexner, *op. cit.*, p. 585.

[23] Lloyd E. Ohlin, "Conformity in American Society Today," *Social Work*, III, No. 2 (1958), 58–66.

[24] *Ibid.*, p. 59.   [25] *Ibid.*

[26] "Tools for Assessing Practice Competence: Reviewed, Revised and Ready for Use," *NASW News*, XVI, No. 2 (1971), 1, col. 1.

[27] Code of Ethics adopted by the Delegate Assembly of the National Association of Social Workers, October 13, 1960, and amended April 11, 1967.

[28] See *Ad Hoc* Committee on Advocacy, "The Social Worker as Advocate: Champion of Social Victims," *Social Work*, XIV, No. 2 (1969), 16–22.

[29] "Eligibility Changes Effective April 1," *NASW News*, XV, No. 3 (1970), 1, col. 3.

[30] Lubove, *op. cit.*, pp. 223 f.

[31] From 1950 through 1962 there was an average of less than one new school every twenty months. From 1962 through 1969, the rate was one new school every four and a half months. See *Encyclopedia of Social Work*, (16th ed.; New York: National Association of Social Workers, 1971), II, 1611.

[32] Ohlin, *op. cit.* See also Willard C. Richan, "A Theoretical Scheme for Determining Roles of Professional and Nonprofessional Personnel," *Social Work*, VI, No. 4 (1961), 22–28.

[33] See Richard A. Cloward and Richard M. Elman, "Advocacy in the Ghetto," in Fred M. Cox *et al.*, eds., *Strategies of Community Organization* (Itasca, Ill.: Peacock Publishers, 1970), pp. 209–15.

[34] See Frances Fox Piven and Richard A. Cloward, *Regulating the Poor: the Functions of Public Welfare* (New York: Pantheon Books, 1971), pp. 256–82.

[35] Zaki, *op. cit.*

[36] See Douglas Glasgow, "The Black Thrust for Vitality: the Impact on Social Work Education," *Journal of Education for Social Work*, VII, No. 2 (1971), 9–18; Joseph Vigilante, "Student Participation in Decision-making in Schools of Social Work," *ibid.*, VI, No. 2 (1970), 51–60; David Wineman and Adrienne James, "The Advocacy Challenge to Schools of Social Work," *Social Work*, XIV, No. 2 (1969), 23–32.

[37] See Chauncey A. Alexander, "National Association of Social Workers Stewardship Report (April, 1969—April, 1971)" (multilith).

[38] See Daniel Thursz, "The Arsenal of Social Action Strategies: Options for Social Workers," *Social Work*, XVI, No. 1 (1971), 28; Richan, ed., *op. cit.*

[39] "Assembly Acts; Reaffirms Priority on Racism/Poverty, Approves Dues Plan," *NASW News*, XVI, No. 4 (1971), 1, col. 4.

[40] *Ibid.*   [41] See, for example, Wineman and Jones, *op. cit.*

42 See Charlotte Towle, *The Learner in Education for the Professions* (Chicago: University of Chicago Press, 1954), especially Chap. 3.

43 See Carl Scott, "CSWE Activities and Plans Related to Ethnic Minority Groups," *Social Work Education Reporter*, XIX, No. 3 (1971), 27–30; *Curriculum Policy for the Master's Degree Program in Graduate Schools of Social Work* (New York: Council on Social Work Education, 1969).

44 See "Prospectus for Change at the CSS," *Social Service Review*, XIV (1971), 205–11; Editorial, "Moving Toward the Future," *Social Work*, XVI, No. 2 (1971), 2.

45 "Responses to CSWE-led Fight for Federal Support of Social Work Education," *Social Work Education Reporter*, XIX, No. 3 (1971), 1–2.

46 From material distributed by the American Federation of Societies for Clinical Social Work (1971). The notion that psychiatric social workers ought to leave social work altogether and join similar specialties in other fields is the thesis of at least one book: William E. Henry, John H. Sims, and S. Lee Spray, *The Fifth Profession* (San Francisco: Jossey-Bass, 1971).

47 Chauncey A. Alexander, "From the Director; Enigma of Unity," *NASW News*, XVI, No. 6 (1971), 10, col. 1.

48 For a statement of the issue from the standpoint of social casework, see Scott Briar, "The Casework Predicament," *Social Work*, XIII, No. 1 (1968), 5–11. See also Martin Rein, "Social Work in Search of a Radical Profession," *Social Work*, XV, No. 2 (1970), 13–28.

49 See Willard C. Richan, "New Curriculum Policy Statement: the Problem of Professional Cohesion," *Journal of Education for Social Work*, VII, No. 2 (1971), 55–60.

50 John B. Turner, "In Response to Change: Social Work at the Crossroads," *Social Work*, XIII, No. 3 (1968), 8 f.

51 *Ibid.*   52 See "Assembly Acts," *op. cit.*

53 See "Grants to States: New NASW Bill for Social Services," *NASW News*, XVI, No. 6 (1971), 1, col. 4.

54 See Editorial, "Moving Toward the Future," *op. cit.*

55 See Edmund H. Volkhart, ed., *Social Behavior and Personality: Contributions of W. I. Thomas to Theory and Social Research* (New York: Social Science Research Council, 1951), pp. 12–14.

Arnold Gurin

❧

EDUCATION FOR CHANGING PRACTICE [1]

Education for practice, under the best of circumstances, is a complex enterprise. It calls for the maintenance of delicate balances between the academic and the practical, the theoretical and the applied, the values of knowing and the values of doing. If there is a fair degree of clarity concerning the nature of practice, its values, goals, body of knowledge, and methods, then the complexities are relatively manageable. Under those conditions, education has some anchors and fixed points of reference. If the premises of practice are themselves in flux, then the educational enterprise is bereft of moorings. "Education for uncertainty" then becomes not a rhetorical expression of a philosophical orientation, but an accurate description of the reality of the situation.

Social work education is today in multiple jeopardy. Uncertainties abound on all sides. On the one hand, social work education is part of the general system of higher education. As such, it is subject to the conflicts and confusions surrounding many different types of efforts to reform higher education. In addition, social work education shares the general undertainties that beset all fields of professional education, because of shifting views as to the functions of the professions in the contemporary world and how best to prepare for them. For whatever comfort that may provide to a profession long suffering from a sense of being different and isolated from others, it is possible to say today that the problems of social work are similar to those of other professions. There are in addition, however, certain unresolved problems that lie directly in the area of social work's own development as a profession and its own educational responsibilities.

The turmoil on the college campuses is too recent to warrant any extensive exposition. The turbulence was a result of many factors, some of which were broadly political in nature and some indigenous to the educational institutions themselves. Perhaps the most important factor is the sheer size of the population receiving higher education. The very rapid and accelerating postwar expansion of higher education has made it obvious that college and university education cannot be devoted to a single objective, nor can it really be conceived as a single system. It is therefore inevitable that there will be growing diversity throughout higher education in regard to all relevant dimensions—goals and objectives, philosophy, criteria employed for selection and evaluation of students, curriculum content, pedagogical methods, and many more.

The need to serve this vast population leads inevitably to certain dilemmas and cross currents. As against a more classical model in which it was the essential purpose of higher education to train a leadership elite, the opening of such opportunities to half the population makes it necessary for higher education to prepare people for a wide range of status positions within the society. The egalitarian strains within the culture, accentuated by at least some aspects of the youthful revolt of the mid-1960s, have pushed in the direction of "anticredentialism," challenging the alleged corruption of the educational experience by its status-conferring functions. On the other hand, given some of the more tenacious aspects of contemporary social institutions in the United States, the purposes of social mobility require that credentials be bestowed. As a result of these conflicting pressures, undergraduate education has tended to become more narrow in its vocational emphasis, while simultaneously and paradoxically being pushed to be less vocationally specific and more broadly humanistic.

It does not seem reasonable to expect that these basic contradictions can be resolved, since the various purposes being served by higher education, although mutually contradictory, are all equally compelling. One must therefore assume a large-scale, probably growing, enterprise that will continue to be marked by great diversity. It may be appropriate to disparage diversity, as Bressler does, as "a symbol of inability to achieve consensus on goals, and the strategem for shifting the burden of educational choice from institution to students." [2] It is nevertheless a rational response to the conflicting pressures being brought to bear by large population groups within the society who need higher education for a variety of purposes. Bressler himself goes on to acknowledge that "in education as elsewhere philosophy is the hostage of inadequate knowledge. Without a comprehensive theory of society and the capacity to predict the shape of the future, no coherent vision of the educational enterprise is possible." [3]

There is indeed no comprehensive theory of society, nor a comprehensive framework of social policy which can act as a guide toward answering the perennial question of "education for what?" Instead, there is a hazardous and uncertain opportunity structure through which persons growing up in the society gain access to status and to resources of various kinds. The chances of being able to use these opportunities to achieve different degrees of resources vary widely for different segments of the population. Although the evidence on the subject is increasingly problematical, it still seems to be true that one of the most crucial factors affecting this process is the extent to which individuals are able to participate in higher education.

The situation of professional education is even more complex. Professional education is almost by definition a channel for awarding status and prestige to selected members of the society. Yet professional education, like higher education in general, has been subject to intense pressure to make these credentializing and status-awarding functions more available to those previously deprived of access to them. One way of dealing with this problem has been to proliferate various subprofessional and paraprofessional categories, thus building more elaborate hierarchies that are nevertheless tied closely to a core profession. Hughes, commenting critically on this development, emphasizes the tendency of each profession to maintain its hegemony by maintaining its position at the top of such hierarchies. [4] However, it is no more feasible to generalize concerning professional education than it is to make uniform statements about higher education. Here too the key factor is diversity.

One of the most crucial dilemmas facing professional education centers on the issue of specialization. On the one hand, the accelerated pace of scientific discovery and the rapid accumulation of knowledge characteristic of the contemporary period have made it necessary for professionals, especially in the scientific fields, to become more specialized in specific aspects of their disciplines. On the other hand, the educational institutions have been faced with the problem of how to keep up with rapidly expanding knowledge in so many specific areas. One finds, therefore, simultaneously a tendency toward greater specialization together with a countertendency representing a search for more general and stable principles and skills that can be transmitted. In other words, finding it impossible to transmit all the knowledge that is being accumulated so rapidly, the schools tend to redefine their function as helping to prepare the professional to accumulate that knowledge continuously as he develops within his field. It is also true, even in the scientific fields, that as specialization becomes more widespread the problems of integration become greater, so that countertendencies come into existence, seeking new syntheses that will improve the effectiveness of professional functioning.

All of this is very pertinent to the current dilemmas in the social professions. In the social professions the issue of "relevance" that has had such wide currency in the most recent period is more pressing and critical than in fields which can make a greater claim to concern with basic knowledge for its own sake. In the social professions, the schools that undertake to educate the future professionals have been pressed very hard to explicate the contributions they are making to the improvement of the society that they are supposedly mandated to serve. For some of the professions the major issue has been defined in terms of values and social responsibility. For example, the major change in the orientation of the law schools has been to highlight the responsibility of the profession to serve as advocates for the penniless and underprivileged in addition to, or instead of, the traditional advocacy they have espoused on behalf of the privileged.

In medicine, which is still the archetype of the "independent" and high-status professions, the issue has been not only social responsibility but also effectiveness. The profession has been asked to concern itself with how well it is serving the deprived segments of the population. It is also being asked with ever greater insistence how well it is serving anybody. Involved in this question is a series of issues regarding the organization of medical care and the responsibility of the profession for the effectiveness with which medical services are delivered to the entire population. Another type of issue relates to the field of medical knowledge itself. Here the central question has been the interrelationship between physical and social factors in the determination of health and illness.

If such pressures have expressed themselves even in fields that are well established and that enjoy wide acceptance in the society, then it is to be expected that the pressure would be even more insistent in newer and less prestigious professions.

During the past fifty years there has been a proliferation of emerging professions that have made some claim to a field of specialized knowledge and to a distinctive area of "practice" or "intervention" in the social field. Until recently, each of them has been characterized by a central consensus as to the basis for its claim. In the field of physical planning, for example, the core subject matter dealt with land use and the spatial distribution of functions within the urban community. Public health has been based on the epidemiological triad of the environment, the host, and the agent, combined with the concept of primary, secondary, and tertiary prevention as the modes of intervention. In the case of public administration, the model was the generic administrator operating on the basis of a set of principles rooted in concepts of organizational and individual behavior and applicable to a wide range of situations. Despite the lack of clarity in social work, it too had an underlying synthesis of sorts. The basic notion in social work was that it represented a helping process using psychosocial concepts to intervene at individual, group, and intergroup levels to improve social functioning.

It became obvious during the 1950s and 1960s that all of these definitions were at best incomplete and at worst constraints that prevented an adequate response to the problems of the time. In each case, the "consensus" did not encompass enough of the important variables that were relevant to the problem being addressed to prove effective in dealing with the problem. Thus, physical planners until recently failed to give sufficient attention to the crucial matters of poverty and discrimination that are basic to any planning for the urban community. The epidemiological model in public health, which had proved adequate for dealing with communicable diseases, turned out to be far less than satisfactory when applied to complex chronic conditions.[5] Field by field, it became ever more apparent that the subject matter would have to become much more comprehensive, incorporating particular kinds of social factors that had been largely ignored in the previous formulations.

As each field becomes more comprehensive, the boundaries between fields become blurred. It has become increasingly difficult in the most recent period for social work as well as for a number of other human service professions to convey a clear image of their central, distinctive areas of expertise. Such uncertainty places an emerging profession, still unsure of its legitimation and status, in a particularly hazardous position. Each of the social professions is caught today in a critical tension between its need to clarify its distinctive professional mandate and its need to transcend earlier definitions and boundaries that have proves ineffective.

Social Work Practice

Against this background we turn now to a more direct consideration of social work education. That must of necessity begin with a discussion of social work practice. Like the other professions, only probably more so, social work has lost its previous synthesis (to the extent that it had one) and finds itself today in considerable disarray. There is uncertainty as to value commitments, goals, methods, and techniques. As one of the newest and least secure professions, social work is particularly vulnerable to the pressures of a rapidly changing period. From its earliest days, the profession has had an exaggerated concern with its status and had not achieved a sufficiently adequate confidence either in the clarity of its own functions or its position in society to be able to withstand very effectively the onslaughts of the attacks on all professions that gained momentum during the past decade. Despite these limitations, the profession expanded considerably during the 1960s as a result of increased public expenditures in various forms of social services. It was therefore faced with the need to absorb a very large number of additional professionals, heterogeneous in background, attitudes, areas of interest, and ideologies. All these factors have tended to add to the general theme of great diversity and to the elusiveness of a common core.

It is therefore difficult to say today what is the essential nature of social work practice. That is indeed the central problematic issue in the entire field. It would seem that several recurring themes are perhaps more pervasive than others and bear very directly on the issues of education for practice. They may be posed for discussion purposes in the nature of dilemmas or polarities, although in truth they cannot be resolved in terms of sharp choices of that type:

1. The issue of the relationship of the professional to the organization

2. The nature of direct client practice, and particularly the strain between "service" and "advocacy"

3. The relationship of direct client service to the functions of policy, planning, and management

4. The relationship of social work practice to the other human service fields.

THE PROFESSIONAL AND ORGANIZATIONS

Schein, in reporting on new directions in professional education, comments on the trend in all professions away from the model of the autonomous practitioner, since most professionals today are employed in organizations. For social work, this has always been the case.[6]

It has always been difficult to separate professional social work practice from the problems, policies, and commitments of the wide variety of organizations in which social workers are employed. The organizations perform many diverse functions and do not constitute a cohesive field of activity. They include governmental and voluntary structures concerned with income maintenance, paramedical services, institutional placements for many different kinds of conditions, protective services for various handicapped and dependent groups, correctional measures to deal with deviant behavior, counseling and therapeutic services to deal with interpersonal and intra-personal problems, and many more. Inevitably, there are many op-portunities for differences and contradictions to arise between the value commitments that are built into these organizations on the basis of their sponsorship and mechanisms of control and the values pursued by social work as a profession. The probation officer with a professional commitment to individualized service to an individual is simultaneously and inevitably an agent of social control. A social worker administering a work test in a public assistance program must reconcile that act with his professional commitment to client self-determination. The question of who is the client that Schein suggests is now becoming more general has bedeviled social work for decades.[7]

The most important point in this context is that the social work profession has very little control over most of the organizations it serves. It has less control than other professions that are also embed-ded in institutions, such as the ministry and the teaching profession. Social work, over the past three quarters of a century, has been able to establish hegemony in only a relatively small portion of the broad and diversified fields that it serves.

A few figures will suffice to document the character of social work manpower problems.

In 1960 it was estimated that there were some 105,000 persons in the United States occupying positions defined as social work. Of these, only some 20,000, or less than one fifth, were completely pro-fessional in the sense that they had completed two full years of graduate education.[8]

Equally significant is the uneven distribution of the professional personnel among the different types of organizational programs. Thus, only 5.3 percent of all professional social workers with two years of graduate education were found in public assistance agen-cies, a drop from the comparable figure of 10.4 percent in 1950. In contrast, over one fourth of all the fully trained professionals were in child welfare work and almost one fifth in psychiatric social work.

Even more graphic are the contrasts revealed by the figures indi-cating the ratio of trained to untrained social workers in the different fields. In 1960 only 3 percent of all the social workers in public assistance agencies had two years of professional education. On the other hand, 36 percent of social workers in other family services (primarily voluntary) had such training. The comparable figures were 41 percent for child welfare, 55 percent for medical social work, and 72 percent for pyschiatric social work.

It is clear that there has been a strong tendency for the most fully trained and, therefore, the most professionalized social workers to gravitate toward specialized functions where the distinctive professional techniques and values have become more firmly established than in the mass services dominated by governmental policies and particularly in the public assistance system. A special paradox reflected in these figures is the high proportion of professionals in medical and psychiatric settings where the dominant profession has tended to be medicine rather than social work. Except in rather small and limited areas, professional social workers have thus been largely ancillary to either politically dominated mass service systems or to medically dominated professional systems.

In attempting to deal with this problem, Richan argues for professional autonomy from the organization.[9] He sees inherent conflicts between the profession and service bureaucracies, and argues for the profession to assert its primacy and to free itself from the imposed restraints. He refers back to Flexner, the specter that has haunted social work for more than five decades, who pointed out that the fatal flaw in social work's professionalism was its lack of *individual* responsibility.

While the Richan position has much to commend it in facing up to the issue of the relationship of professional to organization, it seems to me to move in the wrong direction. The term "autonomy" is particularly troublesome, since it suggests the possibility of a professional practice independent of its organizational base. The only model of practice that fits such a description is the therapeutic relationship. In all other respects, whether as advocates, opponents, or functionaries of established organizations, social workers are dependent upon organized resources in order to perform their functions of service provision. The stress on autonomy tends to blunt this central issue.

Rather than autonomy, the problem for social work practice would seem to be that of contributing to the improvement of the organized services, by assuming a greater rather than lesser measure of responsibility for their functioning. Such efforts may have mixed success, but there seems no escape from the inextricable linkage between the profession and the services.

DIRECT CLIENT SERVICE AND SOCIAL ACTION

It is in the area of direct client practice that social work is faced with the most difficult problems of reconceptualization. With the loss of faith in the earlier consensus based on a helping, therapeutic relationship, the nature of the front-line practitioner's service is elusive. Two contributions to the present volume reflect alternative approaches to that problem. Grosser, adopting the stance that was particularly popular in the late 1960s, makes the case for "advocacy." He argues for a type of advocacy that will not be limited to the case level but "will represent the case for an alternate social system—a bona fide welfare state." Even more explicitly, he calls for the organization of a political constituency as a social work responsibility and asserts that ideological advocacy is an inherent responsibility of the social worker's job. Rein takes a somewhat similar view in his arguments for a "radical casework." [10]

The difficulty with these positions, as Specht points out, is that it is hard to operationalize large-scale system change as a case-level function.[11] Carol Meyer offers an alternative view that seems more realistic as an approach to direct client service. She advocates a systems approach that will somehow build into the professional helping role components that take account of remediable elements in the organizational structure as well as in the client's relationship to his environment. While that formulation obviously needs considerably more specification, it seems at least to be posed at the proper level of abstraction to permit an answer to the question of how to define case-level services.

Whatever differences may exist on other issues, there is widespread recognition today that direct-service functions cannot be considered the exclusive domain of fully trained professionals. The persistent discrepancy between the numbers of fully trained workers and the total personnel in the mass-service fields has made it necessary to think about alternatives to the traditional definition of the master's degree as the *sine qua non* for professional practice. For years it had been said that several different levels of practice should be identified, with appropriate differentiations as to the type of education and training required for each. The implementation of this obviously necessary policy has foundered, however, on the difficulty of clarifying the differential elements of knowledge and skill on which the policy would have to rest. In a situation where both trained and untrained workers have frequently been called upon to do essentially the same tasks in many areas of direct client practice, this has proved, thus far, to be an impossible assignment. Differentials continue to be defined as they have in the past by level of educational requirements rather than by job content.

While many issues are thus still unresolved, a modification in the basic definition of professionalism has taken place. The major breakthrough came in 1970, when the National Association of Social Workers (NASW) agreed to admit to full membership individuals who had obtained a bachelor's degree in an undergraduate program of social welfare, provided only that this program would meet criteria established by the Council on Social Work Education, the accrediting body for graduate programs.

The change was by no means a casual one nor had it been easily achieved. Indeed, proposals to relax the membership requirements in the professional association had been under discussion for at least twelve years before the new regulations were instituted formally in April, 1970. The major significance of the change was that the master's degree in social work was no longer the first professional degree, but its position in this respect was replaced by the baccalaureate degree. In addition, NASW established, for the first time, an associate membership category that was made available to individuals who had a baccalaureate degree in a field other than social work or social welfare but who were employed in some social work capacity. Provision was made for the possibility of shifting members from associate to regular membership after at least two years of experience and some further education, still to be specified.

It will be some time before the full implications of this significant shift in the professional structure of social work become apparent. Despite the actions of NASW, it is by no means certain that the large numbers of personnel who have manned the mass-service agencies as "untrained" workers will now seek identification with the social work profession. The number who have joined NASW is still very small. Despite the assumption for many years that great shortages of personnel would continue, retrenchment in governmental service programs during the early 1970s revealed how quickly shifts in governmental expenditures can affect the labor market in the human services. The demand for trained personnel—whether with masters' or with baccalaureate degrees—was less pressing in 1972 than in the latter half of the 1960s. Whether the achievement of professional status will provide workers with the baccalaureate training a sufficient market incentive to warrant professional investment and the payment of dues to a professional association is still uncertain.

What seems more certain is the fact that the nature of the direct-service function at the case level will be redefined. The most important long-term significance of the shift in professional requirements is the official recognition by the profession that intensive casework service is not expected to be the prevalent mode of direct client service in the future. The earlier emphasis on the master's degree as the minimum requirement for professional status had been based on the rationale, at least implicitly, that a graduate level of training was required for workers to acquire skill in handling interpersonal counseling relationships, and that this was the essential professional service required by people in trouble. That basic notion had prevailed continuously since the earliest days of professional social work, whose very emergence as a profession had been based on the argument that the needs of each individual had to be met in terms that were peculiarly suited to his own requirements and aspirations.

Not only the shortages of professional personnel during the 1960s but, perhaps even more importantly, the drive to employ "indigenous" personnel in the human service professions served to bring these assumptions into question. The renewed emphasis on poverty and social deprivation served also to shift the emphasis away from individual disabilities to the malfunctioning of institutions as the major source of social problems.

A dominant theme of social work practice in the past decade was the emphasis on social action. Community action programs financed by the federal government provided the means, for a period of time, for the organization of citizen groups in low-income urban neighborhoods to engage in protest activity of varying degrees of militance. Professional social workers, among others, became involved in the organization and leadership of these groups as community organizers and consultants. Such activities called for new definitions of professional roles. The idea of "advocacy" as a professional responsibility became very popular not only in neighborhood organization but as a prescription for social workers in service bureaucracies. The notion of the social worker as a change agent received widespread approval, but there were many different conceptions of how the role was to be performed.

A radical position called for militant attacks upon the existing service systems, such as public welfare, education, housing administrations, and the like. The welfare rights movement was an effort to organize recipients of public assistance to bring pressure upon public welfare administrations to correct faulty implementation of the welfare laws and regulations or, more broadly, to bring about improved benefits. Some professional social workers were actively involved as organizers of this movement. Others were advocates and helpers of its cause, providing not only their expert knowledge of the welfare system but also guidance on the strategy and tactics of protest.

These trends were notable particularly in that segment of social work practice that had been identified as community organization. Prior to the expansion of the 1960s, it had been customary to view social work as a single profession in which there were three discernible *methods* of practice: casework, group work, and community organization. All were conceptualized as a client-oriented helping process directed toward the achievement of client-determined goals. There had always been a value framework that combined concern for the improvement of social conditions with help to the client in achieving better social functioning and self-realization. It is generally recognized that the drive for professionalization had the effect of stressing the individual adjustment elements in that value framework, while the social change commitment frequently received only lip service. It was always more prominent, however, in some segments of the field than in others, and the commitment to a reform ideology was never completely absent.

At the point when the profession began to feel the impact of new postwar demands stemming from the racial tensions and the renewed awareness of poverty and deprivation in the disadvantaged segments of the society, it was dominated overwhelmingly by casework practitioners. Community organization, planning, and policymaking constituted a very small segment of the total professional personnel. These latter functions were performed for the most part by administrators, managers, or expert consultants in the public and voluntary service organizations. The community action programs opened up new types of positions in the area of community organization, quite different in context, style, and basic objective from those that had been characteristic of community organization practice previously. It became necessary to differentiate several different "models" of such practice, ranging from grass-roots organization of disadvantaged groups at the neighborhood level to broad policymaking functions in large-scale governmental bureaucracies.[12]

Simultaneously, there were parallel modifications in the conceptions of practice at the level of direct service to clients. Even before the expansion of programs in the 1960s, indeed during the entire postwar period, there had been a gradual broadening of the theoretical foundations of casework practice and the development of a wider range of intervention approaches than the traditional one-to-one therapeutic practice model based for the most part on psychoanalytic theory. Work with multiproblem families was receiving attention some years prior to the rediscovery of poverty, and agencies began to recognize an obligation to reach out to clients more aggressively so that those who needed services would in fact receive them. Family treatment, group therapy, and crisis intervention were some of the newer modalities of treatment that were described and advocated. Such a modification in the casework model did, however, continue to rest on counseling as the major component of the professional service to be rendered by social workers. It was not until more recent years that the efficacy of counseling came sharply under question by those who advocated that social workers devote themselves to the effort to secure greater resources for people in need and that they try to change the conditions under which the disadvantaged live.[13]

It is very difficult to state in any general way what professional social work practice comprises at this point in history, after some two decades of ferment and adaptation. Present practice encompasses a wide range of roles, functions, and tasks, with many differing views held by professional social workers as to the rationale for their activities. Nevertheless, it is possible to identify two major tendencies that exist simultaneously within the profession. One is the tendency for the profession to become divided on the issues of "practice" (which refers primarily to direct services to clients) *versus* "social action" or "social policy." Sometimes this division may take a philosophical form, as in the arguments over whether the role of the professional should be to help individuals adjust to an unjust social system or to help people to change that system. It also enters into disputes as to where the professional association should place its efforts—whether in the improvement of professional standards of work and the protection of practitioners, or in political and legislative activity.[14]

The opposite tendency is to attempt a redefinition of practice that would resolve the supposedly contradictory strains between practice and policy in a new, integrated view of a broadened conception of the social worker's professional role and responsibility. Such a reconciliation is not too difficult to achieve at the level of broad ideological and value commitments. Thus, NASW has committed itself to certain reformist policy objectives and constantly has become more active in pressing its views through legislative and administrative channels. Such positions have the broad support of its membership, regardless of their particular commitments to one or another professional method.

There is great conceptual difficulty, however, in the attempt to build action objectives into the actual practice of the professional.

This is difficult to achieve even in the field of community organization, where problems have arisen in trying to distinguish between professional and strictly political types of activity. It is even less feasible at the level of direct client service. Recent attempts either to rethink the common professional base for all of social work practice or to find a professional framework for a social change orientation in casework are interesting but still very preliminary formulations.[15]

The polarization of discussion along the lines of casework or counseling *versus* advocacy or social action has obscured what may be more significant problems in attempting to clarify the nature of professional practice at the level of direct client service. The service organizations in which social workers are involved are designed not only to provide counseling but also to distribute certain resources of a supportive and supplementary character to make it more feasible for people to function successfully in their communities. We refer here to group care of various kinds, services provided in the home, special training for persons with disabilities of various types, and many more. These are, of course, over and above basic financial assistance, which is still tied to services but presumably soon to be separated administratively. One orientation toward social work practice is to view the central function as one of service provision rather than as the traditional mission of helping individual clients to achieve those changes that will make it possible for them to cope more successfully or more happily.

The emphasis on advocacy has been prominent, at least in part, because of the inadequacy of both financial and service resources, thus making it necessary for individual practitioners to struggle with and/or on behalf of their clients to secure scarce resources. As we have seen, this may take the form of individual client advocacy, or of organized movements to wrest resources from those who control them. However, apart from the issue of adequacy, the focus on services and resources leads to at least two other kinds of differentials in determining the nature of practice. If one assumes the existence of resources and takes the position that the essential function of practice is to provide those resources effectively and efficiently, then the professional tasks tend to be of an organizational, planning, and administrative nature. The actual front-line delivery of the service, in many types of service structures, would call for some understanding of human behavior and positive, human-attitudes, but not for a high level of skill in the management of interpersonal, therapeutic transactions. It is this general line of thinking that provides one approach toward the differentiation of varying levels of professional requirements.

It should be noted, however, that such a differentiation along lines of administration *versus* direct client service is quite contrary to the major tradition in social work, which has been to define professional functioning primarily in terms of therapeutic rather than administrative skills. There continues to be a strong drive in some segments of the profession toward the achievement of higher levels of skill in various forms of therapy, although the repertoire is much broader today than in earlier times. In this case the basis for differentiating among levels of practice would be the degree of therapeutic skill achieved and therefore the amount of training in such skills.

There are thus at least three different kinds of emphases in attempts to define practice. They may be characterized loosely, on the basis of the foregoing discussion, as administrative, advocacy-social action, or therapeutic. How these can be combined in whole or in part is not at all clear at this time.

RELATIONSHIP TO OTHER FIELDS

One of the consequences of this growing diversity in social work practice is a widening network of interrelationships between social work and other fields of activity. The traditional fields of social work practice, such as family (and children), medical, and psychiatric social work, had been related in the past to other major therapeutic professions such as medicine and clinical psychology. In the expanded community action and antipoverty programs of the 1960s, professional social workers became more involved in broader service structures that included administrators and planners who came from fields of education, urban planning, and public administration, or from no well-defined professional discipline.

One of the uncertainities for the future is the potential emergence of a new field of human services that would incorporate many different disciplines, professions, and vocations, including some segments of social work. As yet, the tendencies in that direction are more evident at the level of rhetoric than in the realities of staff structures and civil service requirements. There are, nevertheless, new city and state departments of human services or human resources which may over a period of time bring about more tangible changes. For social work, as for other professions, these tendencies pose something of a conflict.

The trend toward a broader definition of the human services is compatible with one of the cherished aspirations of the social work profession to become identified as a profession serving basic and universal needs rather than being tied exclusively to those segments of the population that are the most handicapped, dependent, or even despised. On the other hand, it does not seem realistic to expect that social work can establish professional hegemony over the vast area of human services, especially if that emerging field is to include major elements of health and educational services. The trend toward a human services framework leads in one or both of two directions: toward interdisciplinary and interprofessional collaboration or toward the development of new disciplines. In either event, the social work profession is challenged to define its particular and distinctive role in that broader enterprise.

The conflict arises from the fact that the broadening human services framework draws different segments of the social work profession into closer collaborative relationships with other fields and therefore tends to blur the social work identity. Those who are concerned with the status of the profession as a whole, while welcoming the broadening of its range of influence and activity, face the difficulty of maintaining the unity of the profession within this growing diversity. That conflict, stemming from recent developments in social work practice, is fundamental to the situation of social work education as well.

Social Work Education

It is obvious from the foregoing discussion that social work education faces the task of preparing students for a rapidly changing, fluid, and very ill-defined field of professional practice. Since there is, in truth, no single field of practice, but many, it is to be expected that social work education will be similarly pluralistic, ill-defined, and subject to a great deal of instability and change. Within less than a decade, the educational system in social work has moved from a relatively uniform curriculum format to a highly permissive and flexible set of options open to schools and to individual students within schools. Increasingly, the view is expressed that schools cannot prepare students for any specific roles in the future, since these are not possible to predict, but that they should try to help students to acquire some basic concepts and tools that will arm them for dealing with the major characteristics of future professional responsibilities, namely, change and uncertainty.

At the graduate level of social work education, attempts have been made to find new and, it is hoped, better ways of conceptualizing and teaching practice. Variations can be found on almost every dimension. One general issue is whether to try to deal with social work as an entity or as a variety of specializations that do not necessarily fit into a neatly integrated pattern. That issue can be subdivided further on the basis of very different approaches both to "generic" social work practice and to the bases for organizing specializations. The result is a rather bewildering spectrum of alternative formulations.

In a limited study made in 1971 several schools were visited, including three that had been established within the past five years. In general, it was found that curriculum built on a single method (casework) or even on a choice among three methods (casework, group work, community organization) was no longer the dominant model as it had been less than ten years ago.[16] Although some groups of students still follow a fully prescribed and traditional program, an increasing number are offered a wide range of choice.

The model that emerges from an examination of the newer schools reflects the broadening mandate that characterizes the social work profession today. While the majority of students are still being prepared for roles involving the rendering of direct services to individuals, families, or small groups, great emphasis is placed on orienting them to the social context of those responsibilities and to the social causation of the problems with which they will be expected to deal. Attempts are being made to prepare them for a great diversity of roles, and there are still many unresolved problems in attempting to combine holistic and specialized approaches. All three of the newer schools emphasize a critical approach to the analysis of society, and all attempt to inculcate analytical skills. Close working collaboration between faculty and students is a goal of all these programs, expressed in a variety of ways, and all seek a diversified student body, including members of disadvantaged minorities who have limited educational background. They therefore have responsibilities not only for graduate education but for undergraduate education and for certain types of nonprofessional training.

Undergraduate programs are even more difficult to characterize than graduate programs, since there is no general information available as to what is actually being done within the very many different programs that are in existence.[17] It is generally assumed that they vary greatly in content and quality. One may also be sure that they are far from stable and very much in process of evolution. There have been, nevertheless, some interesting attempts to formulate models for pursuing the tasks that face the undergraduate educators, and these help at least to clarify the issues.[18]

Many of the issues discussed earlier in regard to social work practice come into focus in the attempt to develop models for undergraduate training. That is to be expected, since the undergraduate programs are devoted to the training of first-level practitioners who will be providing direct client services. Most of the undergraduate curriculum developers are therefore involved in an attempt to reconceptualize practice.

The starting point for such efforts is a rejection of the traditional model of three social work methods—casework, group work, and community organization. Instead, an attempt is made to find some way of interrelating the purposes of the practitioner with the activities that he undertakes and with the set of problems that he is trying to affect. A range of roles or methods is suggested under labels such as "advocate," "broker," "mobilizer," "behavior changer," "community planner," "care-giver," and others. Most of the writers on undergraduate education also try to relate such roles and methods to the organizational systems in which practice is lodged and to the functions of those systems. Bisno, for example, divides them into "micro" and "macro" systems.[19] Others talk more descriptively of specific community and societal structures, the political system, and the like, along with paying attention to the specific service fields in which practice is conducted.

There is obviously a heavy bias in all of these proposals to the generalist approach. The baccalaureate level of social work practitioner is viewed as a generalist who has experienced a curriculum in which the elements of knowledge, value, and skill receiving emphasis have been those that are not tied to specific specialized fields but that presumably underlie all social professions. The range is, however, extremely broad. Knowledge is very extensive, calling for some depth in social sciences that cover micro-and macrosystems. Individual personality development, social structure, economics, and politics are all represented. In addition, the history, background, and structure of the human service systems must be covered. Skills to be mastered range from interviewing, observing, and recording to using oneself professionally both to change individual behavior and to change major social institutions. It is recognized that not all workers will perform all of these functions in equal measure, and that some of the roles form clusters. It is clearly suggested, however, that all such competencies need to be included in a generic repertoire upon which the practitioner can draw as needed.

The recent literature on undergraduate education abounds in ambitious formulations of this type. Thus, McPheeters and Ryan assert that the generalist practitioner produced by undergraduate programs should "be prepared to work with individuals, groups, organizations, and communities." Increasingly, "the BSW graduate is assumed to be the major provider of direct service to the target population," and direct service is broadly defined to include a very wide range of intervention methods.[20]

There is, however, a substantial gap between the aspirations of professional education at the undergraduate level and the realities of the service areas to which the training is directed. The market situation is extremely uncertain, as already noted. It is also uncertain whether there will be opportunities for the pursuit of stable careers based on undergraduate education in social welfare, as in other professions such as nursing. Thus far, positions manned by workers without graduate training have been marked by a very high rate of turnover. For those desiring to pursue careers, these positions have served primarily as transitional experiences toward graduate professional education.

The rapid expansion of undergraduate education, if it is to have lasting importance, presupposes continued expansion and development of the human services to the point where they can absorb large numbers of baccalaureate graduates and offer them reasonably attractive careers. It also presupposes greater clarification than now exists of the nature of the professional responsibilities to be assumed. The generic models that have been projected for the educational task seem to this writer too global to serve as answers to those requirements.

If there is to be professionalization of the direct-service tasks at a level that can be manned by workers of "beginning competence," armed with an appropriate undergraduate education, then it seems reasonable to expect that there will be the same trend toward specialization in these occupations that has occurred in all fields.

There are several ways in which this specialization may take place, and it is not possible to predict what the ultimate direction will be. It is possible, however, to indicate some of the alternatives that may develop on the basis of trends that are already in evidence. Undergraduate education will probably never fall into a single pattern, but will be made up of a wide diversity of programs fulfilling multiple objectives.

Perhaps the most general statement that can be made is that undergraduate education for social welfare is not likely to represent a simple transfer of the traditional social work educational cirriculum to the undergraduate level. To begin with, that traditional pattern is no longer dominant at the master's level. In addition, the various influences and demands impinging on undergraduate education will require a broader range of responses. One of the recent trends in graduate social work education that offers particular promise at the undergraduate level is the shift from an emphasis on methods to a problem-oriented approach.[21] A curriculum that is organized around particular problem areas such as aging or children and youth lends itself to the needs of particular service systems for workers who will have specialized backgrounds in their areas of concern. That kind of specific vocational orientation is one pattern that is already present in undergraduate programs. Given the prevailing patterns of organization of governmental programs into categorical service fields, one may anticipate that the demand for such specialists will be one of the continuing pressures to which undergraduate education will need to respond.

On the other hand, service structures are not fixed for all time, but are subject to continuing reexamination. There is also a continuing tension between the need to obtain more skillful specialists in particular areas and the equally compelling need for professionals with skills in linking different specialized fields in order to obtain more comprehensive and, it is to be hoped, more effective service patterns. There is probably no ultimate solution to these contradictions but a need to seek optimum solutions for a particular period of time by redressing gross imbalances in one direction or the other.

For the immediate future, it would seem that undergraduate programs will not be emphasizing traditional social work methods such as casework, group work, and community organization, but will probably be organized along programmatic lines that are related to major service structures. This poses the educational problem of how to maintain some integrated and stable core of academic content against the pressures of shifting styles and tastes in the development and funding of human service structures.

At the present time the undergraduate programs in social welfare are related to a very considerable extent to professional social work education at the graduate level. On the national scene, the Council on Social Work Education is the major instrument for the promotion, development, and standard-setting of undergraduate programs. To the extent that this situation continues, the products of undergraduate education will be identified as social workers regardless of how different they may turn out to be from the professional social workers of the past.

There is, however, at least the beginning of an approach to undergraduate education that attempts to transcend existing professional lines and to substitute a concept of human services as a new and potentially more generic professional entity. This is still in a rudimentary stage of development and the concepts are quite vague. Here again, what is happening within the educational institutions reflects practice in the outside world. In a number of state and local governments the concept of human services or human resources has taken the form of the creation of superdepartments which bring together various functions, particularly in the health, welfare, and correctional fields. The motivation for such developments has been the attempt to seek improvement in human services through greater integration, comprehensiveness, and continuity. In reality, many of these superdepartments have not brought about significant changes at the operational level, but have at most instituted certain processes of joint planning and budgeting across a number of program structures.

The situation in regard to education is rather similar. Although some undergraduate programs describe themselves not as preparation for social welfare or social work but for "human services" or "social professions," these tend to be combinations of existing professional training programs. One program, for example, combines nursing, social work, and health education. At the present time, the program prepares people separately for these respective careers, but the faculty is working on a common core curriculum and on the extension of field training for all of the professional specializations, so that the area of overlap is growing constantly. Ultimately, the objective is to develop a much larger area of common training built around the concept of a human services clinician. The core content consists of material in human growth and development, human service systems (including social services and health), and social science material relating to intervention at individual, group, formal organization, and community levels.

Because of the great emphasis on undergraduate education in recent years, there has been a tendency to think about the master's level of professional social work education as of declining importance. Indeed, there are some suggestions that it might virtually disappear,[22] being replaced on the one hand by undergraduate programs for the training of pracitioners and on the other by doctorate programs for the preparation of teachers, researchers, and administrators.

Such predictions seem premature and indeed quite hazardous. There is no obvious decline in the number of students seeking a graduate education in social work, nor is it at all clear that, given a competitive market situation, people with undergraduate degrees will be able to obtain positions in preference to those with masters' degrees.

At the present time, the master's level of education continues to be the major channel for entry into the types of occupations that have established professional status in social work. The main shift in graduate social work education in the past decade was clearly away from the concentration on casework. One important change was the development of concentrations in community organization and planning which increased the proportion of social work students in that field from about one percent to nearly 10 percent during the 1960s. However, a much larger shift quantitatively was represented in the development of new types of curriculum for the teaching of social work methods, known variously as "combined methods," "multi-methods," or "problem-centered" curricula. The purpose here was to break away from the predominant emphasis on one-to-one treatment and to help students acquire a wider repertoire of methods for dealing with client needs.

More recently, as greater attention has been paid to undergraduate programs, the master's level of training has come to be defined increasingly as preparation for administration and management. Thus an official document of the Council on Social Work Education, in listing the purposes to be served at various levels of social work education, describes the purpose of the master's degree as "to prepare students for specialized practice, administration, staff supervision, policy development and social planning." [23] The same emphasis on administration, planning, and policy is evident in the definition of the purposes of doctoral programs, except that research and teaching are added as major elements in the careers for which doctoral students are being prepared.

What continues to be a problematic element in the "new look" of social work education is the place of education for clinical types of practice. It will be noted that the definition of purposes of the master's program speaks of "specialized practice," and the definition of the purpose of the doctoral degree includes "advanced practice."

It would be very useful to have at this time definitive data on what positions social workers with various degrees of training actually occupy today. At best, only partial information is available. Ultimately, the definitive answers as to the future impact of social work education will be obtained through current manpower studies and later follow-up studies. There is every reason to believe, however, that for the moment most professional social workers with graduate training are, in fact, engaged in clinical types of services either as front-line practitioners or as supervisors. Despite its recent emphasis on broad aspects of policy, planning, and administration, social work education is subject to continuing demands to produce skillful practitioners for therapeutically oriented services.

Because of this, it seems to this observer that there is still an important need within graduate social work education to prepare people differentially for two major types of responsibilities. These may be described roughly as "clinical" or "therapeutic" on the one hand and "administrative" on the other. Admittedly, this is an oversimplification, and many variations are possible. The essential point, however, is that social work is a profession that will continue to be called upon to render a disciplined and highly skilled service to that portion of the population that needs intensive counseling service from time to time. In this respect, it will be tied to other clinically oriented professions as it has been in the past and will participate in the evolution of newer and more varied methods of therapeutic intervention, including the use of group as well as individual techniques.

On the other hand, there is clear need for growing numbers of professionals in the social work–social welfare–human service fields who will have a high level of knowledge and skills in the organization, planning, and administration of such programs. The emerging developments in undergraduate education and in the manning of the human service structures will serve to accelerate the need for this type of professional leadership.

In the area of planning, administration, social policy, and related aspects of the social professions, social work education faces problems that are of equal concern today in many other areas such as urban planning, public affairs, public administration, and public health, to name just a few.[24] Like social work, these professions are concerned with the need to identify a core curriculum that will help to clarify the nature of their enterprise. There are many different patterns, but those programs concerned with policy and planning seem to gravitate toward a few subject areas that provide at least the beginnings of such a core. Conceptually, economics, and particularly microeconomics, seems to lead, occupying a position roughly analogous to psychoanalytic theory in the old social work model. In addition, the curriculum leans heavily on statistical and analytical methods, such as operations research. Different approaches toward systems technology are also represented.

Also present but less clearly formulated are more qualitative aspects of policy and planning. In this area, all fields find themselves struggling with the interplay of values, knowledge, methods, and skills in conceptualizing the subject. While economics provides the conceptual framework for the analytical methods in policy and planning, many different conceptual frameworks come into play in teaching the social processes of policy and planning. Politics certainly plays an important role, but so too do organizational theory and many other subtopics of sociology and psychology. The identification of a strong, systematic, coherent, and rigorous core of theory continues to elude curriculum planners not only in schools of social welfare but in many other professional schools concerned with social policy.

As in social welfare, the answer to that inadequacy seems to lie in building a specialized curriculum that will help the student at least to master a body of knowledge, experience, and know-how in some defined area of substantive activity. The specific subjects tend to be different from those one finds in schools of social work. In urban planning there is a great deal of specific material on housing and transportation and similar matters. In the more general schools of public affairs or policy science, there will be much more substantive material on governmental structure and finance. Increasingly, of course, the substantive areas overlap. Today, welfare and health are a focus of interest for virtually all policy and planning programs.

As a result, the training being provided today is highly variable and individualized. There are very few required core courses, and almost as many curriculum profiles as there are students. No matter how many different types of courses are available, students are always seeking new and different combinations, sometimes including offerings in other schools than the one in which they are enrolled. A human services profession may be emerging, but it will be made up of professionals each of whom has taken a unique educational path to arrive at the same place.

In the preparation of leadership for the human service professions, social work education will not be able to claim an exclusive domain. Its distinctiveness lies not so much in concepts and content, or even in ideology, but in the institutional structure. Social work has a different network of relationships, reference groups, and institutional responsibilities from that of other professions.

We thus return to the point with which we began. As yet, the profession of social work has not made a clear commitment to accepting responsibility for the future lines of development of major organized social services in American society. Social work education, like social work practice, still finds itself largely committed to an independent practitioner model rather than to the assumption of administrative responsibility for the direction of those organizational structures through which social services must be provided. If the social work profession is to continue to play a role as an organized entity in the future of the human services, it will need to accept less equivocally the responsibility for managing significant portions of the organized human services structure. In order to do this, it will have to embark on a period of serious and assiduous experimentation involving all levels of education in close interrelationships with service structures. It is only in this way that the social work profession in both its practice and its educational roles can deal with the basic task on which barely a beginning has been made—the restructuring of social services and of professional practice within them.

It seems to this observer that it is entirely possible for social work education to accept this challenge without necessarily relinquishing its traditional commitment to clinical practice. It is neither possible nor desirable to impose a uniform model on an extremely diffuse field. Social work can remain most true to its traditions by trying to meet needs as they exist and develop. It should be the last profession to seek simple and monolithic solutions to complex problems.

Notes

[1] This article is based in part on a report prepared by the author and David Williams for the Carnegie Commission on Higher Education. That report is to be published in Everett C. Hughes, ed., *Education for the Professions of Medicine, Law and Theology; Education for the Profession of Social Welfare* (New York: McGraw-Hill; forthcoming).

[2] Marvin Bressler, "The American College: Some Problems and Choices," *The Annals*, July, 1971, p. 68.

[3] *Ibid.*, pp. 68–69.

[4] Everett C. Hughes, "Higher Education and the Professions," paper prepared for the Carnegie Commission on Higher Education (1971; mimeographed).

[5] For an excellent discussion of these issues see *Public Health Concepts in Social Work Education* (New York: Council on Social Work Education, 1962), particularly the paper by John M. Cassel, "Potentialities and Limitations of Epidemiology," pp. 69–85.

[6] Edgar H. Schein, *Professional Education: Some New Directions* (New York: McGraw-Hill, 1972), p. 15.

[7] *Ibid.*, p. 22.

[8] *Closing the Gap . . . in Social Work Manpower*, report of the Departmental Task Force on Social Work Education and Manpower (Washington, D.C.: U.S. Department of Health, Education, and Welfare, 1965), p. 34.

[9] Willard C. Richan, "A Policy Base for Social Work Practice: Societal Perspectives," in this volume.

[10] Martin Rein, "Social Work in Search of a Radical Profession," *Social Work*, XV, No. 2 (1970), 13–28.

[11] Harry Specht, "The Deprofessionalization of Social Work," *Social Work*, XVII, No. 2 (1972), 3–15.

[12] Jack Rothman, "Three Models of Community Organization Practice," in *Social Work Practice, 1968* (New York: Columbia University Press, 1968), pp. 16–47.

[13] Early in 1971 the Community Service Society of New York, one of the oldest and most traditional casework agencies in the country, decided to shift its program from casework counseling to rendering service

to indigenous neighborhood organizations. Further changes are pending.

[14] For a representative cross section of views on these issues, see Willard C. Richan, ed., *Human Services and Social Work Responsibility* (New York: National Association of Social Workers, 1969).

[15] The following represent alternative approaches toward integrating a number of these different directions in social work practice: Harriet M. Bartlett, "Social Work Fields of Practice" in *Encyclopedia of Social Work* 16th ed.; New York: National Association of Social Workers, 1971), pp. 1477–81; Rein, *op. cit.*, Ivor Kraft, "The State of the Social Work Profession," in Richan, *Human Services . . .* , pp. 343–66.

[16] Arnold Gurin and David Williams, "Social Work Education" (unpublished report prepared for Carnegie Commission on Higher Education, 1971).

[17] A document prepared by the Council on Social Work Education entitled *An Analysis of Undergraduate Social Work Programs Approved by the C.S.W.E., 1971,* by Alfred Stamm summarized 158 undergraduate programs approved by the Council under a set of standards that became effective July 1, 1971.

[18] See particularly Frank M. Loewenberg and Ralph Dolgoff, *Teaching of Practice Skills in Undergraduate Programs in Social Welfare and Other Helping Services* (New York: Council on Social Work Education, 1971); Harold L. McPheeters and Robert M. Ryan, *A Core of Competence for Baccalaureate Social Welfare* (Atlanta, Ga.: Southern Regional Education Board, 1971).

[19] Herbert Bisno, "A Theoretical Framework for Teaching Social Work Methods and Skills," in Loewenberg and Dolgoff, *op. cit.*, pp. 72–78.

[20] McPheeters and Ryan, *op. cit.*, p. 99.

[21] For a description of this approach see Henry S. Maas, "Purpose, Participation, and Education," in Lillian Ripple, ed., *Innovations in Teaching Social Work Practice* (New York: Council on Social Work Education, 1970), pp. 9–21.

[22] Alvin L. Schorr, in an editorial in *Social Work*, XVI, No. 2 (1971), predicted that "in time, graduate schools of social work will replace the Masters degree with a doctoral degree" (p. 2).

[23] *Undergraduate Programs in Social Work* (New York: Council on Social Work Education, 1971), p. 6.

[24] For instructive reviews of curriculum developments see *Policy Sciences*, Vol. I, No. 4 (1970); *ibid.*, Vol. II, No. 1 (1971); *Journal of the American Institute of Planners*, Vol. XXXVI, No. 4 (1970). The entire issues of these journals were devoted to educational matters.

Alfred J. Kahn

❦

EPILOGUE

Here the editor speaks only for himself.

I deliberately chose contributors for this volume from different points on the political spectrum, with different perspectives on method and theory and of different professional "generations." I expected and received articles which reflect conflicting theoretical viewpoints and priorities for social work. However, I did not predict or expect that at least three of the contributors (Polansky, Grosser, Richan) would consider seriously the possibility that social work as a profession would disappear. A similar view recently led off an issue of the profession's major social work journal at about the time the papers were completed.[1] Surely, this is a challenge to shape a relevant, effective, attractive policy and practice stance for social work. Obviously, the strategy of the profession vis à vis the society demands debate and action.

Some years ago, in some sentences which were to be subsequently quoted in a number of places, I said:

> Social work in the coming years either must formulate and test its own knowledge on a substantial scale, supplementing it with critical use of social science knowledge, or it must surrender its professional functions to new and more rigorous disciplines . . .[2]

The issue of social work's unique knowledge base remains and takes on new urgency: What is our expertise? Where resides our skill (differential use of means)? To some extent we made progress in the decade between 1954 and 1964. More recently, we have put aside the issue of expertise and professional specificity by widening our scope and taking on new tasks in an era of great social change.

Within some service contexts, generally quite circumscribed, there has been delineation and testing: working with the child in foster care or child guidance; marital counseling through casework.

For the most part, however, expertise and skill have been under-played in favor of commitment and concern, as social work has ex-panded into the many new arenas of practice which have devel-oped during the heightened attention of the past decade to a rediscovered (and redefined) poverty, racial and ethnic injustice, in-creased antisocial behavior, the prevalence of major addictions, par-ticularly drug abuse—and so on. Social work has labored in these fields, but its knowledge-skill-expertise have been modest. We have also advocated policy and legislation consistent with our value com-mitments and have sought to increase consumer involvement in and/or control over programs which affect their lives.

But "cause" both generates and defers "function"; it is no substi-tute. If it is to continue and thrive as a profession with a recognized domain, social work must define and establish its knowledge-skill. This involves not only the borrowing discussed by Kamerman, Dol-goff, Getzel, and Nelsen, but also the development of professional science—theory of the use of knowledge in action; elaboration of what logically can be derived from social science, but nonetheless awaits professional development because only practice gives it prior-ity.

To elaborate practice in new fields and improve it in the old will be no small task because, today, social work aspires to a very broad domain. We would undertake the direct practice discussed by Meyer and Polansky, but also seek major roles in social research, so-cial administration, program development, policy analysis, and plan-ning. These latter fields are as yet underdeveloped, and the unique social work competence is only now being shaped; but we aspire to the roles since we would define the social work profession as going beyond treatment and control of the deviant and the needy and as contributing to urban amenity, more adequate societal provision, so-cial justice, and the shaping of all institutions in this welfare state era in accord with human values not limited to economy, efficiency, and economic growth.

The task of professional definition and development will be intel-lectually difficult because it is broad and ambitious. It will be politi-cally and organizationally difficult because there are competing groups: urban planners, economists, "clinical" sociologists, and others. It will be internally difficult because social work as a profession has been in disarray for half a decade.

Richan offers perspective on the dilemmas of the organized social work profession. Specht widens the "diagnosis." [3] Can we define, capture, and develop a domain adequately? Do we have the power, the credibility, and the internal coherence and qualities required to shape task, methods, knowledge, and professional accountability? It has been alleged, and with reason, that in our eagerness to undo our past overemphasis on the psychosocial, we turned to naïve environmentalism. In our impatience with injustice, we joined unrepresentative activists or gave them disproportionate power in our professional institutions. In our impatience with "irrelevance" we allowed the anti-intellectualism of the era to contribute to a crisis of confidence for social workers. [4] To which we might add: In our guilt at excessive credentialism we undid many professional prerogatives and sanctioned the view that distinctions by level of education of practitioners had no place in agencies or professional associations. In our search for democracy we denigrated expertise and accountability.

This would appear to be a formula for the liquidation of social work or the capture of its domain by competing occupational groups. There are different views about how deep-seated the problem is. It appears to me that in some service fields a process of social work retrenchment and decline is well under way—particularly in the era of curtailed budgets at the time this volume was nearing completion. Richan is optimistic because he assesses our organization networks as sufficiently strong to assure new tasks and roles for social work. This remains to be seen. I would be more sanguine if our future could be secured as well:

1. By facing the need for professionalization and determining that professional self-interest is not inconsistent with social responsibility
2. By the strengthening and development of new practice conceptualizations, modalities, and skills, along the lines of Meyer's suggestions
3. By the development of educational and practice models shown

to be effective in social administration, program development, policy analysis, social planning, so that our entry into these activities may be considerable and substantial

4. By the enhancement of social work research competence and the assurance of behavioral and social science foundations which will encourage continued development and testing of needed knowledge.

Institutional Context

Our volume does not explore adequately the organizational context for the new social work. Clearly, old patterns are undergoing change. Public welfare, long a major social work locus, is separating the administration of monetary benefits from nonmonetary services, and the place of social work in the former is now uncertain. At the same time, an emphasis on work seems to require manpower services which are close to eligibility operations. Will social work be excluded from these new services? On the other hand, child welfare, long separated from public welfare in its delivery system, may now be united with other general social services.[5]

But larger issues are at stake. If the society continues one social service system (public welfare, corrections, many state hospitals) for the poorest and most stigmatized, another system (voluntary agencies, much of community mental health, public child welfare) for the lower middle class and working class, and still another, a market-based system, for other service users, social work may well be forced to continue—with exceptions—to allow a correlation between client status and social worker credentials to prevail.[6] Then there can be no new professional manpower strategy. On the other hand, if the social service philosophy is "universalism," nonmeans-tested programs good enough for any American, it may be possible to plan delivery systems on other principles. Then, too, rational manpower policies will become possible.

Such a process would precipitate review of the entire nonsystem of social service delivery: the issue of "free-standing", social work sponsored services *versus* social work as an adjunctive discipline in factories, schools, hospitals, medical facilities, and so on; the issue of the integration of general social services with the remainder of the social sector; the hierarchal pattern of social welfare programs from neighborhood, to district, to area, to city, to state, to region. The patterning of social sector programs to enhance delivery will have many implications for social work. New roles will evolve for a profession which has stressed liaison and service integration skills. New operational models will emerge because the system, in Meyer's sense, will have been redefined!

NEW ROLES

Other forces, too, will reshape social work roles. If the profession's manpower strategy encourages definition of tasks by levels of professional responsibility for the fully credentialed, for the paraprofessional, and for the volunteer, there will need to be autonomous "master" practitioners, team leaders, consultants, programmers, supervisors, to carry out the direct service and have impact on other service networks; as there will be planners, social administrators, practitioner-researchers, and general researchers to carry out the macrosystem tasks and represent professional venture capital. While the politics of the day creates concerns of the type described above, it also promises the arrival on the scene of new minority and female personnel who will take part in and help develop these new responsibilities.

Advocacy

Advocacy can and should be a component of direct-service roles and a specialty within social work, both in its case and its class manifestations. However, the profession will want to debate Grosser's call for "ideological advocacy"—what I interpret to mean the building of political action into the role of the social worker. Grosser holds that nothing less will meet our commitment to the goals of the welfare state. My viewpoint is that social work has permitted too uniform an ideological perspective to take over in the National Association of Social Workers and the Council on Social Work Education; has demanded intellectual conformity, as though scholarly and real debate would defeat fragile policy goals; and has used confrontation and rhetoric in its assemblies to the detriment of the diversity and experimentation out of which professional advancement comes. Social work practitioners probably should more often see an advocacy component as part of their ongoing client-servicing roles; social work advocacy specialists are also needed for class advocacy activities of several kinds.[7] However, I doubt the appropriateness of a narrowly uniform political commitment for the profession. Shared values, goals, and perspectives can help bind professionals and inspire them. These are needed. But narrow, ideological commitments and political ties rigidify professional organizations and institutions.

There is little choice. The instruments of sound decision and professional development will need to be our professional associations: the National Association of Social Workers, the Council on Social Work Education, the National Conference on Social Welfare—or similar organizations. Their task is to develop and strengthen the profession as a vehicle for social welfare, not to serve narrow ideological and partisan purposes. A humanistic message and social concern must characterize all we do. Balance is not easily developed or achieved.

Social workers will not be able to do any of this unless they recognize that the evolution of professional associations in support of an improved and broadened professionalism is as much in the interest of blacks, Puerto Ricans, Chicanos, American Indians, and other disadvantaged groups as it is of those more traditionally involved. If our guilt about social injustice leads us to forgo social tools which offer greatest promise to the social sector, we shall have enshrined a new knownothingness whose rhetoric may have momentary appeal but which cannot deliver just social policy, comprehensive programs, or competent practitioners.

Society in the United States is not yet seriously attacking either its major social problems or its growing environmental crisis. Most of its citizens are not yet considering the full implications of a real attack on inequality and want. Few are aware of the possible demands of a real attack on pollution, a serious effort to conserve limited physical resources, a possible zero population growth. Lack of understanding and concern constitute a crisis, yet the crisis is not widely acknowledged and perceived. But if the projections are correct, the country must during this decade launch a new debate in the search for a political, economic, and social policy which recognizes that ours is one country and that we shape our society in close interaction; ours is one earth and it is thin-skinned. It will be necessary to debate proposals to counter property rights and social justice and amenity rights; to conceive of an international economy; to review national sovereignty; and to seek the core values by which our world shall guide itself. Only a renewed social work will have anything relevant to say in such a debate. And only a self-assured and competent social work will be capable of shaping the social practice with which the society will need to move from the 1970s into the 1980s.

Notes

[1] Harry Specht, "The Deprofessionalization of Social Work," *Social Work*, XVII, No. 2 (1972), 3–15.

[2] Alfred J. Kahn, "The Nature of Social Work Knowledge," in Cora Kasius, ed., *New Directions in Social Work* (New York: Harper and Bros., 1954), pp. 210–11.

[3] Specht, *op. cit.*

[4] *Ibid*.

[5] For elaboration, see Alfred J. Kahn, *Social Policy and Social Services* (New York: Random House, 1973).

[6] These generalizations are not precise. But despite community differences in detail and many local exceptions, there are three social service systems, and they are stratified in a fashion which parallels the stratification of their clientele.

[7] See Alfred J. Kahn, Sheila B. Kamerman, Brenda G. McGowan, *Child Advocacy: the Report of a National Baseline Study* (New York: Columbia University School of Social Work, 1972).

INDEX

Simon, Herbert A.: on information in management decisions, cited, 117

Skinner, B.F.: cited, 109

Smalley, Ruth: on function and process in the casework model, 27; on Freudian view of man, 104

Small group concepts and practices, 100 ff.; general systems theory in, 106; sociological contributions to, 113

Social Darwinist theories: in service goals, 32-33

Social intervention: relative feasibility, types, and levels of, 130

Socialization: concepts and models in social work practice, 107, 115

Social justice and reform, 98, 99, 204; *see also* Advocacy

Social planning, *see* Community organization approach

Social poverty: concept of, 122

Social psychology: social work use of knowledge from, 104, 107

Social Science Research Council: cited, 112

Social services: strategies challenged, 3; decentralization in, 9; expectations of, 10-11; help, provision, and advocacy of, 17 ff.

Social stratification concepts, as potential contribution of sociological knowledge, 117

Social structure: awareness of in human fulfillment, 104

Social Welfare, *see* Social work practices; Welfare establishment; Welfare services

Social Welfare Workers Movement, 155

Social work career, *see* Professional status in social work

Social work clinicians: *see* Clinicians

Social work education, *see* Education for social work

Social Work Education, Council on: *see* Council on Social Work Education

Social worker relations: intra-professional contention with colleagues, 82-83; with other professions, 115, 147-49, 171-72; with clients, NASW 1969 position on, 153; *see also* Advocacy; Client-social worker relations

Social workers, identity problem of, 149-52

Social work practice: challenges for, ix, 199 ff.; policy role of, x; definition of, 20-21; in relation to world views, 26; types and specializations of, 27, 38 ff.; apparent ambiguities about the integration of, 28 ff., 33-34; affecting social controls, 31-32; in public against voluntary settings, 34; clinical approach in characterized, 38-39; medical model for, 38-40; definitive role of efficient services, 40-42; the role of social science knowledge in, 97-134; contributions of general systems theory to, 105; communications concepts and techniques in, 107-9; behavioral concepts and techniques in, 109-10; alternate re-adaptations to emergent problems, 161-64; education for change in, 169-98; aims of a redefinition in terms of action objectives, 182-83; redesign of in the light of undergraduate training, 188-90

Social work profession: historic emergence of, 18 (*see also* Historic developments in welfare services); individualized versus integrative approach in, 20-21; summary of component approaches in, 20-21; problem versus method definition of, 22-23, 99; diversity of models for, 27-29; separation of eligibility from service within, 42-43; in terms of the general systems approach, 47-53; institutional integration within, 152-54; future realignments with organized welfare, 163 ff.; future perspectives for, 196 ff.; *see also* Challenges and tasks for the new social